Inside Chabad Lubavitch

Who are the explosively growing branch of Orthodox Jews? What do they want? How are they getting it? A case study in Argentina

A.J. Soifer, Ph.D.

Copyright © 2023 by A.J. Soifer

All rights reserved.

No portion of this book may be reproduced in any form without written permission from the publisher or author, except as permitted by U.S. copyright law.

This publication is designed to provide accurate and authoritative information in regard to the subject matter covered. It is sold with the understanding that neither the author nor the publisher is engaged in rendering legal, investment, accounting or other professional services. While the publisher and author have used their best efforts in preparing this book, they make no representations or warranties with respect to the accuracy or completeness of the contents of this book and specifically disclaim any implied warranties of merchantability or fitness for a particular purpose. No warranty may be created or extended by sales representatives or written sales materials. The advice and strategies contained herein may not be suitable for your situation. You should consult with a professional when appropriate. Neither the publisher nor the author shall be liable for any loss of profit or any other commercial damages, including but not limited to special, incidental, consequential, personal, or other damages.

Book Cover by GetCovers.com

Illustrations by the author.

1st English edition 2023

Contents

Preface to the first English edition   1

Epigraph   3

1. Prologue   5
   Who Wants to be a Lubavitcher?

2. Chapter One   21
   Who Fears Chabad Lubavitch?

3. Chapter Two   37
   Life and Afterlife of Menachem Mendel Schneerson, Chabad's Last Rebbe

4. Chapter Three   53
   Proselytism

5. Chapter Four   73
   Conquering the Next Generation of Jews

6. Chapter Five   109
   God's Salesmen: Chabad's Communication Machine

7. Chapter Six   115
   Reborn from the Ashes: Chabad's Revived Synagogues

8. Chapter Seven   125
   Educating in Torah

9. Chapter Eight   143
   Chabad is Everywhere

10. Chapter Nine   169
    No Jew Left Out: Chabad's Social Assistance

11. Chapter Ten — 179
Queen Esther's Heiresses: Women in Chabad

12. Chapter Eleven — 186
The External Front: Chabad's Public Affairs

13. Chapter Twelve — 198
Masters of Repentance: The Baalei Teshuva

14. Chapter Thirteen — 215
The Rabbi Who Didn't Believe in God

15. APPENDIX — 226
Brief History of Chabad Lubavitch and of its Arrival in Argentina

16. Epilogue — 239

Glossary — 245

Bibliography — 249

About the Author — 255

Preface to the first English edition

A few years ago, my wife and I were walking through Times Square in New York City on a Friday, Christmas afternoon, when a random person asked me if I was Jewish.

I would generally be wary of such a question, but I saw where it was coming from and said: "Yes." The person who had asked me further questioned me: "Have you put *tefillin* today?"

I smiled. "Here we go again," I thought. Of course, I hadn't put *tefillin* that day, the previous, and so on. I never put *tefillin*. Unless I'd been asked the same question by people like the guy who had just asked me. He was a Lubavitcher, as evidenced by his attire, which included a black coat, a black hat, and a clean white shirt. He was accompanied by a few other yeshiva-bound teenagers, all asking random Jewish-looking men passing by if they were Jewish and had put *tefillin* on that day.

My wife is not Jewish, and this was her first meeting with a Lubavitcher, so I had to explain the situation to her. I told her I'd probably never have another chance to put *tefillin* in Times Square during Christmas. I decided to go ahead. One more time, for old times' sake. So, I told the young Lubavitcher that I hadn't put on *tefillin* that day and would be delighted if he helped me put them.

I knew exactly what was going to happen and why it was happening, although my research about Chabad Lubavitch had taken place in my home country of Argentina. I knew all this because Chabad Lubavitch works almost the same way worldwide. Of course, each country creates its own institutions and employs its own people, but they all share the same global mission, the same goals, and use the same tools. Lubavitch teenagers have approached me on a Friday afternoon (I really have a Jewish physiognomy because all of my grandparents and great-grandparents were Jewish immigrants from Ukraine, Russia, and Lithuania) in my hometown of Buenos Aires, New York, and Toronto, Canada, where I've been living since 2017. I experienced exactly the same situation each time. Once you know one specific Chabad Lubavitch, you know all about Chabad Lubavitch.

The author putting on tefillin on New York's Times Square. December 25, 2016.

This book was written between 2009 and 2010 and is focused on Argentina. However, its testimonials, anecdotes, research, and conclusions remain as valid and valuable as they were when and where it was first published. Also, as explained, they can be universalized to understand how Chabad Lubavitch, one of the most well-known and fastest-growing Orthodox Jewish congregations, works worldwide.

Chabad Lubavitch is all around the world, and some of their Hasidim have even gained political notoriety during the last few years. Knowing who they are, what they want, and how they are achieving their goals is as important today as it was when this book was first written and published.

While some people mentioned in this book have either departed from Chabad Lubavitch or are no longer in this Earthly realm, their stories, testimonials, and life experiences are fundamental to understanding and answering the questions Chabad raises.

A.J. Soifer, Ph.D.
Toronto, Ontario
August 2023

How would you define the aim of Chabad Lubavitch? What would you say is the raison d'être of Chabad?

It has several facets. The first is to ensure the continuity of the Jewish people by strengthening the connection with their roots: the observance of the *mitzvot*. And to help, motivate, not impose, not preach, but to stimulate, to excite the Jew to connect with his origin through fulfilling the precepts in their daily life. We do not believe in the once-a-year Jew. We do not believe in the "Jewish experience." We believe that what defines a culture is not what is done in a particular way. What defines the living culture of a community is their daily routine: a *kasher* McDonald's, going to play soccer wearing a yarmulke, a *kasher* barbeque. That represents the living Jewish people. Holding a congress of scholars and intellectuals on Judaism does not represent the Jewish people.

We seek that the Jewish people LIVE, and that is achieved through the daily observance of the *mitzvot*; we seek to bring them closer, and we understand that patience, help, encouragement, and support are needed. And we are there for that.

The first aim is to strengthen the Jewish people through observing the precepts and studying the *Torah*. The dissemination of the knowledge of God, the dissemination of the knowledge of the soul, of the soul of the *Torah*, is the second aim of the Chabad movement. A Lubavitcher is a person who works on his person to strengthen his connection with God every day and his relationship with other Jews, but this starts from personal work through study and personal observance. So that a person can become a genuine servant of God, this is developed through a trinomial integrated by God, the *Torah,* and the people of Israel. Then comes a part of Chabad's work that aspires to unite the entire Jewish people. To work so that we are one and connect with our roots, the *Torah*. Let us not discard a single Jew. Let us not lose a single Jew.

Finally, another aspect of Chabad's work, considering that we are very close to the arrival of the *Messiah*, is to foster faith and expectation of his coming and to prepare the world from authentic Jewish sources, not from cheap words, but from the texts.

A.J. SOIFER, PH.D.

Rabbi Tzvi Grunblatt
General director of Chabad Lubavitch in Argentina, in an interview with
the author on January 8, 2010.

Prologue

Who Wants to be a Lubavitcher?

My first contact with Chabad Lubavitch was one afternoon in April or May 2008 at the "Alberto Gerchunoff" Library of the *Sociedad Hebraica Argentina* [Argentinian Hebrew Society], a secular Jewish community sports and cultural club where I worked for seven years. Until then, my knowledge about Judaism was between basic and null. I knew that I "was Jewish" only because my parents had always told me so, because when the months of April and September arrived, I attended family gatherings to celebrate the Pesach and Rosh Hashanah holidays, and because we had to juggle to see which day we would celebrate with my paternal family and which day we would celebrate with my maternal family.

Beyond eating the traditional stuffed fish (*guefilte fish*) and unleavened bread, matzah (my paternal grandmother, who, until a few years ago kneaded the fish with her own hands for hours, was not afraid of committing the heresy of putting braided bread, next to matzah on the same Pesach table, something wholly forbidden according to Jewish customs), we did not comply with any tradition.

The door of my house does not have that little box with parchment written with biblical blessings (mezuzah); I did not receive a Jewish education; I had only visited a synagogue twice before starting this research (and always for tourist reasons); I was not circumcised; I did not have an official celebration of bar *mitzvah*, and my family has had a tradition of atheism for at least two or three generations (except, perhaps, on my maternal grandmother's side, who has her own ideas about God, although far from the precepts of the canonical Judaism.)

Within my family circle, being Jewish was always an amorphous set of vague ideas of belonging: an anecdote about my grandmother's starvation in her birthplace of Vilnius, then Poland and now Lithuania; some distant relatives who died during the Holocaust, and a matter of blood: "You are Jewish because your blood is Jewish," my mother told me when I asked her as a child.

Judaism was never explicitly discussed in my home. Any knowledge I had was filtered through Zionism, in which the State of Israel appeared vaguely and nebulously as a second home, a place to worry about and read the papers for news about it.

My Judaism was by opposition: I grew up with the anguish of feeling persecuted by irrational hatred, ashamed to say that I am Jewish because I didn't understand what it was about other than that it was an excuse for people to despise me.

When I was fifteen years old, I saw Schindler's List on TV, and it reaffirmed my fear and anchored my perception that to be a Jew was to be persecuted.

For the rest, being Jewish has always connoted to me both an ideal of belonging to an educated minority and, perhaps because of my ignorance and naivete, the notion that "being Jewish is synonymous with being a good person" and that "there can be no Jews of bad faith."

Naturally, I gave up that naïve dream as I started interacting with my community. This didn't happen until 2008, with my trip to Israel for Taglit-Birthright Israel, the first time I interacted with other Jews.

I began working at the Sociedad Hebraica Argentina in 2003, but not even there, in the library, amidst the great works of Jewish thought and in regular contact with community members, did I feel the slightest glimmer of interest in anything I considered being just folkloric.

Orthodox Judaism did not interest me even superficially; I saw it as the ways of some crazy strangers, people who did not represent me, with whom I felt such a weak bond that they appeared to me as distant, lost cousins with whom one has no relationship.

In 2008, I traveled to Israel and met a new version of my own Judaism, which I understood as belonging.

One noon, gathered at my paternal grandmother's house with my family, six months after starting this research, I wanted to inquire about my origins. Rabbi Tzvi Grunblatt, general director of Chabad Lubavitch in Argentina, had asked me if I had any relation with the Jewish sage who lived in the XVIII and XIX centuries, Chatam Sofer. Rabbi Grunblatt told me that all of us Soifer would be his descendants. From then on, something that would typically not have piqued my interest became so intense that I began comparing family trees. When I found a portrait photo of Sofer on Wikipedia and saw that the eminent scholar and myself bore a strong resemblance in profile, my interest became even more intense. I wanted to find out where my family came from, whether any ancestor might have been an observant Jew, and why not, even Lubavitchers.

My aunts Helena and Lila told me that my great-great-grandfather was the last religious in my grandfather's family line. He was a Torah scholar who devoted all his time to it without worrying about other duties and occupations. As a result, my great-great-grandmother had to provide for her large family and ended her days exhausted.

They were poor. The couple shared a bed with their children in a modest house in a remote village between Ukraine and Russia.

When my great-great-grandmother came home exhausted from working all day, she would fall on the bed, crushing several of my great-great-uncles, who died of asphyxiation.

This re-enactment of the myth of Cronus, the Greek God who ate his children, apparently prompted my forefathers to seek advice from their local rabbi about how to stop losing their children.

The rabbi ordered the family goat to be tied to the bed. My great-great-grandmother would faint from exhaustion after working all day. With the goat tied to the bed, the animal would bleat when she fell over her children, saving their lives.

I owe my existence to the goat then and to a hollow table where my other great-grandfather hid during a pogrom that killed his entire family.

He was twelve when he embarked on a journey with other orphans to Argentina.

All that, for me, is my Judaism.

But that afternoon in 2008, when I was in the library, I saw a lady come in to ask me for Hebrew-Spanish and Spanish-Hebrew dictionaries; I was still uninterested in anything to do with Judaism.

I knew by ear some things that had been told to me about Chabad Lubavitch: that they paid you to take Judaism classes with them, that they were retrograde fanatics, that they brainwashed you and turned you, out of nowhere, into an ultra-fanatic like them.

I had never seen the lady before, nor did I assume she was Orthodox, much less Lubavitch.

She came a few days in a row; she would ask me for the dictionaries and sit at one of the first reader's tables, where she would consult and take notes. After a week, she felt confident and would go straight in to fetch the heavy dictionary volumes. Up to that point, we exchanged nothing more than a few polite words until one afternoon, after spending about an hour reading and taking notes, she got up, left the dictionaries resting on the top shelf, and approached me.

"Excuse me, can I talk to you for a few minutes?" she asked.

I put the book I was reading on my desk and smiled at her.

"Of course."

"How are you? How are you? How are you? Nice to meet you. My name is Rivke, and first, I want to clarify that I have a degree in political science, a doctorate, and… well… I don't want to give you all my credentials so that you don't think I'm overloading you with information, or that I'm arrogant, or I don't know what…," she told me. "Besides, I was a teacher, a school principal, and, well… First, let me tell you that ten years ago, I used to see all these men dressed in black with those little curls (and she made a gesture like a curl falling behind her ears) and the hat. I thought: 'These guys are crazy!' Then, one day, I was surprised by something I never thought would happen to me. I heard another voice, another reality. I started to attend the synagogue and celebrate Shabbat, and then, look, today my son is dressed in black, with a hat and curly hair! Thank God! And I dress in long stockings and wear a wig, you see?"

Until that moment, I had not noticed that she was wearing a wig. I barely distinguished her as another person who showed up daily to look for information or research in the library.

"I don't want to be tiresome or bother you or anything like that," she continued. "There are different ways of seeing reality. To decide, one has to accept the idea that the other exists and get to know it. So, what I say to you, just like that, without commitment or anything. I do not want money or anything from you. No rabbi put a gun to my head and told me what to do. I discovered it by myself. I say the same to you, if you want to come one day and see, I do not know, for example, on Shabbat, you come to the synagogue, listen to the rabbi, a very cool nice guy, and you see. And then you stay for a while, and you can have dinner with him or with us, and that way, you get to know a new way of seeing reality a little better."

I nodded, a little confused and overwhelmed by her speech, which had been quick and unexpected. It was the first time I had spoken to an Orthodox person, and I had never crossed a single word with a rabbi, so what she was telling me sounded extreme and strange.

"Do you know that God," she continued, "has a plan? That I have come here and that you are here is not by chance. I am not telling you that God sent me or anything like that.

I say there is a reason we converged in this space so that I could give you this message. I hope you can hear it. I will bring you the magazine for which I am translating when it comes out. I will give it to you for free!"

"All right, I'll think about it, okay?" I said.

"Yes, yes, don't worry. I hope you think about it. I will keep coming here. You can tell me and come with us to the Shabbat dinner whenever you want."

I told her that someday, maybe, I would go to the Shabbat dinner with her, and I kept thinking that I didn't know why, but maybe the lady was right with the idea that things happen for a certain reason. But as soon as she had left, I had already forgotten about the whole thing and discarded the idea that there is a destiny.

***

Rivke didn't show up again for a while, and I had forgotten about it until she called me at work.

"Hello, it's me, the religious lady. I wanted to ask you if you have decided to come to spend the night of Shabbat with the rabbi."

I politely declined the proposal, making up some excuse, and forgot about the whole thing again. She came again a few days later, puffed out her chest as if to speak, and greeted me. Before she could say anything to me, I told her I would not go to her dinner that Friday either. I apologized, and she replied I did not have to apologize for anything; it was not a problem.

"When you can come, you will see that the blessing from heaven is incredible," she told me.

She rummaged through his wallet and pulled out a nylon pouch.

"Oh, it's a little damaged... I hope it's okay. Here, I brought you a little present because I was passing by," she said, handing me candy and a can of soda.

I received them and thanked her without understanding what I was supposed to do.

"I'm bothering you with something else," she said. "I don't know if I already asked you... I don't know how to ask you.... well, I must. What is your mother's last name?"

I frowned. Because Judaism is "inherited" through the maternal line, if my mother wasn't Jewish, I wasn't Jewish either.

"Samoilovich," I said.

"Ah," she said and sighed, "Do you know why I asked you that?"

"A Jew is the son of a Jewish mother, according to the law of the womb."

"Exactly. Can I tell you something?"

"Yes."

"How old are you?"

"Twenty-four."

"Do you know there are kids your age who wear black clothes and hats and get up every day at six in the morning because they must be at synagogue from seven in the morning and spend the whole day studying? I mean, it must be fun, right? Because if not, they wouldn't do it, don't you think? I'm not telling you this to convince you to become an Orthodox Jew. I'm just telling you. Well, Alex, I'll spend today working on my translations."

I handed her the Hebrew dictionary and went back to my business. She stayed in the library a while longer and said goodbye.

Over the next few weeks, she insisted on inviting me to a Shabbat dinner with her and the rabbi, and I kept declining.

I told my boss, Debora, who told me Rivke had also approached her with the same proposal. She had accepted, gone with her husband and children, and spent a Shabbat dinner with Rivke, the rabbi, and his family.

"It is an interesting experience. My children had a lot of fun with the rabbi's children," Debora said.

As I started to consider it, I realized I had no trouble accepting the dinner invitation and that it might even be interesting for me to view Judaism from a different angle than the one I had been taught about my entire life at home.

***

"Genius! You are a genius!" shouted Rivke from the other end of the line. I had just accepted her invitation to join her and the rabbi for a Shabbat dinner. "You'll love it. HaShem, our Lord, will be so happy! Shall we meet at seven o'clock in the evening at 1164 Agüero Street? After that, we go to the rabbi's house."

When I finished work that Friday, I walked to the "Agüero synagogue," Chabad's headquarters in Argentina.

I passed a brief interrogation at the security checkpoint and went inside.

At a counter, in front of an open door, stood Rivke, praying with her eyes closed. She saw me enter and approached me with open arms.

"Alex, you showed up!" She spoke while keeping a safe distance to avoid touching me, then vertically bent her knees. "I'm so glad you came. Do you feel like listening to a class with people your age? After the class, we will head to the rabbi's house."

"I'll do whatever you say," I said.

"Perfect, come with me then." She led me to a room across the reception area, next to some armchairs where a couple of Orthodox Jews were chatting.

"Do you need a yarmulke?"

"No need," I said, taking out of my backpack one my grandmother had lent me to attend a Taglit-Birthright Israel meeting.

I entered the classroom, and Rivke disappeared, leaving me in the middle of a bunch of young faces that turned to look at me.

At the head of the table, a rabbi was teaching a class, holding a boy only five years old or so on his lap.

For a long while, I sat there, not understanding the rabbi's words. He was talking about ideas I didn't understand, using Hebrew words I didn't fully comprehend, and tending to his infant, who kept wriggling around on top of him, kicking and thrashing, and falling to the ground only for him to pick him back up again on his lap.

After a few questions from the students, they passed around a booklet of printed sheets, on each page of which there was a Kabbalistic concept explained and graphed with some basic drawings.

The rabbi explained:

"Judaism is a religion with many rules. If you are disorganized, you will be a bad Jew. For example, in the Shulchan Aruch, the book that codifies Jewish laws, by the great rabbi Josef Karo, everything is written: from how Jews should tie their shoes and cut their nails to the laws governing punishment for serious crimes."

Someone asked him to explain how Jews should cut their nails.

"Nails are impure elements. They are associated with death because they continue to grow after a person has died. As a result, they are impure and must be treated differently. They must not be cut as they are cut for the dead. A Jew must cut his nails by skipping a finger: one finger, yes, one finger, no. And first the right hand and then the left. The right hand is always better in Judaism. And with shoes too, put them on in a certain way, tie them differently..."

Some laughs were heard.

"You laugh, but it is a matter of faith. If you are a Jew and don't do this, it's not that God will send you a strike of lightning. But you are committing a fault. It's not as serious as eating ham, but it is still a fault. Well, boys, we'll leave it here for today," said the rabbi. "Of course, you are all invited to stay for the Shabbat celebration."

My classmates got up, and I thought I would follow suit. So I exited the classroom, removed my yarmulke, and returned to Rivke, who was still reading a prayer book and moving his body in quick bows behind the front desk.

"Alex! Alex! Alex! What happened?"

"Nothing, the class is over, and I wanted to see if we were leaving…"

"No! Please come back. Kabbalat Shabbat is about to begin," she said, leading me back to the classroom.

I put the yarmulke back on my head, sighed, and went inside.

I sat at the table as the last woman crossed the threshold into the other half of the room, now divided by partitions. A rabbi I had not seen until then pulled them aside and separated us by gender.

They handed out siddurim (prayer books) with one page in Hebrew and a facing page, half in Hebrew phonetics with the Latin alphabet, and half translated into Spanish.

Two rabbis facing west followed the reading with their own books. Then, one shouted a prayer, and the other pounded the table.

The rabbis started shouting out the page to read.

"Page nineteen, where it says: 'God, King of the Universe.'"

We quietly read the passage until the other rabbi pointed to another page.

I tried to follow what was being read, but I didn't understand a single word, and the part that was in Spanish didn't make sense to me.

I still did not understand what exactly was happening when one rabbi said:

"All rise up!"

"Now we pray aloud!" cried the other rabbi.

A line began forming around the table when we finished reading that prayer. I saw myself in the mirrored window, wearing a yarmulke and not praying because I didn't understand anything, following the little human train and being followed from behind by a rabbi with a long white beard in the middle of a religious manifestation I'd never seen before. I felt strange.

We did a few laps around the table, and when we finished, we returned to where we were before we started the rounds.

The rabbi in the lead ordered a standing prayer facing Jerusalem.

We stood and stayed like that for a while. I didn't know when the prayer was over, so I stood fixedly facing east until a new order called us to sit down.

Then, another man in black came in with a silver tray containing a chalice and a bottle of ceremonial grape juice. They served the juice in little plastic cups. Yet another Orthodox man came in with a tray containing chocolate doughnuts, pastrami, cucumber, and palm hearts.

The officiating rabbi poured the wine into the cup until it spilled over and then raised it while reading a prayer.

When it was over, we were invited for a toast.

"Make yourselves at home, boys," the rabbi told us. Then they pulled out the screen separating the room, and the women returned to join us for the toast.

The rabbi, who seemed more experienced, stood in the middle of the room, remarked that there were many fresh faces at the ceremony, and talked about debt in Judaism.

"A Jew must lend an ear to another Jew, but that debt must be repaid."

He then commented that the land must be given a year of rest every seven years and not be farmed. However, this does not excuse the Jew before God from paying his debts because God does not forget. If someone tries to take refuge in the law of the seventh-year rest not to pay a debt, a council of rabbis intervenes to solve the conflict.

"God does the same," said the rabbi. "You can ask God, and he will give you. He is pure love, but you will have to give him back. And how does God want you to give him back? By fulfilling the Jewish law. We are his most beloved people, so he wants us to continue our customs and educate your children in his law. You will tell me: 'But I was born into a secular family! I didn't know!' No problem! God forgives you! God erases that debt; he cleans the slate, and now that you know, he starts counting the debt."

Upon hearing these words, I thought the rabbi was turning around the infamy that makes the Jews greedy creditors, presenting them as eternal debtors to God instead.

I helped myself to a sandwich and a glass of soda when I felt someone tap me on the shoulder from behind. I turned around, and there was the rabbi who had just spoken.

"You are Alex, aren't you?"

"I am, yes."

"How are you? I'm Moshe. I understand you're having dinner at home tonight?"

"Ye... yes," I stammered.

He smiled at me.

"Perfect. Shall we get going?"

***

Rivke, the rabbi, another gentleman, and I walked out of the synagogue together.

"You know, rabbi, I always wanted to bring Alex here with us for dinner."

The rabbi nodded calmly. He was inviting me to eat at his house on a Friday night without knowing me. Nothing like this had ever happened to me before.

We walked down Agüero Street a few blocks, but not so many that the prescription of riding in transportation during the Sabbath rest could not be endured. I wondered what the dinner would be like, if it would be anything like the ones I'd had with my family for holidays like Rosh Hashanah and Pesach.

"I told Debora to come with her family, but I really wanted to bring you, Alex," Rivke told me happily.

As soon as we left the synagogue, I took off my yarmulke. The other man who accompanied us still had it on his head and was now talking to Rabbi Moshe.

We walked for a while in silence.

"Did you know I am traveling to Israel soon?" I commented to Rivke.

"Really? Oh! I knew the blessings were with you! What a thrill, Alex, and who are you traveling with? "

"With Taglit-Birthright Israel."

"With whom?"

"Taglit. Birthright Israel."

"What is that?"

"Taglit is a charitable organization whose main tenet is that every Jew has a right to know Israel, so they offer a ten-day tour of the country for a very low cost. All included." It seemed odd to me that someone as involved in the Jewish community as Rivke had not heard of Taglit.

"That is amazing!"

We crossed the street.

"Yes, it is."

"It's great, Alex! You're going to get to know Israel!"

We arrived at the intersection between Santa Fe Avenue and Agüero Street. I went ahead and spoke briefly with the rabbi.

Something in his investiture attracted me, his wisdom, his knowledge about issues that I felt distantly affected me but that, in the end, belonged to me by cultural heritage.

"So, Alex...," said the rabbi, "you are going to honor us with your presence at the Shabbat's table."

I blushed.

"Yes, well, thanks for inviting me to participate and...."

"Don't even say it! The table will always be served and open. And tell me, Alex... how did you get interested in coming?"

"I am looking for my roots, rabbi," I said, surprised by my answer. I wasn't sure if I felt compromised with him or if something about my origins led me in that direction.

"Judaism is like a boomerang: the farther you throw it, the stronger it comes back. So, you know, we encourage young people to re-encounter their Judaism... that is why we have study groups like the one you saw. They are very nice, aren't they?"

"Indeed."

"Did you know that those who take our course can travel on a scholarship to New York City at the end of the year? It is an enriching trip, very educational... they get to know the Chabad headquarters there and visit the Rebbe's tomb..."

"I heard something about the program, yes."

"You can come. Today, you've seen more or less how it works."

"I will think about it. As I was saying, I am still searching."

"A Jew will always be a Jew. He will always be drawn back to his essence, no matter how well-hidden and assimilated he is in the Diaspora."

I didn't know what to say.

"They call us Orthodox," he told me as he directed me to turn at the corner of Beruti Street. "I don't know why. We prefer to call ourselves 'observers.'"

"There are many divisions in Judaism, aren't there?"

"Many. It's a real shame. That's because, at a certain moment in history, it was said that Judaism was a religion with too many rules, too strict, that no one could follow. It was said that if we wanted to preserve ourselves as a people, we needed to loosen some of our rules. Thus, the Conservatives were born. It's a real shame. We think just the opposite. We think we must remain faithful to our customs to avoid being assimilated by other cultures and other people. And they call us Orthodox. But as I told you, we are 'observers.'"

We walked silently with the rabbi for a while, and suddenly, I felt observed by everyone passing by on the street. I was next to a guy in black with a hat and a beard that reached his chest.

"We don't accept conversions either. You are born a Jew. If you are not born a Jew, you cannot choose to be one. That's why we are also against the burials of converts in the sacred cemeteries of Judaism," the rabbi finished saying.

***

We arrived at his apartment building.

Moshe removed a key from his belt, placed it on his side, close to his body, and without stretching his arm, inserted it into the lock, turned it, opened the door, and invited us in.

"By stairs," he said.

"Yes, it's twenty-four floors," said Rivke, and without wasting time, she clarified. "No, no, it's a joke, it's a joke, it's on the second floor. It's just that we can't use the elevator during Shabbat."

We climbed the stairs and were met at the open door of the second floor by the rabbi's wife, accompanied by some of her seven children.

"Shalom! Welcome."

"Make yourself comfortable," Rivke told me.

I left my bag on an armchair.

The rabbi removed his hat (he wore a yarmulke underneath) and jacket, leaving him in a suspender shirt.

There were huge bookshelves full of Hasidic books all around us.

I was introduced to Esther, another woman wearing a wig.

We sat in the armchairs, and the man who had walked with us told us he was a pediatrician who had recently read a poem dedicated to the Prague golem by Jorge Luis Borges.

Moshe explained the legend, which he said was an actual historical fact.

"A rabbi created the Prague golem to protect the city's Jews from attacks by Christians who persecuted us and accused us of witchcraft and other things," explained the rabbi.

"They said that our matzah was made with the blood of Christian children," added the doctor.

"Exactly," nodded Moses. "Well, using a very secret Kabbalistic formula, and through God, this rabbi could give life to the golem, a living clay statue. But since only God can create humans, the golem could not speak," he said and looked for some books. One was The Story of the Prague Golem, written in Portuguese, and the other was the same book but written in English. He opened them and looked for a page with pictures of the statues.

"It is time for supper," said the rabbi's wife, entering the kitchen.

Moshe said something in Hebrew to one of his sons, who nodded and followed his mother into the kitchen.

Then the rabbi grabbed a yarmulke resting on one bookshelf, sat down next to me on the armrest of the armchair, and said,

"Alex... we are going to have dinner, and I need you to wear a yarmulke... do you have one or want to borrow this one?" He said while tracing his finger along the yarmulke's interior.

"No need. I have one of my own." I told him.

"Alex, the Rabbi will show you where to sit," Rivke told me.

And so it was. The rabbi told me to sit between the pediatrician and one of his children on the right. He sat at the head and Rivke, Esther, his wife, and two daughters in front.

The table was divided into male and female sectors, all under the rabbi at the head and all of us under the scrutinizing gaze of Menachem Mendel Schneerson, the last Lubavitch Rebbe, whose portrait, in various modalities (serious, reading the Torah, smiling at his followers, his facial expressions protruding from a mountain), decorated the room walls.

"Before we sit down to eat," said the rabbi, "we must wash our hands. It is not a matter of hygiene but part of a prayer. Then we will break the challah, and until we are done with the ceremony, we cannot talk. So come with us to the kitchen."

The doctor went first; the ritual involved throwing three squirts of water from a pitcher with two handles. The pediatrician complied without difficulty, and I got nervous when it was my turn. I felt I would probably do it wrong, which could offend the people there.

I started to throw the water on myself, and the rabbi said:

"Now repeat with me," and he made me repeat sentences in Hebrew, which I followed by phonetic imitation.

When we finished, we went to the table while the women continued the ritual.

The rabbi ordered silence, broke the bread, threw salt on the table, and passed it around. Then he poured sweet wine into a metal cup until it overflowed, as had happened earlier in the synagogue, and then recited a prayer.

He gave each of us a piece of challah and gestured for us to eat it.

We finished that first piece of bread, and Rivke told me,

"You can relax, Alex. When I came here for the first time, I thought they were all crazy. I didn't know anything about what I was doing, either. You take it easy."

The rabbi's wife went into the kitchen and returned with two enormous platters of gefilte fish and a beef stew. I felt at one of my family's Jewish holiday celebrations. Still, with a level of observance, I had never experienced before. That wasn't Judaism to me. Or the Judaism I had experienced was not Judaism. I was confused.

The pediatrician reflected,

"I don't know why they hate us so much. Just imagine: a hundred Nobel Prize winners were Jews."

We nodded silently.

"The State of Israel must be defended with our blood. Not an inch of land for the Arabs," continued the man.

The rabbi asked him how he had arrived at his table that night. He told us he had just divorced his wife and had been looking for a place to spend Passover because he no longer had a family. Also, in Lomas de Zamora, where he lived, there were no collective celebrations like in Buenos Aires City, and by chance, or better put, by God, he had arrived at the Agüero Street synagogue.

"Alex, we have heard little from you," said Moshe.

"I am listening and learning."

"I don't understand atheists," said the pediatrician as he put a piece of fish in his mouth.

"Don't worry about atheists, as they are not to be pitied," replied the rabbi. "In fact, it is impossible to be an atheist."

I chewed silently, feeling touched by his comment, wanting to defend my atheistic Judaism but not daring to do so out loud.

"No one can deny God because no one has such knowledge!"

Afterward, the rabbi told us he had been born in Venezuela. His father was Cuban, and he had been a right-wing religious hero in Israel. He had even been on a ship sunk by Ben Gurion, a leftist. He was retired and now lived in Miami. For his part, the rabbi had previously lived in New York, Paraguay, and other countries.

"At Chabad, we always say: 'Join Chabad and travel the world.'"

"Why is it like that?"

"It's that we carry Judaism all over the world. It is our mission. Imagine that in Paraguay, we founded the first synagogue in the city where we settled."

"Interesting."

"You know, for example," the rabbi introduced a new topic of conversation, "Darwin's theory of evolution has already been disproved, don't you?"

I chewed slowly.

"No, no, tell us, rabbi," said Esther.

"Of course, since the genome of man was discovered and compared with that of the monkey, it has been discovered that they have nothing to do with each other."

I wished my friend, who has a Ph.D. in genetics, was at the table right then because I would have liked to hear the conversation.

The rabbi's eldest daughter said,

"I was taught in school that the monkey descended from man."

Rivke and Esther looked at her with affection. The pediatrician next to me had a glass of soda. The other children of the couple had gone to rest on the couches.

"It turns out that the monkeys are the men who were left out of Noah's Ark. They degenerated into monkeys," added the little girl.

"Of course," nodded the rabbi, smiling.

"Actually, the gorillas," the girl finished.

The rabbi's wife returned to the kitchen and brought lemon brownie ice cream for dessert.

"Alex, I'll speak on behalf of the rabbi because I know he'll agree; if you want to continue the conversation from tonight, send him an e-mail."

"Yes, of course. It has been a pleasure to have you here, Alex," he said.

"Well, thank you."

We finished dinner and did another prayer that ended with a small symbolic finger-washing ceremony to get the salt off.

"Rabbi, we are leaving," said Rivke.

"All right, all right."

He escorted us to the door downstairs and dismissed us.

"I hope to see you again soon," he said.

I said goodbye to them.

"Do you know how to get home?" they asked me.

"Yes, I live nearby. It is a short walk from here."

"Well, Alex, see you soon. I'll call you during the week, okay?"

"No problem," I said.

I crossed the street and was about halfway down the block when I realized I was still wearing the yarmulke. So, I took it off and threw it into my purse.

Chapter One
Who Fears Chabad Lubavitch?

> "I discovered that no one in the Jewish world is neutral about Chabad. Everyone has an opinion, and much of the time it's not very flattering. One editor of a Jewish newspaper called me to say Chabad was 'taking over the city' where she lived. What does that mean? Are they running the other rabbis out of town with shotguns? Are they multiplying so quickly that they're skewing the Jewish demographics? Hardly. And yet over and over I've heard the same warning, sometimes delivered in a whisper, sometimes in an exasperated shout: They're taking over. But what exactly are they taking over? And who's letting them do it?"
>
> Sue Fishkoff, *The Rebbe's Army*

"Your grandma told me you are writing a book about Chabad. How are you planning to approach the subject?"

"I have not thought of a particular approach yet. I aim to be as unbiased as possible."

"You should aim for a critical approach."

"Why is that? What is there to criticize about them?"

"What is to criticize? Well, that they brainwash you, of course. I can accept that they also get you nice things. They will not give you money but get you nice things. For example, the son of a friend of mine was without a job. His life was a disaster, and suddenly, he got involved with them, and they took him to the United States and got him a job. But they brainwashed him, of course."

***

"He was a good guy, but they poisoned his head, and now he's with the Lubavitch."

***

"I am writing about Chabad."
   "The Lubavitch?"
   "Yes."
   "Be careful…"

***

"They traffic drugs, precious stones. Where else do they get so much money? I know people who became rich overnight. They have two houses, one in the city and another in the suburbs; they have four cars. Where did they get the money from? Nobody will tell you, but that's how it is. They take drugs before doing the religious service, and thus, their hearing is sharpened. How else can they hear so well? Before giving service, they will sniff a shot of cocaine. But nobody will tell you about this. There were Chabad rabbis imprisoned for passing drugs. That is well documented, but nobody will tell you about it because nobody wants to get caught. It is not documented that they pass drugs, but everybody knows that. Their Rebbe, who was in prison, was taken out because they put money in. I have acquaintances who saw it. I saw it. They are thieves, outlaws, and drug addicts. They sell drugs; they live off theft. Are you going to publish that? No one will believe it, but I saw it. They are a sect. Religious Jews are sects. You'd better do something about it. Are you going to publish that?"

   "Well, why don't you give me your testimony so I can put it into the book?"

   "No, I can't. I don't want to. I don't want to. What for? They won't let you publish it."

   "Let me be the one who deals with the publisher. Just give me your testimonial."

   "No, no, I can't. I have rabbi friends who will come to me to…"

"But I won't put your name on the book."

"I rather not. And you, you'd better stay out of it because they'll stick a knife in your back. Be careful."

"Give me your testimonial. I will record it and then investigate your allegations."

"Forget it. I can tell you they are drug addicts and drug dealers. I was a sympathizer for many years. I went to New York on their trips. I went to the Rebbe's grave. He has been dead for over two decades. Still, they worship him as if he were Jesus Christ. For that, let them become goyim. Everything is the Rebbe this, the Rebbe that, and they show you videos of the Rebbe in every public event they perform."

***

The above are some actual comments I received from people when I mentioned the name of Chabad Lubavitch on different occasions and places.

No one seems indifferent to the Chabad phenomenon; fear usually comes first. So why does a group of Orthodox Jews generate so much fear among secular Jews?

The impressive worldwide growth of Chabad Lubavitch from 1978 until today can be considered a trigger of susceptibilities. This is particularly true in an era that has seen decreased the influence of religious discourses in most of the Western world.

The rise of secularism and other problems that have plagued Judaism since the State of Israel was founded don't seem to have hurt Chabad Lubavitch. Instead, they are present and influential in the Jewish community in a way that would have been unthinkable for an orthodox religious group in the past.

Their Chabad Centres (*Beit Chabad*) have expanded worldwide and continue to grow.

Damián Setton is a sociologist who studied the Chabad Lubavitch phenomenon for his master's and doctorate degrees. He analyzes the phenomenon of the prejudices generated by the Lubavitch: "I believe it is not because of a Chabad issue that this fear is generated. In principle, they are power struggles in the Jewish community. It is logical, and examples can be found in any other social collective. For example, suppose a group within a social collective grows. In that case, it is logical that other community sectors will feel afraid. They're going to say, 'Well, how far are these guys going to advance? What's going to happen to the people who are with me? Are they going to go with them?' At the same time, there's competition for money. Because the Jewish community largely depends on benefactors."

Jewish Orthodoxy is a sizeable global movement that brings together different and sometimes contradictory ideas about Judaism. In general (though broad statements about such a broad field are difficult to make), these movements can be identified by their literal, non-metaphorical readings of the Bible.

According to tradition, God dictated the Torah to Moses on Mount Sinai following the Jews' escape from Egypt. Moses then communicated the Torah to his disciples. Judaism's sectarian nature comes directly from the prophet's teachings being spread to many people. With so many disciples, each one understood God's complicated rules in his own way.

Jewish Orthodoxy has the most extreme and, to a large extent, fundamentalist view in this field of reinterpretation. It believes that the Old Testament is an accurate record of history and a guide for living.

The Torah (the biblical Pentateuch and the Talmud) has a series of 613 precepts that God is supposed to have commanded the Jews to fulfill. Orthodoxy is known for following God's laws precisely as they have been written for thousands of years. This is because they take the Torah and the *mitzvot* (precepts) to heart. Orthodox Jews believe that the context is immutable; the same rules that applied to a nomadic tribe that crossed a desert 3,000 years ago also apply to a Jew who lives in New York City today or a Russian Jew who lived in Siberia during the Bolshevik revolution.

The Jewish emancipation movements and the so-called "Jewish enlightenment," followed by Zionism, created a Jewish identity that differed from this view and the more "religious" version of Judaism. These movements saw Judaism not only as a religion but also as a nationality and a transnational identity that includes customs, rites, ancestors, mythology, and at least three mother tongues (Ladino, Yiddish, and Hebrew). In its absolute rejection of modernization and non-religious Judaism, Orthodoxy has permanently erected high walls against any influence from the secular world that might push its members away from the path of the Torah.

From there, Jewish Orthodoxy imposed its laws on contemporary media such as television, motion pictures, music, non-Jewish books, and other items.

However, Chabad Lubavitch plays in much more complex territory. Their interpretation of Judaism means many things don't work the same way as they do for other Jewish Orthodox. They maintain a good part of the prohibitions but do not reject some particular use of technological tools.

Lubavitch men don't stop wearing black or take off their yarmulkes, and Lubavitch women never wear pants. However, that doesn't mean they can't have a Facebook page or a Twitter account if they can use these ultra-modern tools to spread Judaism and serve God.

However, people who look at the phenomenon from the outside don't know about these differences within Orthodoxy. Instead, they see a group of obscurantist fanatics who look identical. This is where a lot of the prejudice against Chabad comes from. As Rabbi Mordechai Birman of Beit Chabad Villa Crespo in one of Buenos Aires' most "Jewish" neighborhoods acknowledges: "I think it is our fault to some extent. For many years, we could not show others they were our brothers and that we were still brothers even though I wore a yarmulke while the other person did not or that I performed a *mitzvah* while the other person did not. We should love and respect each other. Still, well, I think there is guilt on both sides. But we, as we supposedly study Torah more, should be more open. We are doing it with all the activities and everything that Chabad does. But for many years, there was an enormous distance between Orthodox Jews and those who were Jewish but not Orthodox, and that remained. Slowly, the ice was broken. Today, I think it is not so much the case".

Without a doubt, no other Orthodox Jewish movement sought to include, rather than exclude, those who were Jewish but not religiously observant, and that made its customs, visions, and practices so visible.

The prejudice is not just directed at Chabad, according to Rabbi Aharon Stawski of another Beit Chabad in the heart of Buenos Aires. The rabbi says, "The prejudice is against everything religious, which is different. Every Jew has two souls. He has an animal soul and a divine soul. They are set one against the other, and the person struggles internally. Every Jew is half schizophrenic by himself. That's normal because he tends towards one thing or the other. That's how it is. That's how God made us. You have free will because there are two equal forces, and you must choose. If we chose only for good, we would be angels, monkeys, or robots. Many non-religious people say about us: 'They are like little monkeys; they are like robots.' But it is not like that. It is a fight inside yourself that you must have. Everything is a struggle. It is not easy at all. The more you want to get closer to questions of spirituality and divinity, the more difficult the struggle becomes. When you see the other person doing what a Jew is supposed to do, and you don't do it, it bothers you. On the other hand, it is more difficult to awaken the one to whom nothing happens, who is indifferent to the religion and doesn't feel the conflict."

Rabbi Tzvi Grunblatt, Chabad's general director in Argentina, aims not only to dispel anti-Chabad myths but also to show the opposite,

"Some people are afraid because they don't know who we are. They are afraid because their organizations are an end to themselves. They believe we are another organization that is scrutinizing them. Instead of incorporating all the positive aspects Chabad brings to their own organizations, they closed their doors to us. They stay in the zeal. But nobody is here to take anything away from them. We are talking about allowing each one to discover his own heritage. There are certain taboos and certain myths. For example, a person once told me: 'I don't want to talk to you because I am not considered a Jew, according to you.' I asked him, 'Why do you think that?' He said, 'I know what you think. You think I am not Jewish enough.' One of the basic things for Chabad is that there are three types of Jews: the Jew, the Jew, and the Jew. There are no different Jews. There is a Jew who goes out and a Jew who doesn't go out. Jews who fulfill more of God's precepts and Jews who fulfill less. So, there is nothing but Jews. One is a Jew or is not. But if you are a Jew, beyond his condition of fulfillment of the precepts, you are and will always be a Jew. The non-religious person thinks that the religious person does not consider him a Jew and that, besides being a barrier, is not true."

Brain Washers

"When they say that we are brainwashing people, we respond, 'Well, we take off a little bit of the dirt they come in from the street with,'" Rabbi Stawski says jokingly.

One of the most significant biases about the organization today is the alleged "brainwashing" that Chabad rabbis would practice on people who approach their activities.

There is an unavoidable truth: there are cases of assimilated, non-religious Jews who have increased their religiosity, spirituality, and observance of Jewish laws and precepts after approaching Chabad Lubavitch, attending its activities, and spending time in the community. Some have even deepened this path and have slowly integrated into the Lubavitch community in a process called "teshuvah." They "return to the certainties" granted by faith and have an assigned category called baal teshuvah: "holders of answers."

The objectives of Chabad Lubavitch are clear, and they do not hide them.

This, however, does not imply a specific mechanism of "brainwashing," even though, as we will see throughout this book, several Chabad Lubavitch devices and institutions are at the service of this process of religious observance restoration. It is also true that Chabad

Lubavitch does not use illegal methods, coercion, or other violent means to achieve its goals: no Jew who does not want to listen to or adhere to the Chabad message will be forced to do so by the institution.

From his role as principal of the Wolfsohn School in Buenos Aires (Kindergarten through Secondary), managed by Chabad Lubavitch, Mr. Gustavo Dvoskin says, "Obviously, one hears criticisms. There is talk of evangelization, of 'brainwashing.' What is clear is that Lubavitchers are insistent people with powerful ideas, very convinced of what they do, and very confident, and in many cases, not all, with an interesting line of argument. They are not crazy people who just come up with an idea. They have substantiated ideas, and they study a lot. Many of them are brilliant people, with a message that can convince."

The process of transformation by which a Jew who has fallen out of observance gradually begins an approach to Orthodoxy, which sometimes can end (and in others does not) with integration into the Lubavitch community, is long and full of ups and downs, but with one constant: the separation of that individual from what had been their group of belonging. A person who begins to observe the dietary laws of kashrut (the food appropriate for a religious Jew) imposes such a significant change in his habits that if his family and relatives do not follow him on this path, a rupture occurs.

Respecting the complex Jewish food rules, with their prescriptions, mandates to have one set of dishes for meat and another for milk, and other issues, entails one of the most visible and radical changes in a person's behavior. Sons and daughters who suddenly refuse to continue getting to their parent's house if not served kosher food is one form of radical change that arouses fear and the common complaint: "What happened to my son? He has been brainwashed!"

Rabbi Birman says about this fear: "As many people entered Chabad and became religiously observant, parents fear their children will also become religiously observant if they come to Chabad. Our goal is to spread Judaism, not to make religious observant people. Once, a person told me: 'You think you are going to make all Jews religious observant,' and I told him: 'No, if you think I believe that, you are taking me for a fool. I want Jews to fulfill more and more *mitzvot*. You don't have to be religious observant to comply with that.'"

The idea that a brainwashing device exists is not observed in any of the activities carried out by Chabad Lubavitch. The percentage of Jews who become religiously observant Jews or join the Chabad Lubavitch community because of approaching Chabad institutions each year is negligible. If a device were in place to brainwash non-observant Jews and convert them to orthodox Jews, its success rate would be so low that it could be considered highly inefficient.

Damian Setton finds this situation problematic for Chabad itself: "As a substructure within the Jewish camp, Chabad Lubavitch tries to build its legitimacy by refuting the stigmas directed towards it. But this legitimacy is built based on two contradictory sources. On the one hand, legitimacy arises from the internal conversion processes of the baalei teshuvah. The one who returns attests to the integrity of the movement's message. The number is, for Chabad, a criterion of legitimacy. The number of members worldwide shows that the group is the bearer of the truth. But, on the other hand, the stigma of being brainwashers is disproved by the same young people who attend Chabad activities and do not convert." (Setton, D., Instituciones e identidades en los judaísmos contemporáneos, p. 102)

Damián Karo is a rabbi. He joined Chabad Lubavitch as a young man barely out of his teens. He spent nearly half his life in the organization, rising to high positions in the general management of Chabad Argentina's operation.

Given his former position, Karo has first-hand knowledge of the inner workings of Chabad and responds to this controversy: "I believe that one of Chabad's success secrets is that it sells truth and happiness in a can. Many people want exactly that, even if they never accept it. The fault does not lie with Chabad, but with the consumerist system we live in, which dehumanizes and objectifies, and whose supreme value is to have rather than be. The positive thing about Chabad is that they are convinced of what they do. They don't sell Coca-Cola and then drink Pepsi. They are very consistent. I don't see the problem if it does a person any good. Once, a mother was sorrowful and said, 'Oh, my son became an Orthodox!' Give me a break! It's not that the kid became addicted to drugs, that he joined a gang to kill people, that he became a skinhead, or that he's become an automaton who spends eighteen hours a day in the virtual cyber world. He is not the plague. If your son chose it freely, what's the problem? If you go into the hairdresser's, you sit in the chair, and they ask you: 'Shall I wash your head,' and you say: 'Yes, go ahead,' then they wash it. If not, they will not wash it. You can't wash the heads of people who don't want to get their heads washed. This is not A Clockwork Orange. Chabad does not kidnap people. They have a free and open system based on talking to anyone who wants to hear them. They will persuade you of their beliefs if what they tell you is persuasive. You are the one who accepts what they have to say. And if you don't find it convincing, they won't convince you of their beliefs. What's the worst thing that can happen if you talk to them? That you may end up liking what they have to tell you? What's the problem with that?! And if you talk to them and don't like what they tell you, well, you will have learned something from someone else."

Let's talk about money

The anti-Semitic myth that associates having money with the very condition of being Jewish is another profoundly ingrained bias against Chabad Lubavitch.

The Lubavitch are said to have significant economic power, funded by donations from their New York headquarters.

The prejudice implies two quick and easy ways to get rich in this life: winning the lottery or joining Chabad.

The popular imagination has created the myth that a person who becomes a Chabad Hasid, joining the local Chabad community and practicing Jewish Orthodoxy, will be financially supported by that community with cash, houses, apartments, cars, and any other luxury goods imaginable.

Simply put, this oversimplifies intricate social dynamics.

I ask Damian Setton his view on this topic, "It is a common talking point that people who get into Chabad suddenly get rich. Is that true?"

"I have observed the case and the opposite: people who could be much better off financially and are not because they are inside Chabad."

"In what sense?"

"For example, there is a guy I know who used to work in tech, earning a good sum. Suddenly, this guy decided to study at Chabad Lubavitch Headquarters at 770 Crown Heights in Brooklyn. He went there for a year, became a Lubavitcher, married, and now wants to manage a Beit Chabad. Managing it will require him to look for funds for his Beit Chabad rather than sitting in a comfortable office, programming and earning the salary he previously earned and being able to travel to improve his skills. It is a job that many people may like. Still, having to ask for donations and live off them all the time is also uncomfortable. He will have to take some donations he receives to live and provide for his family. Now, if I were to live on donations to maintain a Beit Chabad, the guy who donates to me would know I live on that as a rabbi. I could not show up someday with a two-story house and a last model car because he will donate me less next time."

"Do you have any references of people who have seen their finances improve just by joining Chabad Lubavitch?"

"Let's do a thought exercise. Let's suppose that I am a merchant and I sell T-shirts. In principle, I will have more business success chances if I connect with people. If I belong to a Jewish community and attend their synagogue daily, among the people I pray with might be a guy in the same business as me, selling T-shirts, and with whom I might collaborate to open a larger shop. Why shouldn't I take that opportunity? Or maybe the Chabad people prefer to buy from me because I go to the Chabad synagogue. If you have a friend who sells something you need, you will probably buy it from him. All these ideas about becoming financially saved after joining Chabad must be de-dramatized. It is not like, 'Yeah, I got into the mafia and made a lot of money.' I did not see any shady deals under the table in my research. Nor did I look for them. They may or may not exist. I cannot be sure. What I can say is that I don't see any problem with a guy improving his business by joining a religious community. I don't see any drama in that. Another guy can do the same thing with the people he knows from a community center, and nobody would start denouncing him. So why do we have to say it about Chabad?"

As a space that brings together people with similar interests and as a community, Chabad Lubavitch offers an appropriate environment for business development. Even more so because some influential businessmen worldwide have joined Chabad. According to a casual comment circulating in the local Jewish community, if it has always been necessary to take part in boring golf matches and other similar social activities for someone looking to expand their business, today, attending Chabad Lubavitch activities and integrating into their prayer groups can provide a better opportunity to get surrounded by businessmen and businesses opportunities.

Rabbi Karo confirms what Setton said and broadens the perspective: "There is indeed firm support for community members. On the other hand, once you are inside Chabad, you are on your own. Once you put on the beard, the coat, and the hat, it is up to you to figure it out. Once you are in, Chabad doesn't have to take special care of you anymore. You are already part of the community. If you need something, they will help you get it because you are part of Chabad, but they will not pamper you anymore. They must pamper those outside so they can come in, just as they pampered you when you were outside."

It's also not entirely accurate to say that Chabad Lubavitch has an endless supply of money from 770, as its New York headquarters are known, that can give to anyone worldwide. Although donations may come from abroad, they are not directly generated by an "unlimited tap" of money that 770 would open.

Each rabbi in charge of a Beit Chabad must secure their own means of securing donations that enable them to continue operating. In this sense, the possibility of obtaining income will depend on the charisma of each one of them. However, Chabad Lubavitch carries a brand recognition that simplifies the process. Each Beit Chabad and Chabad institution begins with an advantage because of Chabad's ability over time to win the favor of wealthy Jews with large wallets who donate lavish amounts for various projects.

The Argentinian businessman Eduardo Elsztain, one of the wealthiest men in the country, for example, has publicly declared that he contributes ten percent of each business deal he makes to Chabad Argentina, without a doubt, a substantial sum. Another factor for Chabad's visible financial strength is, as put by Rabbi Karo, Chabad's continuous expansion: "Chabad's approach is opposed to that of more traditional businesses. Nobody would embark on a new venture if they didn't have the funds to do it. Chabad is different. When the situation is dire, and they have no money, they build new institutions. They spend more money than they have and end up in the red. This is because they don't consider what they do as a business plan. They believe in the power of what they do. There is a real will to help others, which is why they do what they do. In the aftermath of a recession or an economic downturn, the system functions like a well-oiled machine: because Chabad does tangible material work, founds social aid institutions, runs community kitchens, and is actively involved in the community, donations flood in as soon as the economy gets back into its feet. Although this approach does not go down very well with Chabad's employees, who often have to live with their salaries on hold, waiting for donations to arrive on time."

Rabbi Birman contributes with his vision of the matter: "I can't speak for all of Chabad; I can only speak for my Beit Chabad, and I know that when I explain how I fund it, not everyone believes me. In my case, 90 percent of the financing comes from Argentina. People from the neighborhood, people from outside the neighborhood who know me or have heard something about me, or someone connected with a philanthropist. I have a donor, for example, who helps me a lot but tells me: 'I don't share your way of life, I am not religious, and I don't want to be.' I find it difficult to put him in the picture whenever I see him. However, he still donates to me because he says he appreciates the work we do here to prevent Jewish assimilation. I often invited him to festivities, but he never wanted to participate. On the other hand, Chabad Central indeed contributes a small portion of its rabbis' salaries. Still, this contribution gradually diminishes until it is eliminated, leaving each rabbi to provide their own means of subsistence. The system is based on a decreasing subsidy. Initially, the head office pays the rabbi's salary for about two years, plus bonuses and vacations. Following this period, Chabad Central deducts ten percent of the rabbi's salary annually until it reaches fifty percent of what he received at the start. The rabbi must raise the rest of the money and any additional expenses like children, community expansion, and other activities through donations. In the meantime, Central continues to provide branding and merchandising services, including brochures, magazines, materials, national campaigns, and know-how."

Regarding the possibility that Chabad Lubavitch is financed through drug trafficking, arms, or prostitution, Rabbi Karo is blunt: "It is not true. At least in Argentina, it is not true. Do I believe it might be in other parts of the world? No, I don't believe it. Absolutely not. Chabad holds deep spiritual values. I may disagree with them, but they are spiritual values. Now, there may be some black sheep here and there. As in any human group. It is like you come and tell me: 'Hey, I know a man from Argentina who is a drug dealer, so all Argentinians are drug dealers.' That's not the case. You cannot generalize in any human group. In Chabad? No, most of them are not involved in illegal activities."

In any case, the origin of the donations with which Chabad is financed has also become the target of permanent criticism, transcending into a political battle within the Argentine Jewish community.

Let's talk about politics

December 2007. A young couple is about to get married. Instead of gifts, they ask their guests to donate money to social welfare organizations. The groom will choose one institution and the bride another. He chooses a school for disabled children. She chooses Ieladeinu, a social aid institution for at-risk children, a project commanded and created by an orthodox Jewish institution. The institution accepts the generous donation that will allow it to continue its pioneering and revolutionary work on children's rights.

The wedding cards are printed and show the two institutions to which the guests can donate on behalf of the couple. When the rabbi who heads the Orthodox Jewish institution behind Ieladeinu learns that his institution's name is on the wedding card, he is adamantly opposed to accepting the donations. The rabbi argues he cannot allow his institution, which opposes mixed marriages or the marital union between a Jew and a non-Jew, to be listed as a sponsor of one.

A few days later, an indignant letter from the bride's father began circulating on the Internet, denouncing the situation. The letter stated: "Chabad Lubavitch accepts donations from unscrupulous people, including bankrupts and criminals, but only if they are Jews. If one donor is not a Jew but is an honest, law-abiding citizen, Chabad will not accept the donation."

The case quickly becomes relevant: the boyfriend is Diego Placente, a soccer player from the popular Argentinian soccer league team San Lorenzo de Almagro.

The e-mail from the bride's father started a series of correspondence, newspaper articles, and a heated debate at the heart of Argentina's Jewish community (one of the largest Jewish communities outside Israel.)

About ten days after the bride's father's e-mail went viral, Rabbi Tzvi Grunblatt issued a statement on behalf of Chabad Lubavitch Argentina. He explained his position and that of the organization over which he presides in it, among other ideas: "The issue, in this case, was not the acceptance of the donation, but the use of our name on the card attached to the invitation to an event that, while perhaps happy for the families involved, is directly at odds with Jewish principles and goes against the continuity of the Jewish people. Chabad Lubavitch works tirelessly to ensure such continuity, which is threatened primarily by assimilation and interfaith marriages. Any action that may cause a different interpretation must be avoided. We ask those who did not understand our actions to reconsider. Perhaps an analogy will help to explain the issue: a cardiovascular disease prevention league can accept donations from smokers, but it cannot appear as a beneficiary or sponsor of an event organized by a tobacco company. It would be embarrassing to do so."

This was not the end of the case. For days, new e-mails circulated in response, along with articles in community newspapers signed by various personalities from Argentina's Jewish community. The discussion lost its focus and eventually turned into a full-fledged clash of ideologies when Reform and Conservative Jews united in opposing Chabad Lubavitch as an advocate of Orthodoxy.

The controversy rekindled a series of debates that had seemed to have died away for a long time: What is a Jew?

On December 27, 2007, *Diversidad Judía* [Jewish Diversity], a blog of a Jewish foundation that groups conservative rabbis, issued its own press release, first signed by politically active Rabbi Sergio Bergman. After clarifying that they did not intend to interfere in issues related to the internal life and beliefs of each Jewish group, they explained,

"Chabad's press release clearly states its convictions, which, presented as an unappealable truth, are a restricted interpretation based on the teachings of what was originally a Jewish sect. The *Tanya*, mystical work penned by the founder of Chabad, states that the non-Jew is not different in terms of his religion or culture from the Jew but that is deprived of the essential attribute of the 'Jewish soul.' It is not a matter of interreligious conflict but of the incompatibility of uniting or linking two species. Based on this view of the intrinsic superiority of the Jewish soul, any bond that compromises anything more than respect and peaceful coexistence with others who are humanly similar but spiritually different is condemned."

Rabbi Tzvi Grunblatt's press release did not mention the work of *Tanya* at any point. However, this mystical text from Rabbi Shneur Zalman of Liady, the basis of Chabad's theology, specifies in its second chapter that the Jew has an exclusive second soul that was "breathed" by God "into his nostrils."

The Diversidad Judía press release for its part went on: "We are among those who do not take part in, authorize, or enable interfaith marriages. We also view them as a threat to Jewish continuity. However, once formed, they can be viewed as both a potential assimilation and an opportunity to increase the Jewish people's demographic base. Some people oppose them, while others welcome them."

The press release finally proposed the construction of an alternative to Orthodoxy using, among other arguments, the accusation of spiritual racism.

Another letter, written by Rabbi Baruch Plavnick, founder of the also conservative Jewish Fundación Pardes [Pardes Foundation], released strong terms against Chabad and Jewish Orthodoxy. Parts of the letter read: "The first fallacy claimed is that Judaism has always been Orthodox. This is false! Moses, Hillel, Rabbi Akiva, or Maimonides were not orthodox! Orthodoxy is a movement created in the 19th century against rabbis and leaders who tried to combine Judaism and modernity. Judaism existed and still exists today because it has not fully embraced Orthodoxy. Every era had leaders who knew how to promote the changes needed during their times. Only that the changes were limited and occurred slowly and were separated by long periods. [...] I defend the right of Orthodox Jews to think and live as they wish, but I object to them pretending that this is the only way to live and think as Jews...."

The Jewish philosopher Dario Sztajnszrajber, a member of the staff of the *YOK* group, which proposes a liberal vision of Judaism, intervened with a text published in the newspaper *Nueva Sion* [New Zion] on January 7, 2008: "Chabad Lubavitch defines its own scale of values by prioritizing the purity of its conception of Judaism over the needs of the most disadvantaged. They would counter that no child was undoubtedly left without assistance because of the donation's refusal, making it clearer than ever that this refusal is unquestionably a political gambit. [...]. If the 'mixed' bride and groom had donated the money without putting the name 'Ieladeinu' on the wedding card, there would have been no problem. Again, the problem is not only not ideological and even not economic: it is political."

The thinker brought to the table the true nature of the case, which was about community politics.

Rabbi Damian Karo was the third signatory of the letter subscribed by *Diversidad Judía*, thus turning against the institution where he spent most of his adult life. He still believes in many of the ideas expressed in the letter. He maintains that his signature was motivated by his dissatisfaction with the way Chabad Lubavitch works, which he has never felt comfortable with. I asked him about the entire situation, "So, the letter from *Diversidad Judía* was an intervention in a broader debate inside the Jewish community?"

"Is there a political component to this situation? Yes, without a doubt. And it is good politics. This situation led to Chabad revealing something that was usually hidden. *Diversidad Judía* highlighted the line that they displayed. Chabad fulfills its mission. Whether you like it or don't like it, agree or disagree, it's great. This entire case brought a healthy discussion back to the scene. For me, it represented an opportunity for the dialogue they deny us. The possibility of shaking the 'community's public opinion,' which remains silent and allows itself to be disrespected because of ignorance."

"What do you think about Grunblatt's press release?"

"Rabbi Grunblatt's issue was not the donation itself. The issue was that it was shown in the marriage invitations. That is specified in his letter. I will not claim that this is a Chabad Lubavitch position. It is a Chabad position in Argentina. The money can be accepted, but it should be disclosed nowhere in public or be known. That is exactly what the letter states."

"What about the racist allegations against Chabad in *Diversidad Judía*'s press release?"

"What the letter states is that in *Tanya*, it is explained that non-Jews do not have a 'Jewish soul'; thus, they belong to another 'species,' spiritually speaking. We could call that spiritual 'racism.' According to *Tanya*, there are different spiritualities based on 'genetic' and hereditary grounds. For Chabad, it is not an issue of different cultures or beliefs but of two different 'species.' Now, what about the donations that are accepted? Intermarriage is not accepted, just as working on Shabbat is not accepted. If you are a Jew who works on Shabbat and donates to Chabad, can they accept that money?"

"That is a valid argument, but we have to consider the scale of the transgression, right? Working on Shabbat is not supposed to be at the same scale as a Jew marrying a non-Jew."

"I can give you the answer given to me when I was part of Chabad. I was a firm believer during that time, yet these questions made me wonder. They would tell me that donors usually have a lot of businesses. Why assume that what they donate to us comes from the 'bad' part and not the 'good' business? Why assume that the donation came from the part of the work done during the Shabbat and not during the week? Chabad's problem is that it has to reconcile its orthodox values with going out into the world to give its message. How did they resolve this issue? Out of fifteen rules, they only display ten. You purchase them, and because you are now a part of the group that can address a few of your existential rather than financial problems, you ultimately purchase the entire package. Not that big brands in the market do not do the same. The problem is that big brands want to sell you a soft drink, a hamburger, or a car. Here, they want to sell you a life format, and they sell it to you from a spiritual point of view. What I question is, why don't they come out and say: 'You know what? The non-Jew is different. He has one less soul.' Let them say it loud!"

"That would clash with their need to expand."

"That is what I am saying. In Chabad's need for expansion, they must cover part of what they believe. That's why we have to show what they cover up. We all lie all the time. But what I wanted to make clear by adhering to *Diversidad Judía*'s letter was: 'You don't want to accept the donation? Don't accept it, but don't come up with the tobacco company analogy because I don't believe it. Because Chabad's issue, as they show with the tobacco company as an example, is with appearances rather than money."

Chapter Two

Life and Afterlife of Menachem Mendel Schneerson, Chabad's Last Rebbe

> "King Solomon wrote the *Song of Songs* to discuss the love of man and woman. The Hasidim say that if Solomon had known about a Rebbe's love for his Hasidim and the Hassidim's love for their Rebbe, he would have written about them rather than about man and woman."
> Rabbi Pinjas Baumgarten

> "Many say Chabad is a multinational corporation, but they are wrong. Chabad is the Rebbe."
> Rabbi Moshe Blumenfeld

The leader

Even to those who do not sympathize with Chabad Lubavitch, the figure of Rabbi Menachem Mendel Schneerson deserves respect and admiration.

The Seventh Rebbe of Chabad Lubavitch, who came from a kind of royal family of six generations of leaders who all came from the same ancestor, became the most loved and feared (because of his political lobbying skills) star figure of Orthodox Judaism in the last 50 years. This has effects on Chabad Lubavitch even today.

His portrait is present at the entrance of every Chaba institution, in the offices of the directors of those institutions, reproduced in picture frames in the home of each of his followers and in images to carry in the wallet as if it were a Christian prayer card. Many Lubavitch Hassidic boy children bear his name, so it is unsurprising that if someone says "Mendy" out loud in front of a group of Chabad boys, several heads turn because they feel alluded to. As for the girls, they are named after Chaya Mushka, the late Rebbe's wife or rebbetzin.

His place as the undisputed leader of Chabad Lubavitch is present in the way he is referred to: unlike his predecessors, he has no nicknames other than "Rebbe," continuing his legacy, assuming him as the current leader of Lubavitch even though he has been deceased since 1994.

How did the last of the members of the dynasty of descendants of Shneur Zalman of Liady earn this devotion?

Menachem Mendel Schneerson was born in 1902 in Mykolaiv, a city south of present-day Ukraine. He was the son of Rabbi Levi Isaac Schneerson and his wife, Chana Yanovsky.

The future seventh Lubavitch Rebbe was born into the extended family of Chabad's founder, Shneur Zalman of Liady. It was a great-great-grandson of the Third Rebbe of Lubavitch, Menachem Mendel Schneersohn (1789-1886), in homage to whom he was named.

In 1907, his father became the spiritual leader of the community of Yekaterinoslav (renamed Dnipro in 2016), also in the current Ukraine.

Accounts of his childhood often emphasize his character as a Torah prodigy and that he had already surpassed his teachers at an early age. Some legends circulating in the Hasidic world show him as an early miracle worker. He was already considered a Talmud prodigy at thirteen. He was ordained as a rabbi at seventeen.

In 1923, Menachem Mendel met the Sixth Lubavitch Rebbe. He started working with him to help oppressed Jewish communities in the Soviet Union. When Yosef Yitzchak Schneersohn moved the Lubavitch court to Riga, Latvia, in 1927, the future Seventh Chabad Rebbe went with him and married one of Schneersohn's three daughters, who was a distant cousin of his. Menachem Mendel was 26 years old, and his bride was 22. The year was 1928. The bride's father led the wedding, which took place at the Warsaw yeshiva.

After the marriage, the couple moved to Berlin. Menachem Mendel received a university education, something completely unusual for Chabad Lubavitch hierarchs.

He studied philosophy and mathematics for a semester and a half at the University of Berlin, where he remained until 1933, the year Hitler came to power.

From there, the couple emigrated to Paris, where Menachem Mendel reportedly studied engineering at La Sorbonne University and the École Polittechnique.

The outbreak of World War II found Menachem Mendel and his wife in Paris. Like many Jews, they moved to the south of France under the regime of the Vichy Republic.

The Sixth Rebbe and a small group of followers left Poland as the Nazis surrounded it. They arrived in New York City on March 19, 1940, after a powerful political lobby at the highest level helped them. This lobby included politicians and government officials from both the U.S. and Germany.

The later Seventh Rebbe and his wife could only escape from Europe on June 12, 1941, via Lisbon, after passing through Marseilles by train. They arrived in New York on June 23.

The Rebbe and his court had already taken up residence in a neo-Gothic mansion with exposed brick in Brooklyn's Crown Heights neighborhood at 770 Eastern Parkway.

Once settled in the United States, the future Seventh Rebbe was employed briefly as an engineer in the Brooklyn Navy. At the same time, the Sixth Rebbe commissioned him to command three newly created Chabad institutions: Merkos L'Innyonei Chinuch (Chabad's central education arm, which grew to become one of the base organizations of Chabad Lubavitch today), Machne Israel (which was and is in charge of social welfare issues) and the Kehot Publication Society (Chabad's flagship publisher.)

Menachem Mendel Schneerson would return to Europe only once, in 1947, when he traveled to Paris after World War II to look for his mother, who had been released from a displaced persons camp. His father had died in 1944 in a village in Kazakhstan, where he had been forced into exile after being arrested and tortured by Stalin's secret police in 1939.

Upon his return to the United States, he would not leave the country again and hardly ever left Crown Heights, except for a visit to a new Chabad boys' camp that was established in the Catskill Mountains, northwest of New York, and periodic visits to the Queens Cemetery, where his predecessor was buried and where he stayed for hours on each weekly visit.

Yosef Yitzchak Schneersohn, the Sixth Rebbe, passed away in 1950, and Menachem Mendel Schneerson refused to become the new leader of the Lubavitch movement for a year until pressure from the Hasidim convinced him to do so. In January 1951, he accepted the appointment after a complex political scheme forced him to compete with the deceased Rebbe's other son-in-law.

As Lubavitch Rebbe, Menachem Mendel Schneerson exercised unparalleled charismatic leadership and knew how to lead his movement with extraordinary intelligence when Judaism was in crisis after narrowly overcoming the almost complete extinction caused by the Holocaust.

Contrary to the Sixth Rebbe, who was regarded as an obscurantist because of his views on the Holocaust because of Jews' lack of religious observance and growing secularisation, Menachem Mendel launched a campaign to modernize the movement while still adhering to Chabad's values and beliefs.

The motto adopted by Lubavitch from the leadership of its Seventh Rebbe was taken from Genesis 28:14, which describes the patriarch Jacob's dream in which God appears to him and announces: "And thy seed shall be as the dust of the earth, and thou shalt spread abroad to the west, and to the east, and to the north, and to the south: and in thee and in thy seed shall all the families of the earth be blessed."

Under this mandate, Chabad Lubavitch began the missionary action that characterizes it, taking Jewish life to every place where there is a Jew. The goal is to awaken the "divine spark" in every Jew by demonstrating that he or she is part of a tradition and heir to customs, culture, and 613 precepts that must be fulfilled.

As a Messianic and Hassidic movement influenced by Isaac Luria's Kabbalah, they believe that every time a Jew performs his or her religious duties, the world becomes a little holier, and the arrival of the Messiah becomes a little closer.

Within the orthodox Jewish currents, Chabad Lubavitch is in the subgroup of those who do not reject modernization outright as long as it does not contradict their faith principles and serves to sanctify God.

On the other hand, they consider that this same modernization — a product of the Jewish emancipation of the 18th century — is the most serious threat to the subsistence of the Jewish people since it entails high assimilation to Western culture along with the loss of traditional customs and fulfillment of the religious precepts. This was already a problem for Jewish Orthodoxy before, and previous Hassidic Rebbes were worried about it. After the Holocaust, which was especially cruel for European Orthodox Jewish communities, it became an even bigger problem. In this context, many Jewish orthodox communities, including Chabad, understood that Jews who abandoned their customs and traditions, married non-Jews, abandoned the observance of the precepts, and did not have a Jewish education were another means to complete the Nazi's attempted eradication of Judaism.

With the belief that if a Jew is taught the essence of Judaism, his "divine spark" will awaken, and he will no longer want to live any other way than the Jewish way of life, religiously observant, of course, Chabad Lubavitch undertook an enormous expansion under the leadership of Menachem Mendel, using an original mix of pragmatism to find the best ways to teach Jews about their cultural heritage and faith.

This is what the Rebbe understood and why he put into practice a vast network of emissaries called sheliach, whom he sent to every corner of the world where there was a Jewish community.

Menachem Mendel Schneerson worked with the firm belief that a Jew must act the same way and do the same mitzvah no matter where in the world he is. He also knew that he had to be patient with the ignorance and initial resistance of assimilated Jews to give up their secular customs and "return" to doing what Chabad sees as their Jewish duties.

Menachem Mendel's charisma to enthuse his followers to fulfill this work, along with his support for the development of actions aimed at opening Chabad Lubavitch towards secular Jews, were some of the most outstanding features of his personality and what, still to this day, generates devotion among his Hassidim.

The most significant change Menachem Mendel was able to effect was the opening of a strictly closed and traditionalist Old World religious community to the technological advances of his time. In the sixties, Chabad began using the radio and telephone to transmit Torah teachings to their followers. Later, they would also expand to T.V. with the advent of cable and were pioneers in using the Internet when the web was just taking its first steps.

In 1967, the Rebbe instituted the tefillin campaign, the first of his well-known *Mitzvah* or *Mivtzoim Campaigns*.

Through these actions, carried out with enthusiasm and conviction by his Hasidim all over the world, the Rebbe tried to get assimilated Jews to practice at least ten of the 613 precepts of Judaism that he considered fundamental and that would open the door for secular Jews to connect with their duties as Jews.

The Mitzvah Campaigns got Chabad out into the streets, as its followers worked nonstop to spread the word and get all Jews, no matter who they were or where they lived, to do ten *mitzvot*: putting on tefillin; women lighting candles on Shabbat; putting mezuzot on the doors of every Jewish home; studying the Torah every day; giving to charity (*tzedakah*); filling Jewish homes with holy books; following the rules of kashrut; love for their neighbors, teaching every Jewish boy and girl about Judaism, and keeping the "purity of the family."

Fishkoff notes that other Orthodox groups never regarded such campaigns well: "Critics from the Orthodox world looked askance at the Rebbe's campaigns, believing that it cheapened religious practice to encourage non-observant Jews to perform isolated rituals without adopting the total lifestyle. What good is putting tefillin on a man who will then go and eat a cheeseburger? Doesn't one cancel out the other? To these critics, Lubavitchers respond that each mitzvah, in and on itself, is a deed of cosmic significance that activates a person's preexisting connection to God. It is a holy act, worth doing for any reason. Not only that, but one person performing one mitzvah could be the key event that tips the scale of universal goodness and ushers in the Messianic Age." (49)

The tefillin campaign, which began two days before the outbreak of the Six-Day War (one of the most significant military challenges the newborn State of Israel had to face in its history), was a way for the Rebbe to call all Jews to pray for the protection of the "Promised Land," gained widespread popularity through images of Israeli soldiers wearing tefillin next to tanks. This helped get the Rebbe's message out worldwide and led him and his followers to believe they had played a part in the "miraculous" victory of the Tzahal over its enemies and the reunification of Jerusalem.

This alleged miracle began to be attributed to Menachem Mendel Schneerson, demonstrating that legends build people, or people build legends.

According to another legend, the Rebbe also had prophetic powers. In late 1960, Ariel Sharon, who would become Israel's prime minister decades later, visited Schneerson. As his guest departed, the Rebbe warned him not to take the flight he had planned for his return, adding nothing else. Sharon listened to the advice, and that same flight was hijacked and diverted to Algeria by the Popular Front for the Liberation of Palestine on July 23, 1968.

According to Rabbi Zev Segal, a prominent orthodox rabbi from New Jersey, this rumor spread throughout the Lubavitch world, so when he had the chance, he asked the Rebbe in person if the story was true. The Rebbe replied he had told Sharon not to take that flight. Segal asked him, "So why didn't you stop the plane altogether?" The Rebbe replied, "Do you think I knew they would hijack the plane? I didn't know that they would hijack the plane. Sharon came to say goodbye to me, so I told him not to go. Why did I tell him? When I told him? I don't know."

The miracles attributed to Menachem Mendel Schneerson have been collected in several books and are frequently recounted at any appropriate time in Chabad Lubavitch publications worldwide and on the Internet.

More intriguing is the story of Rabbi Mordechai Birman, one of the Rebbe's emissaries in the Lubavitch community in Argentina, who witnessed a miracle propitiated by the Rebbe. According to his story: "In 1987, I had my first children. Twins. A boy and a girl. They were born prematurely, weighing just two pounds. They had to be put in an incubator. And when they came out of it, two or three weeks later, my baby girl got terrible meningitis. She was in a coma for several days. The doctors told me there was no hope but recommended we pray. And I wrote to the Rebbe from the very first moment. The first week, I didn't receive any answer. One day, Rabbi Grunblatt came to visit me at the hospital. He asked me if I had written to the Rebbe. I told him yes. 'But did you tell him you are one of his envoys?' he asked me, and I told him: 'No, I didn't tell him because he knows.' Rabbi Grunblatt emphasized: 'No, tell him you are his emissary because the Rebbe once said that he will protect the children of his emissaries.' So I faxed him to New York, telling him my case again and clarifying that I was one of his emissaries. The next morning, my wife went to the hospital. Since we had two babies, she and I took turns taking care of one at a time, and it was my turn to go in the afternoon. At about ten or eleven o'clock, I received a reply from the Rebbe saying to add a name to my baby. It's a customary thing to do when a person is in danger; a name is added. In his reply, he gave me a list of three names to choose from and also asked me to check the mezuzot in my house. The ones I had were new. *Mezuzot* are checked once every year, year and a half. I was surprised because they were good. I bought them especially when I got married. I took all I had out of my house. I put a little piece of paper showing where each was from: the one in the kitchen, the one in the living room, the one in my room, and the one in the children's room. I went to the hospital and met my wife, who had just come out of the medical report. They gave us two reports daily, one at eleven o'clock in the morning and another at seven o'clock in the evening. In that first report of the day, they told us that the baby was still in a coma. I told my wife that the Rebbe had asked me to choose another name for her, and we chose it right then and there. I went to the Chabad yeshiva, and we made a minyan. I gave her the name and took the mezuzot to the sofer (scribe.) I asked him to review them urgently because of the seriousness of the case. He already knew my situation. At seven o'clock in the evening, we returned to the hospital to receive the second medical report of the day. Before going to the hospital, we again saw the sofer. I went upstairs for a minute while my wife stayed downstairs, and he told me: 'Look, all your mezuzot are excellent, except for this one,' and it was just the one in my children's room. It's not that it was wrong. It's just that they had forgotten to put a letter in it. And the wrong word was 'your children.' He changed it for me. We went home quickly, put in the new mezuzah, and rushed back to the hospital. We were at the door of the intensive care ward when the doctor came out with a smile from ear to ear. We approached her, and she said: 'Look, a little while ago, your daughter came out of danger. We must assess any neurological damage that may have occurred, but she is out of danger.'"

Rabbi Birman pauses and finishes the story in his deep voice, "You can tell me it is a coincidence. Believe whatever you want. But for me, it was no coincidence. A little over a year later, we traveled to see the Rebbe with my wife and baby girl. When the time came to see him, my daughter went speechless and just looked at him. The Rebbe looked at her, gave her a dollar, and said, 'May you be in total health.'"

Stories like this are widespread. Generally, the Rebbe's miracles have, as a component, the prescription of the observance of some mitzvah and thus serve as moralizers.

The alleged miracles and prophecies, along with his charisma and desire to advance Judaism, led to the development of the Rebbe as a point of reference, a real rabbi in the sense of a "teacher" to be consulted for the widest range of questions, from individual guidance to Judaic and Hasidic philosophy.

Initially, he would receive people who needed private audiences in his home three times a week (Sunday, Tuesday, and Thursday evenings). People from all walks of life passed through them, from the humblest to influential politicians and businessmen.

Later, as his popularity increased, a schedule was implemented whereby he would attend to the most urgent cases first, and the others would have to wait months for an appointment.

However, because of the impossibility of attending to all cases, the Rebbe began to receive a large amount of correspondence, which he first answered personally and then with the help of secretaries. There are currently thousands of letters that make up entire volumes edited with what was sent to him and his responses.

In 1978, the Rebbe suffered a heart attack while celebrating Simchat Torah with his Hassidim, despite which he refused to end the service early.

He refused hospitalization and spent his recovery in his home, limiting his public appearances and personal interactions with fans and visitors after 1981. However, he continued to send messages to his community.

In 1986, he introduced a new method of communication with his followers: Sunday Dollars. Every Sunday, he would sit in his office and give a dollar to charity to each of the thousands of people who came from all over the world. His followers would queue for hours to have that brief moment of contact with him, taking advantage of the opportunity to ask him for a blessing.

On February 10, 1988, his wife passed away. The funeral procession gathered fifteen thousand people who accompanied the coffin to the Jewish cemetery in Queens.

His political influence was not only limited to his followers and the United States, where campaigning candidates would often stop by to ask for his blessing.

Although the Lubavitch rarely meddled in the political affairs of the State of Israel, in the 1988 parliamentary elections, Menachem Mendel ordered explicit support for the religious party Agudat Israel in response to a campaign that had attempted to erase the influence of Hasidism within the Parliament. As a result, the party won three more seats in Parliament than it already had, bringing it to five.

These legislators helped to prevent Shimon Peres from forming a coalition government in 1990. That coalition sought to establish talks with Yasser Arafat's PLO, which the Rebbe feared would jeopardize Jewish security in Israel.

On August 19, 1991, a motorcade carrying the Rebbe, a police car escorting him, and a third vehicle carrying followers of the leader returned from Montefiore Cemetery in Queens, where Menachem Mendel had gone to pray at the graves of his father-in-law and wife. On the way back to 770, an accident occurred: the caravan's third car collided with a private car, killing the seven-year-old son of Guyanese immigrants, Gavin Cato. This triggered the eruption of religious and social tensions that had always been latent in Crown Heights.

For three days, groups of African Americans attacked, harassed, and destroyed Lubavitch property, including the stabbing to death of Yankel Rosenbaum, an Australian Orthodox Jew from outside the community who was in Crown Heights, to conduct Holocaust studies.

During the uprising, African American and Latino community members marched through the neighborhood streets, burning Israeli flags, chanting anti-Semitic slogans, and assaulting police officers.

The Lubavitch Rebbe received intense criticism for his attitude regarding the child's death and the riot. He did not express condolences or apologies to the victim's family. In an incident that seemed to overcome him, he did not behave appropriately for a leader of his stature.

The T.V. docudrama (later released on DVD) *Crown Heights: Nothing is as simple as black and white* recalls — in a format that mixes interviews with African-American neighborhood residents and Chabad Hasidim — those terrible events and focuses on how community leaders from both sectors joined forces to achieve peaceful coexistence in the same city.

The film is subtle about the Lubavitch Rebbe's non-direct intervention in the confrontation, showing how his personal secretary delegates that task to one of his Hassidim. Through talking, getting to know each other, and starting a basketball team and a hip-hop band with people of different races, the neighborhood returned to a tense calm, still threatened by the fundamental differences between the two groups that must live in the same space.

By the time of the 1991 clashes between Jews and African Americans, the Rebbe's health was already failing. He was almost ninety years old and in poor health. He had a stroke in 1992 while praying at his predecessor's tomb, which left him with severe speech difficulties. Nothing would ever be the same after that. He spent his last years in a wheelchair, surrounded by a great expectation of the imminent messianism he had been responsible for generating. His inability to express himself after his stroke, as well as his lack of offspring, worried his Hassidim, who began to cultivate an environment in which it was assumed that their leader would reveal his true essence at any time: he was the long-awaited Messiah.

That never happened; instead, he passed away on June 12, 1994.

Asked about what this meant for the Chabad Lubavitch movement, Rabbi Tzvi Grunblatt answers: "It was the worst moment in history. It was a tremendous blow. It is irreplaceable. If the Rebbe were with us today, the Lubavitch movement would be three times what it is. Let's do the math... it would be unimaginable... unimaginable."

Death and Transfiguration of Menachem Mendel Schneerson

> My father sighed. "Reb Saunders sits and waits for the Messiah," he said. "I am tired of waiting. Now is the time to bring the Messiah, not to wait for him."
>
> Chaim Potok, *The Chosen*

The death of the Lubavitch Rebbe signaled a schism in his community, which was also felt outside of Chabad Lubavitch and reverberated throughout the Orthodox Jewish world.

At first, some analysts considered the Lubavitch movement finished with the disappearance of its leader. Rabbi Birman says: "We were brought up thinking that his passing would never happen. We never thought that we were going to reach that situation. Because the Rebbe was the leader, the one who drove us, the one who guided us, and no one was thinking, 'What will happen next?' There was no after he died. There was no such thing as an after. We assumed that when the Rebbe died, the Messiah would appear. Nothing else was available. At that point, we all thought we were doomed. But I believe that's part of the strength that the Rebbe instilled in us: to put our heads down and keep going. Seven days later, after the mourning, they put the tombstone in his grave, and one of his first sheliach, an emissary in California, was going to speak on behalf of all the other emissaries. They all agreed with what he would say: 'Rebbe, if the Messiah doesn't come, we all leave and do nothing else.' That was what they were going to tell him, that we couldn't go on without him. And yet, when he spoke, he told him: 'Rebbe, stay calm. We will continue the work.' The opposite of what he was going to say. Thank God because that was what we all felt at that moment. That we had to continue. And so we went on."

The Lubavitch Rebbe was not only the leader of his community, but he was behind all the decision-making, managing the affairs of all his Hasidim, living as their leader and servant. His followers dress very similar to how he used to dress. This is the only reason we can still see them walking the streets of any city where they have a presence, even when it's boiling or freezing, and wearing warm black clothes to show grief for the destruction of the Second Temple of Jerusalem in 70 A.D.

What happened after Schneerson's death within Chabad is a complex subject to discuss with Chabadniks, who usually refuse to talk about the matter or prefer to talk about the Rebbe when he was still alive. In general, a sense of deep sadness is relieved when they refer to him as a presence that, while not physically present, is still behind each of his Hasidim and the Jewish people.

After his death, great turmoil took hold of the Lubavitch movement. Not only was it a matter of determining how to continue without the leadership of their Rebbe, but encouraged by a series of statements and beliefs stimulated by the Sixth Rebbe and taken to paroxysm by the Seventh Rebbe, many Lubavitch Hasidim believed, and still believe today, that he was the Messiah awaited by the Jewish people.

Indeed, consulted on the imminence of the advent of the Messiah, Rabbi Tzvi Grunblatt responds,

"Is there any sign that can be observed of the imminent arrival of the Messiah?"

"There are many telltale signs, all of which occurred in the last hundred years of history, with the significant changes in the world, which appeared to be dominated by communist atheism, which suddenly and unexpectedly fell. Countries dominated by communist dictatorships were liberated from one day to the next, achieving their positive freedoms towards the spiritual. The world came to the awareness that war is not the way, the awareness to use budgets to ease hunger as never existed before in all of history; the spread of Jewish mysticism, the capacity we have today to spread wisdom as never existed before: there are no more limitations of time and space."

"All these issues show we are moving towards a change: ideologies have fallen. Not that we are moving to a world without ideologies. We are entering a world with ONE ideology, the true ideology. It is not true that because all ideologies have fallen, we will be left without ideology. The path to THE ideology is a transition."

"Which ideology would that be?"

"That of the Kingdom of HaShem on Earth."

"You speak of the 20th century, but that century also saw the Holocaust."

"The Holocaust was part of the pre-Messiah arrival suffering mentioned in the Talmud. Is it rational that Jews from all over the world can now freely return to Israel? That was something unimaginable fifty or sixty years ago. These are actions that show that we are preparing for the fulfillment of the Messiah's prophecies. Although we have not yet met the Messiah, the world is preparing for his arrival."

"But the State of Israel is a secular state."

"The secular would have existed with or without the State of Israel. What is new is that the Jews are in Israel."

What precisely would the Messianic era comprise? The work of Jacob Immanuel Schochet clarifies it:

"Mashiach shall restore the Beit Hamikdash in Jerusalem. This refers to the third Beit Hamikdash that will stand forever, fulfilling the Divine prophecy of Ezekiel 37:26- 28... Through Mashiach shall be effected the gathering of all the exiles of Israel... This Divine promise of the return and restoration of Israel is unconditional. It will occur even if the people do not want to return... The Messianic era will mark the end of evil and sin... The Messianic era will be a time of universal awareness, perception, and knowledge of G-d... The awareness and knowledge of G-d will remove the narrow minded dispositions that lead to strife and war. It will be an era of peace and harmony in the Holy Land and throughout the world." (19-27)

The dead would be resurrected, and men would be assured of maximum physical and spiritual happiness, with all the sick being healed and the annulment of death, fertile lands, and liberation from all the impediments that face man today to fulfill the *mitzvot*: "Our aspirations are to be free to devote ourselves to Torah and its wisdom, with no one to oppress or disturb us. We long for that time because there will be an assembly of the righteous, an era dominated by goodness, wisdom, knowledge, and truth. It will be a time when the commandments of the Torah shall be observed without inertia, laziness, or compulsion..."

"The sole preoccupation of the whole world will be to know G-d. The Israelites will be great sages: they will know things that are presently concealed, and will achieve knowledge of their creator to the utmost capacity of human beings." (32)

According to Jewish theology, all generations have a tzaddik (sage) capable of revealing himself as the Messiah. This will be a man and descendant of King David, through the line of his son King Solomon. The Messiah has existed in the Garden of Eden since before Creation and will incarnate in the tzaddik when the time comes.

During the Sixth Rebbe's tenure, the hope for the imminent arrival of the Messiah became one of Chabad Lubavitch's most ardent beliefs, fully embodied during their Seventh Rebbe.

Suppose we add up all the things we know about the Messiah, that Jews can speed up his arrival or prepare the way for it by doing good deeds, and Menachem Mendel Schneerson's leadership. In that case, it's easy to see why so many of his followers believe he could reveal himself to be precisely the long-awaited savior. The Rebbe's mitzvah campaigns, leadership in spreading Jewish religious customs to all corners of the globe, and personal charisma reactivated the messianic fervor, as it had done with Sabbatai Zevi and other false Messiahs.

The messianic theme had begun to appear more frequently in Menachem Mendel Schneerson's speeches and public addresses since the 1960s, which excited his followers, who began with some cautious proclamations that he would indeed end up revealing himself as the one sent by God.

The movement then grew, and petitions calling Menachem Mendel the King Messiah were published in the most important newspapers in the United States. Stickers, posters, and books that called him the Messiah were also widely distributed. As part of this "marketing campaign," the old biblical chant Yechi started to be sung by the Chabadniks with new lyrics: *Yechi Adoneinu Moreinu v'Rabbeinu Melech haMoshiach l'olam vo'ed*! which translates as "Long live our Lord, Master, and Rabbi, King Messiah, forever and ever."

The messianic controversy did not end when Schneerson died in June 1994. His followers would worship his image, and this became one of the most troublesome things about Chabad Lubavitch's relationship with the rest of Judaism and the rest of the Hasidism movement. Various reactions were elicited among Schneerson's followers upon his death. A branch of Lubavitch was tasked with finding explanations for Menachem Mendel Schneerson's death so that it did not interfere with their messianic assignment to him.

Just as an attachment to the deceased leader's figure continues to be expressed in the present, many Lubavitchers believe he is still the Messiah despite his death, which they justify with Torah and Talmud readings. A position that is clearly contrary to that of normative Judaism, which clearly states that the Messiah will reveal himself during his human lifetime.

Rabbi Damian Karo confirms that some sources of the Jewish tradition assign the possibility that the Messiah is someone already dead and revived: "There is a source," he explains, "that says: 'If the Messiah is alive, he is such, and if he is dead, he is such-and-such another.'"

The rabbi explains how it is possible to find justifications that differ from the normative or what is thought to be established in Jewish tradition, an essential feature of Judaism itself: "I can come and show you a quote while I cover another, contradicting one. So, I can back up anything I want to believe." He even ups the ante, placing the Jewish tradition as the product of an endless and maddening series of literary criticism by which anything can be justified, even the idea that a dead and buried leader can rise from the dead and become the Messiah of the Jewish people: "Orthodoxy justifies everything with 'The Torah says...' But the Torah might say something and also the opposite. Because the Torah can have a thousand different interpretations."

As is clear, the interpretative possibilities are broad and flexible. The method of over-interpretation was already present even in the messianic assignments made to Sabbatai Zevi, even when he had converted to Islam. These reinterpretations are the basis for the belief system developed by sectors of Chabad that allows them to affirm that a resurrected Jewish sage will be revealed to be their Messiah. The conflict between those who believe and those who do not believe Schneerson is the Messiah has spawned two camps inside Chabad: "messianists" and "non-messianists." A tiny group of Lubavitchers maintains the Rebbe is indeed, and without a doubt, not the Messiah. Then there are more radical sectors that publicly affirm, launch media campaigns, and seek justifications in Jewish tradition (such as attempting to prove that he was a direct descendant of King David, one requirement that the Messiah must fulfill according to tradition), to maintain that Menachem Mendel Schneerson is the Messiah and will be revealed soon. Within this group are those who maintain that he indeed died but will revive to reveal himself and those who affirm that, in reality, he never died. In the intermediate positions are those who do not rule out that the Rebbe may be the Messiah but do not affirm it either, and last, some prefer not to talk about the matter.

The most visible manifestations of messianic positions are the waving of the messianic flag (yellow with a blue crown in the center and the Hebrew word Mashiach in orange letters) on some festive occasions and the addition of the prayer "We Want Messiah Now" at the end of the prayer performed at the tefillin putting, which some Chabad rabbis propose.

Lubavitchers are mainly reluctant to discuss this matter with outsiders. They are cautious with their words to make clear their admiration for the Rebbe and belief in his presence, even if not in physical form.

Rabbi Karo describes the phenomenon's manifestation in no uncertain terms: "What's the difference between the messianists and the non-messianists? Many people think the Messiah will come, that the Messiah is the Rebbe, and that the Rebbe died but will return. Then, what's the difference between them? Whether they should say it aloud. Whether it is good enough to show. If it's true, why would it be up to debate if it is worth showing? Because it is an issue that either brings people closer to Chabad or pushes them away from Chabad."

Within Jewish Orthodoxy, the issue has taken a political turn, where it is used as a pledge of legitimacy that involves much more than the Judeo-theological debate over whether the Rebbe is or can be the Messiah, with some scholars even pointing out that believing the Rebbe can rise from the dead to reveal himself as the Messiah means abolishing one of the fundamental differences between Judaism and Christianity.

Beyond the discussion about Menachem Mendel Schneerson's messianism, his tomb, erected in Montefiore Cemetery in Queens, next to that of his father-in-law, the Sixth Lubavitch Rebbe, is a site of worldwide pilgrimage by the Chabad Lubavitch Hassidim.

The place, known as *Ohel* (tent), receives thousands of pilgrims who gather yearly, especially on the 3rd of Tammuz (the anniversary of the Rebbe's death.) The Ohel Chabad Lubavitch Center, next to the tomb, houses a synagogue, a library, and "a comfortable place where people can write letters to the Rebbe," according to its official website. It also provides appropriate footwear to respect the tomb's expected standards of conduct. It is open 365 days a year, 24 hours a day.

For those unable to travel to the cemetery, several Internet services offer to send letters by e-mail to be deposited in the Rebbe's tomb. The Ohel Chabad Lubavitch Center receives hundreds of messages for this purpose, and those in charge deposit them at the tomb every two hours.

The ultimate nature of Rabbi Menachem Mendel Schneerson — whether he is the Messiah — may still appear unknown to many people. Still, his influence and presence remain determining factors for Chabad Lubavitch worldwide.

Chapter Three

Proselytism

"Chabad Lubavitch uses formulas of proven effectiveness in spreading their spiritual project. And they go straight to the heart. They listen and advise. They listen, and they give. They listen and talk, offering millenary answers. They do not promise what they do not believe in. They say what is written in the Torah and live as God commands. They have the means, that's true. They soothe anxiety and offer a scenario in which everything makes sense, an explanation that obeys a higher sense of justice... They provide a kind of escape route amid the values and meaning crisis. They appear to be something that grows, is successful, and lives Judaism with confidence and joy, which is no small feat in this day and age."
Diego Melamed, *Los judíos y el menemismo* [Jews and Menemism]

Awakening the inner spark of each Jew: How does Chabad Lubavitch bring assimilated Jews closer to Orthodoxy?

With a total area of four hundred and forty square meters and space for seven hundred people when used as an auditorium, the Emerald Room is the largest and most stylish room of the *Dinastía Maisit* event center in the dense Jewish-populated Villa Crespo neighborhood in Buenos Aires City.

The dark mustard-colored columns contrast with the planned symmetry of the light walls, and their smooth decoration is interrupted by some plaster moldings of circular shapes.

There are few people yet; only the comments and murmurs of the women can be heard filtering from the other side of the cream-colored fabric *mechitza* screen, which separates the room in two according to the Orthodox mandate, which does not allow men and women to share a prayer or meeting spaces to preserve modesty and decency.

Above the stage, a rectangular sign reads:

> Great Farbrengen
> Kislev 19 Celebrating Hasidic Joy and Inspiration
> Chabad Lubavitch

In the left corner is a picture of the Seventh Lubavitch Rebbe. In the parallel corner, a portrait of the First Lubavitch Rebbe.

Today's Hasidic gathering (*farbrengen*) is to commemorate what Hasidim consider the *Rosh Hashanah of Hasidut*, a holiday that not only coincides with the date of birth of the Maggid of Mezerich (the successor of the Baal Shem Tov, founder of the Hasidic movement) but also, and especially, with the release of the First Rebbe of Lubavitch, Shneur Zalman of Liady, from the Czarist prisons.

The security guard held me for a moment while he checked my bag and asked me why I was there, what Beit Chabad I usually go to, and what the name of its rabbi was.

In a hurry to improvise, I only told him I was actually "getting closer" to Chabad and that I had come because the invitation sent by e-mail said that it was an event open to the community. That was the key for him to let me in because it meant more people approaching Chabad. They would not refuse me entry on that basis.

I can see a row of heads with yarmulkes in the first row of chairs in front of me. I accept they are the faint periphery of Jews sympathetic to Chabad, Jews who came for some reason I can't discern. I am amused by the yarmulke of a guy a few chairs away from mine, fastened with a little metal hair buckle whose tip ends in a Star of David.

Some Lubavitchers are moving in, like a tall, thin man who looks like a doctor.

An older lady walks across in front of the stage, where they are still testing the sound and video. The lady waves to a man on this side and soon slips back on the other side of the modesty wall.

Now, a boy is sitting next to me. He wears a grey coat and hat, a blue shirt, a salmon-colored tie, black leather shoes with rounded toes, and slight mustache hair. He is also wearing *tzitzit*, the strips or bangs that observant Jews wear around their waists to keep in mind the 613 precepts they must fulfill.

Other women peek out behind the screen, spy on the male sector, and disappear again.

The boy beside me runs off and gives way to a man who knows him. They talk and are dressed very much alike. They could be father and son, but they don't look much alike.

The young man tells him about a brochure we were given when we came in, a promotion from a healthcare company that advertises itself as "For you and yours." The sale is for a "five percent discount for the entire community." The older man replies, "I don't need them. I have *HaShem* as my health provider," and then complains that he doesn't get to read the translation of what they are showing on the screen to test the video. The man now complains about the air conditioning: "It's on minimum," he says and fans himself with his hand.

The image of the Rebbe invades the screen, and a round of applause comes from the women's sector.

"Thank you, thank you," says the man next to me as if the applause were for him.

Some Lubavitchers sit in the back seats.

A man prays with his back to the stage, leaning his body back and forth.

I hear someone say that they will put together a *minyan*, and soon after, a small group of people praying, also with their backs to the stage at the same level as the row I am in.

The man next to me talks to me,

"Do you know who is coming here?" he says.

"No, who?"

"The President," his tone is serious, but he immediately laughs at his joke, "No, I am just kidding! How did you expect her to come if she is the country's leading anti-Semite?!"

I look to the side.

"If they distribute food, it will become crowded. Notice how there is no one here? That's because they are not giving food," the man continues.

And he keeps going. He says he's attending the meeting because his wife is Orthodox. In reality, it is not his wife. It is his fiancée. Technically speaking, she will be his second wife. His first wife abandoned him fifteen years ago.

"We are going to do it. We are leaving. We are doing *Aliyah* and getting to Israel. I will go next May, and she leaves in June."

"You're just leaving?"

"Yes, yes, off we go," he says with a look of circumstance.

Then he tells me he had a tumor in his brain: "That's why I can't see or smell. See? I can barely distinguish you as a set of shadows", he tells me.

I listen to him as the room fills and the video and audio systems are calibrated.

"During my time as a conscript, I was assigned to serve in the federal police. Do you have any idea how many anti-Semites there were?"

Then he tells me about when an American rabbi was visiting and, for some reason, stopped by his house and met his fiancée.

"When he saw I wasn't wearing *tzitzit*, he asked why I didn't have them. I told him I had no money to buy them. He took out of his pocket a hundred dollars and gave them to me. For them, it's an obligation to give money to charity. Did you know that?"

A rabbi with a long beard and a few gray tips comes on stage. He does not introduce himself, and there is no need to. Everyone present knows that he is Rabbi Tzvi Grunblatt.

"Today we celebrate the energy, the strength of what Hasidism represents," he begins his speech in an accent that is a potent mix of Yiddish, English, and Spanish.

"Rabbi Israel Baal Shem Tov was born in 1698, just after the Cossack pogroms that had wiped out a third of the Jewish population of Europe. The Jewish people were fallen, discouraged materially and spiritually. That's where he came and awakened, breathed a soul into the entire Jewish people by founding the Hasidic movement." His tone is seductive. He speaks not like a preacher, but like a scholar or a university professor. He holds the attention of a silent room. "What did Israel Baal Shem Tov do? He revealed the secret. The secret of what? The secret of what a Jew is. The secret of what the Torah is. And the secret of what God is. There is no more darkness when those secrets are in front of someone's eyes. 'Whoever knows the secret,' said the Baal Shem Tov, 'can illuminate.'"

Chabad Lubavitch's communications can be linked to New Age language forms. One of the most powerful of these is the idea that the initiates have a secret and that knowing it brings light to life and the possibility of waking others up. Part of Lubavitcher's logic is based on this: a Jew who has awakened that inner light can help another to find it and kindle it. Grunbaltt continues his speech: "The people of Israel, God, and the Torah are three parts of a whole that can't be separated. Each of these has two sides: one that is shown and one that is hidden. The Jew's intelligence, feelings, and the person we know are all shown. But there is a hidden side to his soul that we don't always see. Then, there is the face of the Torah that has been shown to us. We know this: the laws, the stories, the text, and how we know what it means. A man like Abraham married a woman like Sarah. They had a son named Isaac, everyone here's grandfather or great-grandfather. That's how it was. Our grandparents, Abraham and Sarah, Isaac, and Rivka, were the same way. They were not mystical beings; they were human beings. That is the revealed Torah. The laws. For example, put on *tefillin*. That is the law. Women have to light the Shabbat candles. That is the law. The Talmud is the concrete body of the Torah. Then, according to the Zohar, there is a hidden part behind all of that. There is a whole spirit and a hidden soul behind every law and tale. It is beyond our comprehension and perception. What action did the Baal Shem Tov take? He revealed the secret. The Torah may look like it has a lot of rules, and it does. It's a list of rules that must be followed. But when the Torah's hidden soul comes out into the light, that law that seems to squeeze us becomes a source of inspiration and light."

The speech aims to persuade his audience to fulfill the *mitzvot*, or the 613 precepts in total (248 positives and 365 negatives), that every Jew is supposed to fulfill to make this world a holy dwelling place for God. The speech skillfully combines the purely mechanical parts of Jewish religious practice with the idea that everyone here is unique because they know a secret that the founder of Hasidism told them. The knowledge of this secret gives the people in this room a firm foundation to plant explanations of the most pragmatic articles of a rule-bound religion, such as the Jewish religion. Many of the *baalei teshuvah* here today would have recognized those same laws as out-of-date and ridiculous remnants of cultural heritage in the not-too-distant past. At least, that's how I feel at this moment. I feel triggered by the false narrative about a mythical belonging tied to biblical times: no one here is the grandchildren or great-grandchildren of the patriarch Abraham.

But in this quiet room, all you can hear is Grunbaltt's strong rhetoric, which includes repeating keywords in a clear tone with a firm voice. A baby's cry doesn't even reach a first wail before it stops.

The rabbi traces the succession from the Baal Shem Tov to Shneur Zalman of Liady. Meanwhile, a Lubavitcher walks through the ranks, handing out small plastic cups with a bottom filled with vodka to all the men present.

The story of Chabad's First Rebbe's imprisonment also lends credence to the concept of martyrdom. To keep the secret of God, the Torah, and the Jew from being revealed to the Gentiles, he was betrayed by the opposition, the so-called *Misnagdim*, and imprisoned by the Tsar.

I get the cup of vodka; I try to pass it to the man sitting next to me who was giving me a talk, and he rejects it.

"No, I don't like it. Give me a good whisky. I won't refuse you that," he laughs. "You know how these Russians drink here, don't you?"

Rabbi Grunblatt now asks for a l'chaim, a toast to Hasidism, which has made it possible for Chabad Lubavitch to exist today in all parts of the world and for Judaism to be once again a secret to share with so many brothers.

I drink the cup of vodka the man refused in two or three gulps and feel that the confinement, the people, the pure alcohol, and Grunblatt's speech are making me bloated.

An organ plays, and from the front rows, there is applause that follows the melody of a Hasidic chant that goes on for a few minutes.

When they finish singing, Grunblatt returns to the microphone and introduces a video: "The Baal Shem Tov of our generation, this is the Lubavitch Rebbe!"

The video shows some samples of the leader's life. Grunblatt returns to the stage where he continues: "Hasid is someone who follows the teachings of the Baal Shem Tov, is not the one who knows the theory. It is the one who applies it, the one who approaches another Jew, the one who awakens his soul, the one who takes advantage of every situation to pull him out of the swamp and help him fulfill a *mitzvah*. Action is the main thing. This is the work of the Rebbe's emissaries worldwide."

Next, he shows a video that was taken at the recent World Congress of Emissaries of the Rebbe, the *Kinus Hashluchim*, in New York City, where he says that about four thousand emissaries of the Rebbe were in the same room: "Three thousand rabbis and one thousand civilians. The Congress of the Shluchim, the work of the Baal Shem Tov, applied to the 21st century."

In the meantime, trays with two kinds of *lekach*, a honey sponge cake typical of Ashkenazi cuisine, are being passed around.

The audio and sound problems continue. Resigned, Rabbi Grunblatt says: "Well, it's just that *Mashiach* has not come yet... we are waiting for him, but he has not arrived yet."

The video shows many Hasidim in hoods, hats, and beards dancing around the tables of what looks like a gigantic wedding. Some carry other rabbis on their shoulders.

"You can count them. You're going to see that there are four thousand," says Grunblatt.

After the video finishes, businessman Miguel Rosental is invited to the podium.

A well-known figure in the province of Santa Fe, Rosental is engaged in the stock market, real estate investments, and hotels, and his holding also owns a currency exchange business.

A powerful man, he stands on the dais with a *yarmulke* covering his head like any other Jew man in the room.

Chabad Lubavitch has always known how to connect with the rich and powerful. The businessman's embrace of Rabbi Grunblatt is an example of this. It also helps explain why Lubavitch gets so much money from donations: they have access to a group of donors with a lot of buying power.

"Why do I say I have to pinch myself to see if it's true?" says the businessman. "Because I can't believe being in this room with so many people listening to what I might say. I see a lot of familiar and beloved faces. I must say that for me, those faces represent feeling alive. I can feel alive materially, alive in my body, but there is a vast difference between feeling alive in my body and feeling alive in my soul. I can tell you I only felt alive in the body until not so long ago. I would say seven or eight years ago. I was a person who got up in the morning, dressed, went to work, and did the life every human being does. But there was something I was missing. It was as if my spirit didn't exist. I see here Tzvi Grunblatt, and Shlomo Tawil, the rabbi of Rosario City. I see great friends who have helped me to be a cheerful person. As I told you, I had never put on tefillin until eight years ago."

The discovery of Chabad Lubavitch by the businessman from Rosario took place in 2002 when he spent a Passover dinner (*seder*) at the five-star Llao Llao Hotel in Bariloche, one of the most world-renowned Argentinian tourist destinations in its southern Patagonia region. The Passover celebration in the famous and exclusive hotel began in 1999 at the request of the businessman, also present tonight, Eduardo Elsztain, one of Argentina's wealthiest men and perhaps one of the most visible faces of the country's influential sympathizers and contributors to Chabad Lubavitch.

As one of the hotel's shareholders, Elsztain had proposed to Grunblatt several times the idea of closing an exclusive hall and filling it with influential Jews, potential donors to Chabad, until the rabbi accepted the idea. The event was a tremendous success and has been repeated multiple times since then.

Since then, special tours to spend the Jewish holiday at the Llao Llao Hotel have been available for booking. The facility has been refurbished to meet all the needs of an orthodox Jew in a clean environment with kosher food menus and even a *mikveh* for ritual baths.

"When I entered that Pesach *Seder* and saw so many people dressed in black, with hats, I didn't understand what was going on, a rabbi stood up and asked me: 'Do you have a place to spend the *seder*'" Rosental recalls his first immersion into Orthodox Judaism. "I wondered what a *seder* was and thanked the rabbi who had made me the offer, having perhaps one of the best nights of my life. Rabbi Grunblatt saw that, over time, I could gradually come to fulfill some precepts he had just mentioned. So, eight years ago, he took me to Shlomo Tawil to have the *tefillin* put on me. The sequence of events that followed was dizzying. Today, it seems incredible to me to be here, wearing a yarmulke and speaking to people who know I don't fully understand everything."

Rosental says that together with a group of businessmen friends, he travels every year to Ukraine, Poland, and other places of pilgrimage for Hasidism, where the principal sages of the movement are buried. He describes the experience as a trip that aims to recharge spiritual energy for the rest of the year, just before the High Holidays, which they spend in Argentina, and then immediately embark on a trip to the International Conference of Shluchim in Brooklyn.

The businessman recreates scenes from his travels as a succession of experiences that brought him closer to the communal aspect of Chabad and spiritual fulfillment. "I remember that the first *mikveh* I ever went into was the one that the Baal Shem Tov owned. My friends were all there, but I was one of the last to walk in because I was shy and a little scared. I went in when they were all singing and shouting with joy because they were going to see the tomb of the Baal Shem Tov. I thought the *mikveh* was a little dirty. The water looked dirty. I went down and got in up to my neck. That's the truth. I didn't have the nerve to stick my head in. When I came out, my friend César Wengrower saw me and said, 'Your hair looks a little dry. What happened? Didn't you stick your head in?' I told him, 'No, César, the water isn't very clean; it is full of loose hairs.' He looked at me and said, 'Come on. Put your head in the water nine times. When you get out, you'll know what it is.' I did what he said, and ever since then, I no longer think a *mikveh* can be dirty. From then on, I started to really like what a *mikveh* is."

What Chabad Lubavitch offers that is appealing to an assimilated Jew is what Rosental emphasizes: hospitality, which allows him to experience a form of intense Judaism and happiness.

He ends his words with thanks "to those who have given me back my spiritual life, those who have taught me what a true Jew is, what a *Yehudi* enjoys by fulfilling the precepts." And then he dedicates a toast to all those present.

Grunblatt takes the stage to tell a brief anecdote before giving way to Eduardo Elsztain, who is greeted with applause and embraces the rabbi on his way to the stage.

The man who now stands in front of the five hundred people in this ballroom is used to appearing before much more demanding and less benign audiences, such as the legendary Anne Krueger (former number two of the International Monetary Fund) at the Davos Economic Forum in 2004. On that occasion, he had to defend Argentina in the face of her economic orthodoxy intransigence.

Contrary to that time, Elsztain is here to defend another form of Orthodoxy: religious Jewish Orthodoxy. But more than that, one of the wealthiest people in Argentina will try to share his experience, just like his friend did just now.

The well-known story goes that this man comes from a middle-class Jew family. He began his career as a manager for his father Isaac's real estate firm. His meteoric rise to the real estate empire he now oversees began in 1989 when he visited New York City. There, he met the Hungarian-Jewish speculator George Soros, whom he persuaded of the profitability of investing in Argentina and with whom he worked for ten years until 2000, when the Argentine economy was already on the verge of its December 2001 collapse.

Elsztain had met Rabbi Tzvi Grunblatt shortly before his trip to New York and had become Jewish Orthodox at the latter's request. Given the close relationship that has existed between both men since then, the suggestion that Chabad Lubavitch has served as an intermediary between the Hungarian Jew magnate and the Argentine businessman is insistent and does not appear implausible, given that Chabad frequently serves as a business space between members of its community.

"I have to admit that Tzvi has a strength in his word," says Elsztain from the stage. "I had told him this week I was unavailable, that I have a friend's wedding, and he insisted until he convinced me to come today, even if it was only for twenty minutes." Elsztain's presence on stage captures the public's attention. It is not a minor thing that he is present here and now. His convening power, by the mere fact of being a successful businessman and one of the wealthiest men in Argentina, separated from the public by nothing more than the stage platform, telling intimate anecdotes of his relationship with the head of the institution, generate a staging of power and the advantages of belonging. Whether it is presented that way.

"The only thing I can say after knowing Tzvi for over thirty years is: thank you very much," Elsztain's voice sounds convinced. "I thank him because, after thirty years of knowing him, I believe that every time he takes someone at his word, he is not thinking about himself but about what else he can do for him." The tribune applauds, and Elsztain continues over the chorus of clapping: "It's giving and giving and giving. And when I prepared to come here, he told me I didn't have to prepare anything. He just wanted me to tell you what this gathering of all the Rebbe's emissaries in New York means to me. For me, it's a dance. It is every *sheliach* representing their small or big *Beit Chabad*. When you see all of them dancing, it is amazing."

Elsztain now tells a business anecdote in which a complicated situation ended up being resolved, at least in his story, through an intervention that could be miraculous. It is the story of a Lubavitch emissary in Peru, and when he finishes, he gets another round of applause. His last sentences bore the mark of that entrepreneurial ideology mixed with the Chabad flavor of new-age discourse. Combining business with extremely rigid religious precepts is undoubtedly one key to Lubavitch's success, and no one better than Eduardo Elsztain expresses it in his presence and anecdotes.

"I believe," Elsztain concludes his speech. "This is what I was telling you: when one trusts in *HaShem*, everything is fulfilled in the word. That is why we must be cautious with everything we say." Grunblatt, who was standing to the side, now takes the microphone and, stepping on the last words of the businessman, takes advantage of the situation to ask everyone to shout: "May the *Mashiach* come now! May the *Mashiach* come now! May the *Mashiach* come now!" The tribune chants the slogan, and the rabbi then invites Rabbi Rafael Tawil, Chabad's emissary in the northern Argentine province of Salta, to take the stage and share his life story.

He uses Hasidic tales as parables of the difficulties of living an orthodox life in a massively Roman Catholic city like Salta, where until three years ago, he and his family were the only ones who respected Shabbat.

Rabbi Tawil, who is young and thriving on stage, is an example of the new generation of rabbis born into Chabad families. These young people work with the conviction of those who have always lived inside the institution. "There are indeed no observant Jewish families, no *mikveh*, and no Jewish schools, but we are there to sit at a Purim table and do the *mitzvot*. To do it where no one else does," says the rabbi.

The experience of the massive gathering serves as community building: "This is who we are. This is what we do." Now, Tawil is talking about the Kinus HaShluchim, which is the annual Chabad meeting that takes place in New York City. During that time, all of Chabad's emissaries from all over the world get together in one room and forget about their worries for a while. Photos of the gatherings show a sea of black hats and coats, grey and young beards, bottles of vodka on the table, and a lot of dancing.

Tawil refers to Gaby Holsztein, a Chabad rabbi who was murdered along with his wife Rivke in the Bombay bombings in 2008. He mentions they met when the young rabbi passed through Buenos Aires City to study. Tributes to the Chabad martyrs were the second primary reference of the evening. "He gave up his life for the *Yehudim*. He didn't have a house or a car. That's the real life, the real *Yehudi* who cares for others. That's one effect, one of the true effects of *Kinus HaShluchim*. If I have to say what it means to me, I will say it means charging a battery. After attending, I feel renewed. It makes me want to go to Salta and explore the city, which is good. I come with a lot of plans and a strong desire to do things, which I think people can sense and that I can pass on to them."

The rabbi tells the story of a French Jewish couple who shared their last Shabbat table in the country with him, recounts how they met while living in Indonesia, and says there must have been divine intervention because of the serendipitous way they met. "I want to end," he says, "by making a l'chaim so that this *farbrengen* may impact on us for the entire year and that *HaShem* will see the effort that each one of us makes and once and for all send the *Mashiach*, send this redemption, and that all of us together may return to *Beit Ha Mikdash* with the *Mashiach*. L'chaim!" The rabbi receives an extended round of applause. When he finishes, Grunblatt takes the stage to announce that a memorial video about the Bombay victims will be played.

The video projection starts, and I get up and walk around away from the man next to me.

I walk through the chairs and see a man standing next to a column. A few weeks ago, he told me loudly that everyone in Lubavitch is a drug dealer, a white slave trader, a drug addict, or sick. He also sees me but acts like he doesn't recognize me.

I leave the main hall. In the lobby, there is a large crowd of men and women mingling. A Chabad Hasid, assisted by his wife and children, sells slices of pizza, waffles, and pancakes from behind a table.

I go back inside when the main lecture of the evening starts. It will be given by Rabbi Nathan Grunblatt, Rabbi Tzvi's brother. I feel dizzy. The small glass of vodka, the heat, the number of people, the noise, the tingling legs from sitting so long listening to the speeches. I cross paths with a rabbi I have already met before. He greets me,

"The journalist!"

I didn't understand his words or who he was, but I gradually recognized him. He appears to have changed since the last time I saw him. He was more "indoors" the last time he wasn't wearing a black jacket, and now he's in full dress uniform and holding one of his children in his arms.

This is a farbrengen. This is a gathering where the community comes together as one extensive family, and those who don't yet belong to it get a good look at what is happening inside.

I finish greeting the rabbi and consider going back to get a seat. Rabbi Nathan's lecture is about to begin. But I'm at a breaking point. I exit the hall, cross the crowded lobby with a tired expression, and sneak onto the street.

Chabad Lubavitch took my baby away

Families torn apart because a son abandoned his secular life to pursue religion. People who go from the most militant atheism to the most fervent orthodox Jewish faith in a single day.

There is some truth to the myth of brainwashing. Many people from secular Jewish families have found an alternative path in life by converting to Jewish Orthodoxy. It is also true that Chabad Lubavitch was the institution that first presented them with this path, assisted them in making the change, and finally welcomed them into the heart of their community.

"Whenever I go to Buenos Aires, I see many new people in our community and ask myself: 'Who are these people?' The community has grown a lot. And it keeps growing," a Lubavitch rabbi who works far from Argentina's capital recently told me.

Why is it in the interest of Chabad Lubavitch that more and more Jews become observant of Jewish laws and precepts? Samuel Heilman and Menachem Friedman offer an excellent synthesis of this point: "The goal of such proselytizing is not just to make believers or bring back prodigal children, or even to make Jewish observance possible for those who have gone far from their Jewish home. At its core, Lubavitchers believe, it is an essential means to fulfill a messianic vision that began with the Ba'al Shem Tov." (p. 2) That vision was described in one of Baal Shem Tov's letters, describing a meeting with the Messiah in heaven. In this encounter, the latter supposedly told the sage that he would descend to Earth once the message of Hasidism had been spread to all Jews.

The goal would be to make our world a holy place where the Messiah can come down and begin his reign in the least traumatic way possible. The theology behind this shows the need to reunite all the sparks of God scattered over the Earth, a basic idea of Jewish mysticism.

Rabbi Moshe Blumenfeld, director of *Leoded*, one of Chabad Lubavitch Argentina's social assistance programs, maintains: "The expectation of anyone in Chabad, anyone who follows the Rebbe, is that the Messiah will come. Everything we do is to realize what in the Torah is considered the goal of creation: redemption. The clock of History has run out; for the first time, we Jews are scattered worldwide. History has ended, and this is a little further. The genuine success for someone educated in Chabad and trying to transmit its message is to return God to the world."

So, how does Chabad fulfill its objectives? What factors are involved in the phenomenon of the *baalei teshuvah*, the returnees, those who become Orthodox?

The messianic idea is not unique to Chabad Lubavitch, but it has been a big part of how it came to be. Scholars who have investigated the subject agree that the process began with the zeitgeist around the beginning of the 1960s when Western society underwent many political and social changes.

The protest and countercultural movements that arose as a response to the Vietnam War and the channeling of that youthful energy by the Lubavitch Rebbe to put it at the service of a revival of Judaism after the catastrophe of the Holocaust seem to have been one pillar of this phenomenon.

The Brazilian anthropologist Marta Topel, who analyzed the phenomenon of Jewish Orthodoxy in her book *Jerusalem & São Paulo: a nova ortodoxia judaica em cena*, explains: "The idea of *teshuvah* in its modern meaning was born as a result of the connection established by Rabbi Joseph Isaac between the physical disappearance of European Jewry and the spiritual poverty of North American Judaism. From his new residence in Brooklyn, the Rebbe appealed to the Jews of the United States to assume their responsibility before the tragic destiny of their co-religionists in Europe and, by process of collective *teshuvah*, to contribute to the immediate redemption and the arrival of the Messiah." (38)

Thus, on the one hand, we find the need for Orthodox Jewish Holocaust refugees in the United States to form a movement to regenerate lost traditions, customs, and lives, and, on the other, a contentious youth in search of answers.

Many theorists regard Orthodox Judaism as an orthopraxis rather than an orthodox religion. That is to say that it has a ritualized series of norms that are placed even above the dogmas of faith. It can be understood as a way or a way of life that also provides answers to existential questions.

As Topel points out: "The orthodox *modus vivendi*, so different from the values and rules of modern 'superficial and materialistic' society, emerged as a seductive alternative for hundreds of men and women eager to change the course of their lives radically." (106-107).

Judaism as a provider of a way of life was the initial impulse that led many young people to join Orthodoxy. They were the first boundary of a movement that can be thought of as having two: an internal one, where members follow all the *mitzvot*, precepts, and laws that govern the way of life for an observant Jew, and an external one, where people who get close may be drawn in by the consistency of the rabbis and members of the community on the internal boundary.

The mechanics of the double frontier is one of the main characteristics of the *keruv* (approach) work of Chabad Lubavitch towards the rest of the secular Jews: they let themselves run the external border as far as they can, always trying to keep the demands of those who are getting close to a minimum level while changing to meet the needs of those who are outside. The sociologist Jésica Azar, who analyzed some characteristics of the institution's operation, points out: "They combine some of what Chabad Lubavitch has always done with the fact that people are looking for places to belong at this time in History. It is a marketing strategy that allows people to enter without precise limits. It is an institutional way to reach new people. In the post-modern world, where nothing is clear, the way for Chabad to grow as an institution is to loosen up a little their strict rules for the outside world. So, the kid who comes to the Chabad courses or activities does not clearly know what he is doing there. Thus, they combine their unique answer and vision of the world with other activities that any secular Jew can identify. It is complicated if you give the kid only Torah and expect him to identify only with that. It's different if you tell him: 'You go about your daily routine, watching TV at night, but while you're at it, study some Torah with us.'"

Chabad Lubavitch's mode of operation for moving from secularity to fulfilling the *mitzvot* is gradual, slow, and not necessarily complete. That means that not just any secular Jew they encounter will eventually become observant.

One of the most effective marketing actions that Chabad Lubavitch carries out, and that affects this process, is more of a branding effort. They are extraordinarily effective at altering the public's perception of Jewish Orthodoxy. Showing themselves to be open, modern, and involved in the everyday world, sharing the same concerns and many of the tastes of those they want to approach. So, a day like Shabbat, where Jews can't touch money, work, light a fire, turn on or off lights, or travel by car, can become, in the words of a Lubavitcher, "one day a week at Club Med": a place to rest where the Jew doesn't have to worry about worldly things and can get some fresh air and find peace with its spirit. The Lubavitch discourse then transforms what appears to be a burden and restriction into an advantage and a means of relaxation. In fact, according to Chabad, in a hyper-technological society full of worries like ours, even on weekends, this appears to be the only correct way to rest.

So, everything looks different in the Lubavitch discourse: a holiday with thousands of rules and protocols is not a burden but a legacy of the Jewish people; a way to connect with customs that the ancestors did in Europe; a memory of the *zeide* (grandfather) or the *bubbe* (grandmother); an instance of reaffirming the individual identity from belonging to a small community in the middle of a much larger collective that is, to some extent, seen as alien, as is the rest of the gentile, non-Jewish society. This also works because it's hard to keep a strong sense of what it means to be Jewish today in other, less Orthodox currents. These seem too rigid and inexpungable to outsiders. Other less strict Jewish identity types also have trouble keeping people in their communities and getting new people to join.

Rabbi Damian Karo knows the mechanics of the double frontier Chabad employs: being open to people from the outside and closed, strictly in compliance within its community. During his time as second in command in Chabad Lubavitch in Argentina, Karo was pivoting between the two borders, bringing people from the external border closer to the internal one. He comments that one secret of the "Chabad method," one formula of its success, comprises gaining the trust and friendship of the subject they want to bring into the observance. He explains the procedure by analogy with the method used in the case of an anorexia patient in recovery. He says: "Let's take the case of a person on the verge of malnutrition who sees herself obese in the mirror. How do you recover such a person? The first thing is to gain their trust, to befriend them. You establish a bond of trust, no matter how long it takes. Six months? A year? It doesn't matter. When I have her trust, I tell her, 'Look, I want you to do me a personal favor. I want you to eat this eighth of a tomato. I swear you're not going to get fat.' It's a long and arduous process. Two months go by, and I get her to accept and do it. The faith in me I built during that time will allow her to eat that eighth of a tomato, and it will allow me to say to her, 'Did you see? You ate that eighth of tomato and didn't get fat. You look the same.' I know this will not save her and that she could have died in the six months that passed until I convinced her. But now that she has eaten that eighth of a tomato, we will get her to eat it again. Twice a week, three times a week, then with a little lettuce, until she eats normally. That's a format that some Chabad people use."

He then gives a concrete example of his way of working during his years in the Chabad *yeshiva*: "I used to run a campaign called *Shabbat Shalom*, which comprised standing on Fridays at the door of the secular Jewish ORT high school to get the kids to read Torah; to give candles to the girls to light; to give them pamphlets. When the kids passed by, they didn't want to talk to us. So, I would say to them: 'Excuse me, excuse me,' and they would say: 'No, no, no.' Then I would answer: 'But excuse me, I just wanted to say, *Shabbat Shalom*. Do you mind?'; 'Not really.' Next week, I would proceed with the same. 'Excuse me, excuse me'; 'Look, I don't want to put *tefillin* or pick up your leaflets'; 'I just want to tell you, *Shabbat Shalom*. May I?' And so on: '*Shabbat Shalom*; *Shabbat Shalom*,' until the kids got used to our presence, they passed by and smiled at us. 'Hey, *Shabbat Shalom*,' they were the ones telling us. Until one day, that boy who didn't want anything to do with me came running to me and said: 'Hey, I have a math test. Shall I put on *tefillin* and see if God helps me?' I answered him: 'Look, that's not why you put them. But if you want to put them, I'll help you."

Pablo Hupert holds a degree in History and is a scholar of contemporary Jewish issues. He understands that the global social configuration is fundamental to understanding the success of the Chabad Lubavitch-led *teshuvah* movements. The historian says: "There is talk today of the uncertainty of contemporary culture, of a permanent crisis, which is the way of being of today's capitalism. It is no accident that in the last ten years, there have been similar economic crises in various parts of the world. Each time they occur, they are cataclysms, and the lulls between crises do not erase the uncertainty. What subjective security can one have when one does not know what will remain in one's life? Security can be achieved when things are more permanent. Still, it is tough to achieve if you do not even know if you will remain firm in your job." The historian recognizes that in the face of these centrifugal forces, others oppose it, which he refers to as centripetal forces and which attempt to nucleate, cohere, and generate community. Chabad Lubavitch is one example. Then, given the context of a lack of vital certainties, the fertile ground for the revival of religions observed in the last decades.

Joining the Lubavitch community can not only solve the vital anguish of many people but also give them a framework of social and emotional support and a space of mutual benefit. Marta Topel states: "Being part of Orthodox life is not reduced to incorporating a new worldview. Above all, it implies integration into a cohesive community that assists all those who wish to join a group but lack the resources to live a Torah and *mitzvah*-filled life." (120).

Entering a community such as the Lubavitch community implies, on the one hand, social integration and grants certainties for a slightly less stressful life while facilitating for the newcomers a soft landing in a host of customs, traditions, and rituals that seem, at first, unmanageable. The increasing compliance with mitzvot and the body's adaptation to a series of rituals ensures a practical way to experience these newfound firm grounds: one puts one's body into the transformation process and lives it. It is no longer an ideal sense or one that only requires dogmatic faith but also includes the body as a channel for religious experience.

Some theorists argue this trait has been lost in the Reform and Conservative Jewish experiences because they propose a Jewish experience that lowers religious observance demands. A model that may have been very effective in the past but no longer determines a sense of life or a series of certainties strong enough for many people who find them in Jewish Orthodoxy. Chabad Lubavitch provides a recipe for contemporary Jews to connect directly with and inherit their Eastern European ancestors' customs and ways of life. The black hoods and hats, the beards and customs all appear as experiences drawn from a past that are recovered as a living inheritance in the present. According to the Brazilian anthropologist: "In a world and an era characterized by ethical relativism and multiple identities, sometimes contradictory, sometimes simply different, that converge in the same individual, it is easy to see the peace of mind that a manual of 'instructions for living' gives to the *baalei teshuvah*, for whom all their doubts and questions have an answer, including what is expected of them as Jews." (244)

Gregorio Kaminsky, Ph.D. in Philosophy and Professor of Social Psychology at the University of Buenos Aires, who has studied issues related to organizations and institutions, insists on the same idea: "These movements plant a shared subjectivity, communally instituted, which is not that of the European rational discourse but the American one. This is very good for many people; it calms the questions of the spirit and implies a certain type of infatuation at the level of subjectivity. They use forms of conviction that imply surrender through schedules, rituals, slogans, noises, shouts, and liberation from the preoccupation with other things. Infatuation and hypnosis. They do not solve your problems but provide you with answers. They have very strong consolations from a conception of the world that has been around for five thousand years."

Without a doubt, Chabad Lubavitch provides answers to the questions. But how does one acquire the customs, rituals, and precepts that an Orthodox Jew must follow? After all, it is difficult to change one's life so radically that one incorporates 613 precepts and everything that makes up a Jewish Orthodox life in such a short period.

The path to religious observance usually begins with respecting the Shabbat and then moves on to incorporating a kosher diet. One thing leads to the other. It is not by chance that the Shabbat marks the beginning of this path, an instance often used by the Lubavitch to show the benefits of an orthodox life. Karo explains that someone outside is invited to a dinner party in a house belonging to one of them: "What are they going to show him? They will show him how they are a happy family and are having a rest and all that. When they get there, many people see that people who didn't know them invited them to the house to eat. They opened the doors of their house. They made them feel comfortable and showed them a happy family. All of this has an effect. The person seeking an answer may conclude that this is what he desires for his life. If they ask me if that image of happiness is accurate, I would say no. They are regular people like us. The man had to go to great lengths to put what they're having for dinner on the table, and the woman had to spend the entire day cooking excessively. They're both exhausted. They might have even argued. They could have had issues with the kids or whatever. Instead, the guest sees that they have an open house and have this idea of toasting because their God told them so. They truly believe they must do this according to their sacred texts. They truly believe that by inviting a stranger to share their Shabbat dinner, they will improve the world and bring the Messiah. Yes, it is true that now they are happy with the guests and with their children. But it is also true that they are tired and bored. Both are true. Of course, I'm referring to specific instances. Each person and family are their world; one cannot generalize."

With all that it implies at the level of observable ritual and values of rest and happiness, the Shabbat dinner is one of the major gateways to Orthodoxy because it allows a glimpse of one of the most pleasant sides of observant life and the Jewish holidays. These two components are the most exploited in the external frontier: invitations to Shabbat dinners, public parties, and massive gatherings.

Chabad Lubavitch has studied carefully how to reach each demographic. They have a form that attracts children, one that attracts teens, one that attracts adults, and one that attracts seniors. All these forms are made to fit what each group might need.

Once the subject approached the Chabad structure and became interested in the new way of life proposed to them, the slow path to *teshuvah* begins.

From his office in Chabad Lubavitch Argentina's most inner frontier, Tzvi Grunblatt offers insight into the *teshuvah* process. Says the rabbi: "Every person is different. Some people have their moment of 'inspiration,' and the light bulb goes on, and they take a turn. Sometimes, you must stop them and make them go slower because they try to speed up too much. In other cases, you must push them and tell them: 'Hey, you can't stay in kindergarten all your life. You must move up.' We work with patience and listen to each person, but we are sure that Judaism is for every Jew. People are afraid to get close to God's law, to Judaism, because they think it will take away their comfort or ability to enjoy life. But it is the contrary. These things will make their lives more enjoyable. It might take some temporary comfort away, but nothing more."

According to Rabbi Damian Karo, accepting the Jewish laws, rites, and customs is slow and starts as a routine: "It is a gradual process. It does not happen from one day to the next. Human beings have a great capacity to adapt. And, when you do it with faith and have the meaning of life solved and placed there, it does not weigh you down. It is more or less difficult, like anything else in life. Who doesn't find it hard to go every day to study or to work? It's like a person tired of dieting, going to the gym, and sunbathing to look good and keeps doing it. Someone who does all that doesn't care much about their appearance. They want to be happy and not have to do all that anymore. But he must do it because that's what the rules of his society say. It doesn't matter if he agrees or wants it; he does it anyway. It bothers him just as much as the system's rules do."

Chabad Lubavitch has a series of institutional devices and trained human teams to fulfill its mission. Still, it also provides a series of facilities for those who wish to enter.

Sociologist Damian Setton argues that the concept of *teshuvah* is challenging to understand in a system of flexible borders and liquid Judaism such as the one proposed by Chabad Lubavitch: "What do we understand by *teshuvah*? Do we define it as starting to wear a hat, eating kosher, and wearing the Chabad hood? Is it when I put on *tefillin* every day but still don't wear a yarmulke on the street? From the sociological point of view, one tries to see what the social actors themselves define. *Teshuvah* is the guy who enters the community. However, for a Lubavitcher, going to a religious class, even if they pay me to do so, means that I am on the right track or that something has awakened in me."

The difficulty of defining what it means to be a *teshuvah* and what it means to be a full Lubavitcher is real. And yet, it can't be denied that every day, more and more men are walking around dressed in Chabad style, and more and more women with baby strollers, skirts that reach their ankles, and wigs for modesty reasons.

In the following chapters, we will examine the institutional structure, campaigns, and methods used by Chabad Lubavitch to attract new Jews to religious observance.

Chapter Four

Conquering the Next Generation of Jews

> "A young person is like fire. With direction and guidance, he or she can change the very shape of the world. Without direction, the fires of youth are wasted at best, while at worst, they can become a dangerous, destructive force. To lead a meaningful life means harnessing the fires of youth; to do so, we must first understand the purpose of youth itself."
> Simon Jacobson, *Toward a Meaningful Life*

The very modern and well-designed web page of the CHAT Group (Centro Hebreo Académico de Torá [Hebrew Academic Torah Center]), which is the youth branch of the Beit Chabad Almagro in Buenos Aires City, explains its objectives and contents in the section *Who we are?* as follows:

The CHAT Center is here to meet two needs that come up among young people in our community (ages 25–39): a sense of belonging that makes it easy to meet new people, socialize, bond, and talk to them, as well as a place to learn the Torah in a dynamic, professional, and modern way, focusing on a wide range of current issues and the fascinating wisdom of our people.

What do we do?

- *Weekly studio meetings | DJ Jew Music | Drinks | Appetizers.*

- *Weekly meetings — Kabalat Shabbat & Kiddush Party.*

- *Conferences and Debates with successful guest speakers.*

- *Outings and social gatherings — Themed parties and events.*

- *Semiannual trips to New York City, Washington, Miami, and Disney World.*

- *Coming soon: Multidisciplinary workshops.*

Upon finishing the course,
End-of-the-year vacations. Did you take part in the course? You won!
Exclusive benefits for CHAT participants.
Did you study? You have your prize! CHAT invites you to enjoy your summer with a dream vacation in New York, Washington, Miami, and Disney World.

After filling out a form on that same page, a few days later, I received a call from a rabbi inviting me to have a personal interview with him before I could attend the group.

I accepted his invitation and arrived at the synagogue a few minutes earlier. The wooden doors were a bit intimidating, but a bright light came from the windows decorated with stars of David. I rang the doorbell, and they opened directly. A security guard wearing a yarmulke asked me why I was there, and after I told him about my meeting with the rabbi. He checked my bag and then went back to make a phone call. I had to wait long until Rabbi Jaim finished a previous admission meeting.

I looked around in the meantime. Several soda bottles were stuck in a plastic container next to a door that led to a hallway in an otherwise neat and clean building.

They made me go upstairs, and I hesitated about grabbing one yarmulke from the pile for the non-wearers. Still, I felt uncomfortable about putting it on, like I was about to commit a desecration or something. But I also felt uncomfortable not wearing it.

Rabbi Jaim vaguely told me about the CHAT project: lectures on Torah focalized on building a group of belonging in Jews from 25 to 39 years old, which at the end of the course, and as "dessert," according to his own words, there was the possibility of a trip to New York, Washington, Miami and Orlando (Disney World), with aerials and lodging at only 999 dollars.

When I told him I was there because I was interested in returning to my roots in Judaism, he shook his head as if he didn't care or thought I was lying.

"As I told you, the trip is the *dessert* of this seminar. The goal is to make friends... and have a good time in a Jewish environment with friends. Are you single?"

I said yes.

"Very good. Here, I tell you, I'm sure you'll get a girlfriend."

He did not ask me for any proof of belonging to the Jewish people. Neither my mother's surname nor any paper that could show I am Jewish. He asked me to write my phone number on a separate sheet of paper, next to those of two boys he had just interviewed.

A class was scheduled for that same day, so he invited me to attend. It was to start in twenty minutes. I then went for a short walk around the block, and when I returned, I felt I would be alone with the rabbi. I got into the synagogue once again. This time, the guard instructed me to follow him through a hallway full of pictures depicting Hasidic scenes of celebrations, prayers, and some pictures of Chabad's Rebbe.

In the back, a room covered with red curtains and a very intense smell of food. I peeked behind the curtains and saw a dining room where some homeless were eating *empanadas* and other things being served to them. The men were all wearing yarmulkes.

I kept going until a girl asked for my personal information again and gave me a pen with the CHAT logo and a notepad with the same logo in the background. Some other people around my age were also waiting to enter the class.

We went up another flight of stairs next to waiters carrying trays of *empanadas*, potato *knishes*, and pastries.

The room had blue neon lights and a white two-piece couch in the center.

In front of the couch, left, right, and center, were rows of red chairs and tables with food and soft drinks in the back.

I sat down and waited for a while. A classmate in the chair next to me talked to me. She told me she was a regular at Jewish groups, especially Chabad. She also told me she had tried several times to complete the program to get a cheap trip to the U.S. but never managed to endure the seminars and dropped out early. This time, she was determined to make it so she could travel cheaply to Disney World.

"An offer like this... It's hard to turn down," she said. "I don't understand those who take this seriously. Even so, I can tell you that there are all kinds of crazy people around here."

"At least we can take advantage of the food for now," I said, standing up to look for a *knish*.

At about 8:30 p.m., the two rabbis hanging around the place sat on the couch. They introduced themselves: Baruj Jaim (who gave me the admission interview) and Ariel.

Baruj began speaking.

"I am going to tell you what CHAT is all about. I can start by saying that CHAT was born in a swimming pool in San Bernardo[1] during Pesach with the event coordinator of Beit Chabad Almagro. The question arose: Why do Jewish study groups end at thirty? The answer is that at that age, a young person is supposed to be married and have already started a family. But the other day, there was an article in the newspaper in which they showed that this was not the case. That you can be thirty years old and still be single. So, CHAT was born: the first group for people over thirty. And many have called us and said: 'Hello, yes, I was calling about the trip.' We answer these calls with a simple: 'What trip? There is no trip here.' Let's be clear: this is a group to make friends or find a partner, but it is not a group to travel. The trip is something extra. It's as if we already knew each other and one day we said: 'Hey, why don't we take a trip, since we are all friends.' That's the idea. That the trip is a way of sharing as a group. We are here to have a good time and to meet people, but this is not a proposal for a trip. CHAT is a place to have a good time in a group. This differentiates this group from other groups in Chabad. We don't want this to be a boring group where you come out of obligation and feel like it's a chore. We want you to look forward to the weekly meeting to have a good time."

After he was done, the rabbi gave the microphone to one of his colleagues.

"The idea of CHAT is to combine containers with content," the second rabbi said. "In other groups, there is a situation where there is more content and fewer containers or less content and more containers. Our idea combines both: the group experience with innovative content, burning issues from the mystical point of view. The idea is to get involved, participate in this, and have fun. We are going to work a lot with group dynamics, with contact and interaction, bringing dynamism to the contents of the Judaism of the twenty-first century."

Rabbi Jaim grabs the microphone again,

"The travel issue... well, here's the thing, you need to have perfect attendance at the talks. This means that to be eligible for the scholarship allowing you to have the trip for US$999, you must attend all the meetings. Lodging in New York will be in homestays, and in Miami, in hotels. The trip is to be a vacation, and although there will be activities we will perform together, you will be free most of the time. Food is not included except

---

1. A middle-class vacation destination in the Buenos Aires Province.

for Shabbat. The idea of the trip is to be a vacation but also a spiritual one, so we will start early every day with an hour of prayers."

When he finished speaking, the meeting was adjourned, and people got up to leave. Many exchanged greetings. They knew each other from other similar Chabad youth groups.

Jewish youth, divine treasure

Study groups such as CHAT, explicitly aimed at young people and with a reward of a trip to the United States at the "course's" end, abound within the Lubavitch community.

The best known of these is ISEJ (Instituto Superior de Estudios Judaicos [Higher Institute of Jewish Studies]), the heir of an earlier study group, Morashá Universitarios [Morasha College Students.]

That earlier group became famous because of their "scholarships" to all interested in attending. Teenagers who attended all classes received a respectable sum for it and had to undergo periodic evaluations to record their learning. Morashá Universitarios became famous within the Jewish community for being the first to introduce this method of payment to its students, which led some critics to point out that a sort of "commercialization" of Judaism was taking place.

The current proposal seems polished by experience: ISEJ offers a trip to New York and Washington at a meager cost to those who attend a minimum of two hours of classes in Jewish subjects per week for one year.

Aimed at young people who have been excluded from traditional Jewish education in Argentina because of assimilation or Jewish education institution's bankruptcy, ISEJ set the standard for other Chabad Lubavitch study groups in the country, which then adapted their proposals to convert monthly financial aid into a scholarship for a trip to the United States or Israel.

Rabbi Damián Karo comments: "Morashá arose during the worst of the (Argentine) 2001 crisis as a kind of help for needy families because it provided the children with a snack, activities, study, and some cash. In the end, the theoretical discussion is: 'Are we selling the content?' To say that Judaism is free is to say it has no value. To say that it is not only free but also that they must pay you for you to study it is something else. Even if they disguise it with the excuse of economic crisis and aid. But, if instead, they tell you: 'Come and study and at the end of the year, we will give you a ticket to New York City,' it is something else. First, not all those who start the program finish it. The investment is in people who have studied hard for a year. And the money is well spent because the effect is so big. Ten days of brotherhood at the Chabad world headquarters, with all its symbols, is a powerful experience for those who attend."

Changing a monthly financial aid for a subsidized trip seems to have primarily blurred the issue's focus since it is now not a concrete payment but a scholarship students receive at the end of the course. However, the "end of the year trip" is not the only form of "exchange" presented in these youth organizations: their events usually include a festive, social side and excellent and free catering for attendees.

The *Centro para la Juventud* [Youth Center] — located in Beit Chabad Palermo, Buenos Aires City — organizes, every other week, several talks on Jewish topics framed in a horizon of interest for young people. A free shawarma or sushi dinner accompanies these meetings.

The expansion of Chabad's practice of providing Jewish education in exchange for money or trips has made other Jewish organizations in Argentina more hostile to Chabad. These institutions see it as unfair competition because they lack the resources to try something similar.

The Jewish study groups offered by Chabad Lubavitch, with their various characteristics and the specific imprints of each Beit Chabad, offer a similar menu, including a visit to the movement's headquarters at 770 Eastern Parkway in Queens, the Rebbe's tomb and the Crown Heights neighborhood.

The classes try to propose a relaxed mood, where the students' critical intervention and the exchange of ideas are allowed, obviously within the framework of religious education.

The ISEJ proposal includes a list of studies that will meet the needs of the participants. Its classes are diverse, and its time slots are flexible. Students sign up based on their interests and have three attendance options: six hours per week, four hours per week, or two hours per week. The level of the "scholarship" that the institution will grant changes depending on their choice: the trip cost will be US$750 for the first option, US$850 for the second, and US$950 for those who choose the option with the fewest hours in attendance.

Organized in thematic modules of free choice (each class lasts one hour), students in 2010 could choose between the following seminars: Kabbalah, Married Couples, Painting, Jewish Cooking, Hebrew, Groups +30, English, Kabbalat Shabbat, Parashat HaShavua, Couples, Messiah, Life Cycle, Frequently Asked Questions about Judaism and Basic Concepts of Judaism.

To attend, prospective students must pass a rigorous ISEJ rabbis' selection. Only those who have previously signed an affidavit stating that they are children of a Jewish mother can take part in the program (children of a Jewish father and a non-Jewish mother and adopted children are excluded from the program because they are not considered Jewish according to Jewish Orthodoxy beliefs.)

At the first ISEJ briefing, a rabbi teaching the seminars and going on the trip summarizes the program and the places they will visit in the United States. These include the main Lubavitch centers, other places of Jewish interest, tourist attractions, and other recreational venues.

In this way, ISEJ is not only a framework for higher Jewish studies in an environment of a similar age range but also a space where the teachings and study of Judaism are mixed with broad topics and interests. It works as if a child had to take a medicine with an unpleasant taste, and his parents had to help him do it by mixing it with candy or food he liked.

A red cow and the end of the world

Wednesday, 19:46. I walk through the Abasto neighborhood to the Beit Chabad Central, on Agüero Street, between Cabrera and Paraguay Streets. I don't ring the bell at the main gate, which is always open, and I enter the small courtyard where the security checkpoint and some guards are.

I already know the procedure and feel comfortable entering the building, which no longer seems as intimidating as the first few times. One guard asks to check my backpack. I open it; he feels it, sniffs inside, and after making me open my toiletry bag, he lets me pass.

The space of the Central Beit Chabad, which is always occupied by Hasidim, is now being "invaded" by secular Jews who walk its corridors with the arrogance of those who take something that does not belong to them.

Upon entering the building and going downstairs, where the classrooms are, men are mandated to wear a yarmulke. For those who do not have one or forgot to bring one, there are piles of old public-use ones made of paper cloth left over from the 2007 Maccabiah Games.

The encounter between people dressed in black, heavy overcoats and hats, and girls and boys dressed in modern secular and Western attire leaves me with an odd impression.

In the courtyard, some boys play table tennis during recess. In contrast, others smoke, and different groups chat with each other. I stand in line to go through the fingerprint scanner, which is how attendance is computed. Next to the machine, a sign warns that if a student is caught clocking in and leaving before the end of class, he or she will be charged an extra hundred dollars for the trip that month. If the behavior is repeated, the student will be expelled from the program. It also explains the policy on excused absences: by excuse only and making up the missed class by attending another day of the same week.

The narrow corridor connecting the classrooms is clogged with people waiting for their next class to begin or leaving their Jewish cooking class with an aluminum lunch box and a nylon bag in their hands, leaning against the red-painted walls. In colorful and modern design, a bulletin board announces different courses and classes that can be taken. There is also an advertisement for getting a Hebrew name for those who don't have it or do not remember theirs.

A flyer with a picture of the Hasidic heavy metal band *Atzmus* is pasted on a corkboard on the opposite wall.

Also pasted on the wall are an announcement of the next class hours, the classroom and rabbi that correspond to them, and a list of recommendations from the Lubavitch Rebbe for these times immediately preceding the arrival of the Messiah. The most essential precepts to fulfill to hasten his arrival are highlighted.

Next to the stack of public use yarmulkes, there are a few piggy banks for *tzedakah* and a stack with copies of Chabad printed and distributed magazines: *Chabad Magazine* and *Kids Vivan el Desafío* [Kids Live the Challenge] aimed at children.

The boys and girls mingle in the hallway. They talk to each other; they know each other; they are the siblings of someone they know, or the cousin of another person they know, or a friend, or acquaintance of some other someone they know. They all appear to have someone in common, either a referent which has already travelled or a friend who will accompany them. They are part of groups of friends from school or the community center. Inside ISEJ, no one is out for himself. The few people who appear to be here alone are clearly here because they want a cheap trip to New York.

I enter Classroom 2 a few minutes before eight o'clock, which is gradually filling up with men and a few women. We sit around a rectangular table in a classroom that is thick with the presence of hundreds of young people who passed through it during the day. There is also a metal blackboard against the wall, some shelves with Jewish books, and two rows of chairs around the table.

The rabbi enters.

"Good afternoon. As few women are here, I see this is turning into a men's seminar."

I am sitting in the *Fundamental Concepts of Judaism* class, which, for someone like me, who received no formal Jewish education, is proving enlightening on terms like Torah, Tanach, and Talmud.

I chose to take only two hours per week and arranged my classes from eight to nine o'clock and from nine to ten o'clock. I will take *FAQ: Frequently Asked Questions in Judaism*.

"I hope you girls don't feel uncomfortable."

"No worries," answered the two women who remained from a course that had maintained a balance of sexes in the previous weeks.

This week's class is all about *mitzvot*. According to the rabbi, there are three types: those whose understanding is clear, as specified by the Torah itself; those considered "testimonies of historical facts," such as the precept of eating *matzah* on Pesach to commemorate the Jewish escape from Egypt; and, finally, those whose motives are not explained in the Torah. A simple example of such is the obligation to eat kosher. Before anyone can object, the rabbi clarifies that the justification that some find for the prohibition of eating pork in the prevention of trichinosis is a possible explanation. Still, since it is not explained in that way in the Torah, it is only speculation, and no one can be entirely sure.

He then comments that, within the group of *mitzvot*, there is one that no one could ever unravel its hidden meaning, its motivation, not even the greatest sage who ever lived, King Solomon. The rabbi announces with suspense that the *mitzvah*, whose meaning could never be deciphered, refers to the sacrifice of the red cow, eliciting comments from those present.

The rabbi explains that at the time of the Holy Temple in Jerusalem, pilgrims were required not to be impure before entering it.

"Impure is he who has been in contact with a dead person. This impurity is contagious. So, if one was impure and touched another who was pure, that other also became impure," he explains.

The only way to purify an impure person was through the ritual sacrifice of a red cow, mixing the animal's blood with ashes and some herbs, and then sprinkling a few drops of the product on the impure person.

"This looks like a satanic rite, I know," says the rabbi and smiles, "but it is not."

I write everything he says. I'm the only one with an open notebook on top of the table. No one seems to take the class as more than a casual chat.

"By red cow, I mean an absolutely red cow. With a red coat. All of it. All of it. They would check it and see that it didn't have one little hair that wasn't red. It's obviously strange that something like that can happen; that a cow of that color can be born. According to the Talmud, only nine red cows appeared from the building of the First Temple until the Second Temple's destruction. You can imagine they sacrificed them and kept the blood for other occasions. Now, why did God ask this of us? No one can know. It is an odd *mitzvah* because the person who throws the drops of blood from the red cow to the impure person becomes impure himself."

A student intervenes:

"Well, but then someone else would throw him the blood."

"Yes, well, I guess so. But then that other person becomes unclean, and so on. And when I say unclean, I mean not even being able to go near the perimeter of the Temple. Can you imagine how difficult it was at that time to be unclean? It was terrible. They became social outcasts."

I had read some of the red cow stories in Michael Chabon's novel *The Yiddish Policemen's Union*. I also recall hearing during a trip to Israel that the Temple can only be rebuilt once a new red cow appears.

The rabbi explains it clearly: nowadays, we are all impure because, in one way or another, we were all infected with impurity. Therefore, none of us could enter the Temple. The appearance of the tenth red cow will signal the imminent arrival of the Messiah, who will rebuild the Temple of Jerusalem and bring about the end of the world.

The class continues and deviates from the non-explanation of certain *mitzvot* to the non-explanation of the existence of God. The rabbi says that faith, in the Jew, comes by inheritance and continues,

"When you use a computer, you use it. You don't know how it's made or why it works. You don't even question it. It's the same with God. You don't question why he made the world or how he made it. You just have to know that he did it. Someone must have made the world, right? How else do you explain everything being so perfect and tight? Just chance? You don't question what you do. You just do it. When you light a stove, you don't think about how the fire is produced. Consider a newborn baby. He cannot comprehend the reality that it observes. He only has evidence of what is directly in front of him."

The rabbi then tells a parable of a wise rabbi on his visit to a foreign king. In the tale, the rabbi asks the king if he believes in God. The king replies he doesn't believe in that kind of superstition. The rabbi in the tale then goes home and draws a magnificent picture, an art for which he was gifted. The following week, he gives the painting to the king, who, surprised by its qualities, comments: "Did you do it?" to which the rabbi answers: "No, all I did was to arrange the painting elements around the frame. Then the paints fell on the canvas by themselves, and this painting was formed by chance." The story ends with the king accepting the existence of God.

People murmur, and the rabbi responds with kindness and suggests that the sciences are not irrefutable either and that, on the contrary, they cannot be bearers of the truth because they are refuted from time to time.

"And if you still need evidence, witnesses, what better evidence than three million Jews seeing the divine presence when God gave us the Torah on Mount Sinai? If God appeared to men constantly, there would be no free will because his presence alone would prevent men from choosing between Good and Evil. Everyone would opt for Good."

"Why did God create this world?" asks the rabbi, "to have a house in this world. And how was that house built? Using Torah and *mitzvot*."

The rabbi uses a metaphor to discuss home and how people act there. He says that when people feel comfortable at home, they are carefree, relaxed, and dress casually. You must act, look different, and talk to others on the street. In the rabbi's explanation, Jews must perform *mitzvot* to make the world like home for God.

"A king," he returns to the subject, "when he appears before his subjects, has to follow a protocol. He has masks. If we do not make God's house comfortable, he will not make Himself comfortable. He will not show himself at home, and He will be hidden behind thousands of masks. By fulfilling our duties, we make the house more comfortable, and he will act less formally when he comes to see us."

He emphasizes that the approach to *mitzvot* begins with practice and progresses to conviction and awareness.

There is always a pleasant word, a parable to understand the unintelligible in the Jewish hero's path. It is the path of the Padawan to the Jedi. To believe in the force, you must experience the force first. There are no lightsabers here. There are *tefillin* and kosher.

Class ends.

We go back out into the hallway. It is a little before nine o'clock at night. Still, I am walking up the stairs to the second-floor synagogue, where my second class has moved because it is a more spacious place that better accommodates the more significant number of students enrolled in the course.

I pass by the counter next to the stairs that have a display stand from which to grab brochures and old magazines; I grab a couple of tickets for the *Lag BaOemer* celebration (a semi-holiday celebrated by mystic groups) to be held at an amusement park and hosted by a very well known T.V. host.

I enter the synagogue. It is the same place where I had my first Chabad experience two years ago, brought here to spend a Shabbat dinner with a rabbi and his family.

Now I understand that what I saw on that occasion was just another class in one of the ISEJ seminars from that year.

The synagogue is filling up, and the rabbi in charge arrives after a while.

So far, he has devoted the first three meetings to giving Judaism's view on abortion. Now, he is going to start with a new topic, he says, a much more positive and happier one: the interpretation of dreams.

He asks if anyone in the room has ever studied psychology. When he finds out that only one girl has, he says that he does not know Sigmund Freud's works but that it is not a coincidence that he was Jewish. According to the rabbi, dream interpretation was already present in the Talmud.

"Does anyone know what it means, according to Freud, to dream that your teeth fall out?"

No one responds.

"That means you're afraid of being castrated," he smirks.

The rabbi talks about the Talmud and shows one book in his hands, from which, he says, he extracted the quotations he will talk about tonight.

"Judaism considers dreams as an attempt of the soul to reach the Creator. When one sleeps, say the sages, he experiences a sixtieth of death."

Then he says that only those who properly nourish their soul can have that moment of approach in dreams to the Creator.

"Did you never have silly dreams? Nightmares? Those are failed attempts of your soul to rise. They try to rise, they can't, and then these ugly dreams appear."

The rabbi speaks of premonitory dreams as a condition in people with an elevated spirit who place their souls with God, where there is no temporality. He also says that a person who does not care for his soul so much can access an elevation of his soul on the eve of holidays, which are special moments.

"Because, believe it or not, you all fulfill *mitzvot* daily," he says, and generates some murmuring among the students, "What? Did any of you kill someone? You shall not kill. There, you have done a *mitzvah*. Do you not honor your father and mother? You shall honor your father and mother. There, you have done another *mitzvah*."

He recounts Bible dreams and focuses on the Dream of Jacob, a Genesis episode in which the character slept and dreamed of a ladder on which angels were climbing. The first angel fell after climbing some steps. A second angel climbed a few more steps before collapsing. A third angel climbed and climbed without falling. Then God would have told Jacob that all would fall, even the one who hadn't yet fallen. The Talmudic interpretation of the dream points out that the angels represented enemy empires of Judaism that rose but would eventually fall. In the Talmudic interpretation, the Roman Empire would be the last angel that rose and did not fall in the dream.

"That it has not yet fallen," says the rabbi, "What? Do we not live in an 'apostolic, catholic, and Roman' country[2] ? When it falls, it will be time for the Messiah's coming and the Temple's rebuilding."

The rabbi then comments that candles are lit to represent the souls of the departed and continues with the theme of the meaning of dreams. Now, he is focused on those dreams that cast deceased relatives or friends.

"If someone dear to you who has passed away appears to you in a dream, you must pay attention to how he is dressed, looks, and speaks. It doesn't matter what they say. What matters is their outward appearance. If you see him well, calm, and neat, that means he is at peace, having a good time in the afterlife, and being happy to be with God. If you see him looking bad, he is trying to communicate something to you. He is asking you to help him. How can you help him from here? By doing the one thing they cannot do over there. You are the arms and legs of those who are not here. You can fulfill *mitzvot* in his name. That is the way to help them."

"I am going to confess something. I am orthodox. Here, you see me with a beard. I believe in the Torah because I believe it is the truth. However, these Talmudic aspects of dreams... never made complete sense to me. As you see me, orthodox and all, to tell you the truth, I never believed in that thing about dreams until one day. I was exhausted and went to sleep for an hour's nap. In my dream, I saw the father of a student who said to

---

2. In chapter 2 of Argentina's constitution the Federal government adopts the "Catholic apostolic Roman" faith.

me: 'Are you coming to see me?' I woke up, and just a second later, I received a message from another rabbi. It was to tell me that the man who had appeared in my dream had just died. He had appeared to me at the very moment he was dying. Believe it or not."

The class remains unfinished. The rabbi says he will conclude it next week.

I think about my dead loved ones who appeared to me in my dreams. The one who appeared to me the most was my grandfather. How did he appear in my dream? Was he looking good or bad? He wasn't even religious in life. Could he ask me after he died to do a *mitzvah* for him?

I go downstairs to run my finger through the fingerprint scanner again and clock out.

I place myself at the end of the queue, and while I wait, bored, I look around me. In the pile of public-use yarmulkes, one, in particular, catches my eye. It is black, with words embroidered in gold thread.

I dislike yarmulkes, but I always carry about three in my backpack. Now, I'm using one of those for public use. I look at the one on the counter, get closer, and recognize it. It is mine. It's the yarmulke my grandmother gave me two years ago, the one with the inscription "Savoy Hotel Jerusalem" that I wore to my first TAGLIT meeting. It is the same one I used to come to that night I met Chabad for the first time. The one that belonged to my deceased grandfather.

I don't understand. That yarmulke never leaves my backpack. I should have it there now. I look inside, and it is not there. That yarmulke lying among the public-use yarmulkes is mine; it belonged to my grandfather.

A strange feeling comes over me, and I think about what I just heard the rabbi say, and I think that putting on my grandfather's yarmulke would be like doing a *mitzvah* in his name. I grab it and think for a moment about putting it on. But I remember him as an atheist, and I squeeze it, put it in a pocket. I check out, and as I walk up the stairs to leave the Beit Chabad, I take out the yarmulke I'm wearing and put it in my pocket.

Clashing or converging spaces?

Damián Setton, who did sociological research on the Morashá Universitarios experience, says that these places where secular Jews and Orthodox Jews can live together lead to a process of constant negotiation because the institution promotes porous and unclear boundaries to get young people to come.

Not only is there a negotiation of spaces, but the classes themselves are made to attract and seduce a naturally distrustful and hesitant public, trying to fit the topics in a way that will spark genuine interest and looking for forms of contemporary Jews. For example, the CHAT Group's 2009 class schedule included seminars such as "Second Life. Unraveling the enigmas of reincarnation of souls and your parallel lives" or "Would you forgive an affair from your significant other? Would he/she forgive you? How do you go on when trust creaks and cracks? A discussion about slips, betrayals, forgiveness, and reparations." All these classes were taught from a Torah perspective, with some other frankly bizarre such as "The little green dwarfs: UFOs and extraterrestrials: Is there life on other planets? Can we contact extraterrestrial beings? Myths and truths of an unresolved intrigue."

Chabad Lubavitch knows how to take advantage of the social context in which it is inserted and is not afraid to raise issues or debates that, a priori, seem far from Orthodox Jewish discussions. For example, its Youth Center organized the talk "Homosexuality and Gay Marriage. What do you think?" on July 22nd, 2009, at the height of the debate on extending social rights to same-sex couples in Argentina.

The themes, names, and descriptions of the classes are in that space of negotiation and convergence, in which the institution appears flexible, as a sort of liquid Judaism that admits a certain openness to the society in which it is immersed and places the Orthodox Jew on a par with any young secular Jew. Chabad Lubavitch uses a method of communication that appeals to young people to spread its mix of Jewish Orthodoxy and pragmatism to a broader, more skeptical public.

"They are not different from us."

The El Lazo Youth Center's Facebook group post suggests a Las Vegas-style Purim party with Texas Hold'em Poker, roulette tables with professional casino dealers, blackjack, American food, and an open bar.

Since it is a requirement, or *mitzvah*, for adults to get drunk on Purim, the offer looks pretty appealing compared to those of other Batei Chabad, which have also used a moderate propaganda campaign for their own celebrations in the past few days. These included "Purim Italian style, with pasta and open bar" at Beit Chabad Almagro-Abasto, Purim with a show for kids at Beit Chabad Once, and so on, with each Chabad branch offering something particular.

Another custom of this festival is to dress up in costumes. With disguised and drunk people, Purim is the closest thing to a Jewish carnival, where social roles are reversed. For example, it is common to see, in communities with a higher observance and tradition, Jews disguised as historical enemies of the Hebrew people, such as Egyptians, Cossacks, and even sometimes nazis.

If, despite its proximity to my home, I had never visited Chabad's Youth Center, it was partly because I had a strange impression of the door leading to a second floor in an old fruit market structure. A door that is not guarded by anyone and that does not invite anyone to pass through appears to be a passage reserved for connoisseurs.

All until tonight, under the excuse of the subversion of values imposed by the carnival and the costume, I dare to climb the stairs whose walls are decorated with glued playing cards and dollar signs cut out of gold and silver plastic.

In the background, a song is playing that is a remake of a popular queer song from this year that has been changed to talk about Israel.

A few guys and girls are before me, settling in at the top of the stairs. Just before the last flight of stairs, two or three girls are taking notes on everyone who walks by and asking them for personal information.

The guests are between 18 and 28 years old. Not all of them are dressed up, but I can tell a Daniel-San from the *Karate Kid* movies and a hip-hop dancer, among others.

I notice a sign in the restroom's window. The sign reads, "Men working for a new Youth Center."

The *Centro para la Juventud Pasaje el Lazo* is directed by the Brazilian Rabbi Shlomo Levy, who, before arriving here, was in charge of a Beit Chabad in the capital city of Buenos Aires Province, La Plata.

When it opened in 1994, this Youth Center had a small offering of activities for Jewish youth. By March 1995, it had weekly Kabalat Shabbat dinners. The neighbourhood quickly learned that in this place, they taught Judaism in a fun and exciting way and that kids could also hang out and meet other kids from the area.

El Lazo, as it is known, is one of the most visible and active institutions of Chabad Lubavitch in Buenos Aires City and organizes activities and thematic parties specifically for young people. It also has a travel program to New York City, as does ISEJ and the CHAT Group.

The center serves as a Beit Chabad for young and modern Jews. It is explicitly aimed at "Palermitanos," or residents of the Buenos Aires' hip and trendy Palermo neighborhood where it is located, just a few blocks from the city's Botanical Garden.

El Lazo usually offers courses for young Jews on topics like "kabbalah related to business" and love and relationships. In this respect, during a dinner with CHAT group participants, some girls told me they used to come here to socialize with other young Jewish boys. They had also recently attended a *pegisha*, a four-day seminar in a recreational center that included study and encouragement to engage between them and other Jewish young men.

The experience of these girls had been positive but boring. They had gone to a hotel in a small coastal town. They remembered the mandatory activities well, but they valued much more the free hours they had in the evenings when the rabbis' rules were more relaxed.

One goal that Chabad youth organizations make no secret of is matching Jewish young men and women. As a result, most of the festivities and activities that they organize for young Jews consciously violate the traditional separation of the sexes that they mandate within their institutions.

Now the music changes to the song *Chop' em Down* by Matisyahu, the American former Chabadnik who makes reggae/hip-hop fusion with religious lyrics.

The line moves, and I reach the girl who records my information in a notebook. Name, surname, mother's surname, phone number, postal address, and e-mail address are all required. After that, I pay a small entrance fee and am ready to go.

I enter a large loft with two divisions, one for offices and a kitchen and another at the back with a glass window. There are still not too many people at the party. It is barely after ten o'clock at night. I spot two blackjack tables, a poker table, and a roulette table where most people gather.

There are also tables with soda bottles and white plastic cups.

Matisyahu's songs continue to dominate the soundtrack. A magician goes around, surprising the audience with simple tricks.

I walk down some stairs to a sort of annex that serves as a library during the week. The room has carpeting, air conditioning, tables fixed to the floor, and windows that look out onto a street with an ice cream shop.

To the right is the drinks bar, which is a real little bar, and to the left are the shelves with Jewish books published by Chabad.

A foosball table is in the center of the room, and a few groups of friends sit on chairs and cushions.

I notice a lot of small groups of friends congregating around the area. People, I presume, know each other from meeting here. There doesn't seem to be anyone who doesn't understand what it's all about or has been enticed by the prospect of an open bar for a small entrance fee.

I approach some guys trying to peek over the bar and ask them how they got here and what they are looking for.

"How did you hear about today's event?" I ask a boy.

"Because Rabbi Shlomo Levy called me, I already traveled with him to the United States."

"Did you know Shlomo before your trip?"

"I knew him from before the trip, but my relationship with him grew at that time."

"And how did you first come to Chabad Lubavitch?"

"Because of my brother's girlfriend."

"And how did you have that first interest that made you decide to keep coming back, take part in the trip, and meet the people?"

"The truth is that I chose to keep coming because I appreciated the human aspect of this place. I found the courses very didactic and did not feel them as a burden. I enjoyed them."

"Did you think the course would be a burden before you came?"

"I didn't imagine anything because I usually study Torah during the week, and I know what a Torah course is. I thought this was a very good one."

I ask the boy's girlfriend,

"How did you learn about this event at El Lazo today?"

"My boyfriend told me, and I found out on Facebook and from a friend."

"Have you been in contact with Chabad for a long time, or is this your first time here?"

"Since last year, I have been coming to the talks to get the trip to the United States."

"And did you go on that trip yet?"

"No, not yet, at the end of this year."

"Beyond the trip, is there any other reason you are interested in Chabad Lubavitch?"

"I think they are cool."

Her boyfriend interrupts her answer and jokes, "She likes it here because I say so!"

"I also like it here because my boyfriend and friends come here too… It's like a big family," she adds. "They make me feel comfortable," she adds. "They are no different from us."

I return to the main hall and see a guy in a suit carrying trays of hamburgers with a slice of tomato. He places them on one table with sodas and napkins.

I grab one and put mustard on it. The only condiment there is.

I feel the meat dry; they are homemade burgers, and for a moment, I try to differentiate their taste, as if the fact that these burgers are made of kosher meat means that they must have a different taste than the burgers I eat in my daily life.

In fact, according to Chabad philosophy, the fact that I am eating a hamburger right now means that I am at least not eating non-kosher meat. Anything goes. Anything adds up. As a Jew, I am fulfilling a *mitzvah* by eating this kosher hamburger, which matters to Chabad. The rest of my context, at least for tonight, doesn't matter to them. It doesn't matter that tomorrow I will eat a ham and cheese sandwich. It matters that I'm not doing it right now. As long as they can keep me here, at this party, eating kosher hamburgers and later also kosher hot dogs, I will not be eating *terefah* (non-kosher.) Even better, if I eat so much kosher food tonight that I get sick, I might skip breakfast tomorrow and thus eat even less *terefah*.

I recognize Rabbi Shlomo Levy by his unmistakably long beard and because he keeps hugging boys who show him great affection. He is dressed in black clothes and a clown-colored wig topped with a yarmulke.

It is ten past eleven at night, and about one hundred and fifty people are at the party.

I walk around the place a little more, looking at the people who now keep arriving. There aren't many people dressed up, but the one that stands out the most is a girl wearing a piece of clothing in the shape of an empanada with the words "Empanada de Soja" (soybean empanada) written on it.

I stop at a billboard near the entrance, around some plastic chairs and a small group of girls chatting.

There are photos, news of the trips to New York, and a chart that catches my attention. It is a comparative table that takes as variables generations, Jewish congregations, and, I suppose, the number of families because there is nothing to clarify what the numbers refer to.

	Secular	Reformist	Conservatives	Orthodox
1st generation	100	100	100	100
2nd generation	36	51	62	209
3rd generation	13	26	38	426
4th generation	5	15	24	911

After eleven thirty, I try to approach the poker table because I am just another victim of ESPN-televised Texas Hold'Em Poker tournaments.

I ask a girl who has been playing at the table since I arrived how I can exchange chips.

"With the little card that they gave you at the entrance."

"What do I do with that?"

"You give it to the *croupier*."

I sit beside him and pass the paper to the man who deals the cards with clear professionalism. In exchange, he hands me three hundred chips.

I win first hand, which I play with a single pair, and then I systematically lose until I get bored and leave.

The loudspeakers play music from the eighties, hybridized with Jewish themes in the main room, while in the small lounge with the bar, there is a more chill-out mood.

It gets boiling and humid here, according to the number of people overflowing the place. The crossover of Orthodox and non-Orthodox people is expressed uniquely. In contrast to a Kabbalat Shabbat ceremony at a Chabad synagogue, most of those in attendance are not Orthodox, and those who are do not present themselves as a threatening figure of authority.

The music stops, and Rabbi Levy takes D.J.'s place to announce over the microphone that the Megillah Esther, the scroll of Esther in the Old Testament that tells the story of Purim, will soon be read in a small adjoining room.

I go down to the lounge and squeeze through the overflow of people crowding around to get a drink at the bar.

While waiting for a drink, I am greeted by a guy I don't recognize until he tells me he is a friend of my brother's, with whom he has just gone to TAGLIT and later to Europe. We greet each other. He is with another friend who tells me he has already traveled with ISEJ and intends to travel with El Lazo this year.

"They are all the same," he concludes.

My brother's friend tells me he will attend ISEJ to learn Hebrew.

"Hey, what's it like there?" I ask the one who has already traveled.

"It is very relaxed, really."

"But isn't there a lot of praying and all that?"

"Well... just a little."

"What about putting *tefillin*?"

"They say that you can wear them if you want to, but, well, being there, it's not that they force you... but they almost do."

A Hasid unrolls Esther's scroll, but the ambient noise is too great, and the microphones do not work. After a few unsuccessful attempts and some consultation with rabbi Levy, he gives up and puts it back in its case.

I get up and walk around the room a few more times. I rest the pile of casino chips left on a table next to the tray with cold hamburgers.

Tonight's religious content wasn't all that strong; in the meantime, the roulette ball keeps spinning, and I start my retreat.

McDavid's and complimentary cocktails: feeding hungry young Jews

Jewish holidays, such as Purim, are occasions when Chabad Lubavitch, as an institution, organizes various celebrations. Each Beit Chabad proposes its own, and the youth groups have their own way of celebrating with their students.

But it is not only on specific holidays that these activities take place within the youth study groups, but also themed parties are organized. The CHAT Group, for example, as part of its 2009 annual activity plan, organized the "*Tu B'Av Mega-Party, the Day of the Jewish Lovers,* in the panoramic lounge on the 24th floor of the Sheraton Hotel. Cocktail, humor show, and romantic music." The same group organized a *Lag Baomer* celebration on a cruise ship in the upscale Buenos Aires neighborhood of Puerto Madero in 2010.

These Chabad youth programs also organize their own Shabbat celebrations, which are presented as a space for settling relationships among course participants, spaces of friendship and exchange. During these occasions, Orthodox restrictions, such as the separation of the sexes, are loosened to the point of disappearance.

The Chabad's *Center for Youth* in Argentina seems to be at the forefront of destabilizing an outsider's image of an Orthodox Jew.

In a study by sociologists Jésica Azar and María Schwartzer, a quote from Rabbi Levy seems to clarify the matter. The rabbi said: "When a young man comes on Friday, for example, he comes not for its essence. He comes to meet boys and girls and to eat well.

In the middle, something of Judaism is transmitted to him about daily life. He then says: 'How interesting, I feel identified,' and, without wanting it, that's when the first flame is lit. If he is a persevering person, later he will want more answers because he will say: 'Here they will teach me how to get along better with my parents, my partner, with myself.' Then he will see that Judaism is a religion that talks about prayer, Shabbat, and his reality."

According to the sociologists, the center proposes a "multi-offering of activities that are clearly adapted to modern times, in which the individual who consumes (who attends the courses) cannot be defined through homogeneous consumption."

In addition, they state it is possible "to find activities clearly linked to religious topics (*Bar* and *Bat mitzvah* courses, Kabbalah courses), related to professional training (courses for leaders, talks with economists, historians) or to social life (events in bars, dinners in hotels with shows.) The courses are very varied and are given frequently, which makes it possible to have enrollment dates throughout the year."

Chabad youth groups work to attract young people by using a borderline language in which everything can be rethought in light of the Torah. The seduction technique is based on a marketing mix of Orthodox and secular elements, and many of the structural visions of the rabbis in charge of these spaces align with conservative political programs.

Researchers Cynthia Fidel and Tamara Weiss state: "El Lazo sets in motion a complex communicational scaffolding, especially focused on transmitting a 'flexible and relaxed' image of the Beit Chabad. These messages, which travel through different channels, let young people know whether they identify with the Beit Chabad. The most used media are the Internet site, www.jovenesjudios.com.ar, e-mail campaigns, flyers distributed at meetings, and telephone calls. We can affirm that El Lazo uses all the resources and applies all the technology at its disposal to reach its target population through colloquial language. The images do not show people clearly identifiable with the Orthodox Jew stereotype. The lively colors and the chosen phrases and photos transmit attributes related to a permanent celebration, fun, friends, novelty, youth, etc. They also employ isotypes, logos, and rebranded common phrases to spread, invite, and 'seduce' their recipients." (77-78)

El Lazo generates a marriage between the secular and religious fields, which gives the assimilated public and the Orthodox rabbis a specific horizon of common expectation.

The work with young people is the space that allows us to see more clearly this kind of contradiction that the work of Chabad Lubavitch offers.

The first three classes of the course *FAQ: Frequently Asked Questions About Judaism*, which I attended at ISEJ during the first four months of 2010, dealt with the Jewish vision of abortion. A perennial issue that was addressed in the classrooms in a non-contentious manner. During the classes, the rabbi teaching the course showed different data sets and statistics and went through some center-right Jewish views on the subject.

Thus, the contents of these courses and studies aim to integrate the Jewish worldview, obviously Chabad's interpretation of the Jewish law and sacred text, and contemporary reality so that participants learn Judaism's answers to today's problems. Azar and Schwartzer cite Rabbi Levy in their work: "People are looking to meet other people. When we in Chabad bring people such as economists, the owner of a big mall, or the director of a fancy hotel, they transmit their experience, and we transmit ours. The aim is to transmit to the Jew that being a Jew is not to change or move to another world but to bring Judaism to his own world... He does not have to stop studying or working; he has to continue working as a Jew, studying as a Jew, and thinking as a Jew within the world where he finds himself. For this, he has to study Judaism."

For Chabad, there is a non-negotiable background, which has to do with the values and convictions of the rabbis: "We do not transmit that people should be the same as us. We want people to be themselves. We do not want people to be like us. But in our private lives, we give ourselves completely to Judaism. According to the Kabbalah, the beard is necessary because beards are special divine emanations. We put on two pairs of *tefillin*. We observe Shabbat slightly ahead of and slightly after its scheduled time. But all this is in our private lives. Young people learning about Judaism cannot be expected to achieve a 'level ten.' Similarly, we cannot transmit a 'level two' to a young person already at 'level six.' In other words, everyone can have his own Judaism," says Rabbi Levy.

The idea of "integrating" first, without preconditions, is one of the most striking characteristics of Chabad Lubavitch. Because if everything is permissible, if it is permissible not to wear a skirt, not to grow a beard, not to wear *tzitzit*, not to travel on Shabbat, in short, not to live an observant life, the very definition of Jewish Orthodoxy appears to be lost. Then, the practice of Judaism leans toward other less strict forms like conservatism or reformism Judaism.

The work of Chabad's *Youth Center* can be felt in a part of Buenos Aires City that used to be like any other neighborhood with a majority of Catholics before Chabad moved in. Instead, things have slowly begun to change over the past few years. A kosher sushi restaurant and a kosher grill opened within two blocks of El Lazo. The ice cream parlor in front of the Beit Chabad incorporated kosher flavors. A long-established American-style barbecue a few meters away changed its kitchen and menu to kosher. Around the corner, a party hall has become the site of Hasidic weddings, Bar and Bat Mitzvahs, and other gatherings for the local Lubavitch community. A kosher grocery store opened its doors just a few blocks from Chabad's *Youth Center*. It is now common to see various Hasidim walking around the neighborhood during the day.

The turn in this area appears to be a prominent feature of a slow but continuous process. Those in charge of the *Youth Center* and Chabad Lubavitch understand that they will not be able to convert all Jews to Orthodoxy. But that is not their goal either. Instead, they will celebrate each of their small victories against Jewish assimilation and secularization.

Shabbat dinners, courses on Judaism and non-Jewish subjects based on Torah reinterpretation, and public events geared toward young people are places where Chabad's religious restrictions are negotiated to appeal to a broader audience. Therefore, Chabad Lubavitch, particularly its youth branches, accepts that their celebrations be held without gender restrictions or excessive control. However, some form of strictness is still applied. The *kashrut*, as well as certain ritualistic aspects of the Kabbalat Shabbat, are non-negotiable.

Following this logic of consumption, it is worth mentioning the group aimed at teenagers, AIEKA, led by Rabbi Ionatan Sirota, and located near one of the secular Jewish ORT High School sites.

This is another of Chabad's youth branches that have developed an innovative approach to persuade young Jews to perform religious acts: the *AIE-KArd*, a kind of "loyalty program" with benefits for its members. Participants in the program can use this card to earn points based on their actions to improve their religious observance. Eating kosher food, for example, or attending talks and lectures given by the group's rabbis. These points can then be redeemed for prizes like video game consoles.

AIEKA is a space that is defined, according to Rabbi Sirota, in an institutional short film as "a meeting place and kosher eatery," where inexpensive dishes and menus are offered to teenagers at school lunchtime, but also talks with rabbis, extracurricular activities, and Jewish studies. Foosball games and soccer tournaments are organized, as well as celebrations and invitations to the children to spend dinners at the various rabbis' homes.

Even with all we have seen, not every Jewish teen who approaches the courses and social activities offered by ISEJ, CHAT, El Lazo, or AIEKA becomes Jewish Orthodox.

Damian Setton says: "Attending an Orthodox group is not viewed as a repentance from a mistaken past, but as another moment that does not imply a radical shift in one's relationship with Jewish institutions. The person who now attends these groups can go back to consuming Reform or Conservative Judaism in the future. This subject responds to the consumer category, little linked to authority and little committed to any ideology or movement." (62)

The range of activities that Chabad Lubavitch offers to young Jews through its groups includes thematic dinners, speed dating among Jews events, traditional celebrations and new ways of carrying out those celebrations, soccer tournaments with rabbis, and a wide range of products that combine the way of consumption of contemporary societies with religion, all presented in a seductive, attractive, uncompromising, pleasurable, and quick format.

Take part in Chanukah and win a P.C.

It is past six o'clock on a Sunday afternoon. A golden chanukiah rises several meters above the ground at the end of Del Libertador Avenue. Alemania Square looks like a return to the fair. In the background, where the play of lights is reflected, are the balconies of some of the most expensive condo suites in Buenos Aires.

The public Chanukah celebrations are a long-standing tradition in Chabad Lubavitch. They spread by the Rebbe's impulse, the same way his emissaries colonized the world. Wherever there is a Beit Chabad, there will be a public Chanukah celebration.

A stage is set up, and an extended rectangular sign in the background wishes a joyous holiday from Beit Chabad El Lazo.

Chanukah, also known as "the feast of luminaries," recalls a miracle at the time of the Second Temple in Jerusalem (2nd century B.C.) At that time, the land of Israel was occupied by the Seleucid Empire, a Hellenic detachment from the fall of Alexander the Great's empire.

In 174 B.C. Antiochus IV came to power. Intending to unify his reign, he attempted a process of Hellenization that eventually led to the prohibition of the customs and laws of the Jewish people.

In 167 B.C., an insurrection began in Modiin when the troops of Antiochus attempted to force the high priest Mattathias to worship Zeus.

Killing a Hellenized Jew who had worshipped the Greek gods in public, the leader and priest started the rebellion. He and his family went into exile in the mountains of Judea. Upon his death in 166 B.C., his son Judah Maccabee led a guerrilla war that not only fought successfully on the military level until they forced Antiochus' army of 40,000 men to retreat but also fought for the survival of Judaism by destroying pagan altars and circumcising boy children.

With the triumph and the return to Jerusalem, the famous miracle of Chanukah took place: the Maccabees recovered the Great Temple, cleaned it of profane idols, and when on the 25th of Kislev 139 B.C. they tried to consecrate it, they found that there was no sacred olive oil that had not been profaned. The only one left was in a single vessel and would only last one night. That oil was used and instead lasted eight nights, the time required to produce new pure and sacred olive oil. That was the miracle that showed God's return to protect his people. The Chanukah holiday is an eight-night celebration in which these events are remembered.

The story is told in Chabad's child-oriented magazine *Kids Vivan el Desafío*, which anyone can take free of charge from the pile on the white tablecloth table that welcomes people arriving at the public square.

In its first pages, the magazine advertises a raffle for 500 *guelt pesos* — it is customary during Chanukah to give money (*guelt* in Yiddish) to boys as a way of reinforcing the charity *mitzvah* — or the chance to win some "Anti-gravity boots" (modern sneakers), a "beeswax candle roll," and a "popcorn maker machine," which is described with the epigraph: "Invite your closest friends to your Chanukah celebration. This authentic hot oil popcorn machine will live on in their memories!"

The magazine explains the essential components of the celebration, the customs (it includes recipes for making cheese *latkes*, a fried snack typical of Ashkenazi cuisine), and the history, with a design full of drawings, curiosities, and relevant aspects of the celebration.

Under the title "Marvelous Miracles: The Chanukah Story," a narration traces the holiday's history in kid-friendly language from the perspective of its miracle and Jewish liberation, with recognizable comic book superheroes transformed by retouching into Jewish superheroes. I can recognize Superman with a yarmulke, a stylized Hebrew letter Shin on his chest, and a long beard; Doctor Doom as "The Evil King Antiochus"; Captain America as Judah Maccabee with a beard and a stylized Hebrew letter Mem on his shield fighting against the Seleucid army, from which the Incredible Hulk stands out. In comics, the character is known as The Green Goliath and was created by a renowned American Jew, Stan Lee. Although I don't believe this has anything to do with his appearance as a Chanukah story illustration.

It's December 13th, and it's hot in Buenos Aires during the last days of spring. Around two hundred people walk around the square or sit in one of the white plastic chairs in front of the stage. While some parents buy popcorn and cotton candy for their children at the *Kol Simcha* (All Joy) cart, some clowns with a poor repertoire for the children.

The same long table that greets the entrance to the square with stacks of the *Kids Vivan el Desafío* magazines also displays Chanukah kits that include a *chanukiah* and a pack of candles. A Lubavitcher, no more than eleven years old, passes between the rows of seated people handing out spinning tops (*dreidels*) for a game typical of this holiday.

A tray at the reception table offers *friar's balls*, a traditional Argentine deep-fried pastry to share among those passing by. Because the feast commemorates an oil-related miracle, any fried food is appropriate for the occasion.

People outside the festivity approach the stand, grab a *friar's ball*, and leave.

Rabbi Shlomo Levy approaches me and welcomes me to the celebration.

He is not the only one. Several Lubavitchers will wish me happy holidays while I browse the tables selling everything from Israeli pretzels to Jewish handicrafts, such as magnets with the inscription *"Bubbe*, I Love You." A table near the popcorn stand sells various toys for children, including stuffed animals and Torah rolls. Everything a little Lubavitcher might want.

The delimitation of the spaces for this event is not marked by any signs. Anyone, Jew or not, can enter and walk through the fair. It is a public place, after all.

At the back of the square, at the monument and fountain *Riqueza Agropecuaria Argentina* [Argentinian Agribusiness Riches], stand the spectators, who I assume are *goyim* — non-Jews — or who watch from a distance, heads down and uninterested in what is going on here.

A Lubavitcher of about fifteen faces me to greet me for the holidays and asks if I put on *tefillin* this morning.

Although the party is open, Chabad style, with no pressure, no man is seen within the perimeter of the party without something to cover his head.

So, I also wear a yarmulke, the passcode that allows the boy to approach and try to fulfill another *mitzvah*. This Lubavitcher who has intercepted me is doing as his Rebbe instructed: "Thou shalt expand," which is the basis of Chabad Lubavitch's operation.

He makes me run to the side, next to the crane that will be used later to climb up to the height of the arms of the giant *chanukiah* and light the candles. He holds back his excitement as he dictates the prayers in Hebrew, which I repeat by phonetic imitation. A man taps me on the shoulder. I give him an obnoxious look, and he tells me I must look to the East and cover my eyes during the ceremony. He doesn't say anything. He is a large, gray-haired man with short hair, dressed in a black yarmulke that covers most of his head and a blue shirt that hangs loosely from his pants.

The Lubavitcher making me comply with the *mitzvah* of putting on the *tefillin* gets a little nervous and chases the man away. Something was disturbing about his intervention. Approaching the complicated web of customs, laws, precepts, and knowledge that a secular Jew doesn't have creates tension: pronouncing Hebrew well, doing a strictly codified act with regularity and established forms of compliance implies violence because it informs that individual that the way he has been practicing Judaism his entire life is incorrect and that there is a better way. Immersion in these rules implies adult learning, which will frighten the candidate for re-entry into Judaism if not done slowly and patiently. Assisting a secular Jew in putting on *tefillin* is part of a Judaism literacy program for adults. This comes with all the difficulties and tensions that entail attempting to educate an adult. The man who insisted with his silent and stertorous gestures for me to look to the East and cover my eyes could have thrown away the efforts of this young Lubavitcher who was helping me fulfill the *mitzvah*. When I finish reciting the *Shema Yisrael* prayer, he tells me: "You have just done a very, very important *mitzvah*. Very important." He asks if I'm lighting the Chanukah candles, and I tell him no because "I'm just getting into Judaism."

"You can go over there, and they will give you a *chanukiah* and candles," he says, pointing to the table where almost no *friar balls* are left to grab.

I go there and ask how to light the candles, in what order, and in what way, and they give me a complete Chanukah kit for a small donation.

People settle in the chairs in front of the mobile screen they now put up.

A speaker says there will be raffles as part of the evening's program and tells people to fill out a piece of paper that a few Lubavitchers gave everyone. It was a form in which people had to fill in their personal information and put it in the contest ballot box. It was an excellent way to get a database of new Jews to bring them closer to their roots.

A DVD on the screen tells the story of the Chanukah miracle.

The video is manufactured in another country and comes in several languages. It is material that can be found on one of the Chabad websites. Educational materials such as this are produced at Chabad headquarters at 770 Crown Heights, Brooklyn. They are distributed to the various sites where Chabad is represented as if they were part of the package or franchise.

The first public Chanukah celebrations occurred in Union Square in San Francisco, U.S. 1975. They were inspired by mass demonstrations like those against the Vietnam War and the hippie years. Music producer Bill Graham was inspired by these public demonstrations to publicize Chabad Lubavitch. He programmed the first Chanukah celebrations in the squares. Soon, the Lubavitch Youth Organization of New York started sending their several-meter-tall *chanukiahs* around the United States in their *mitzvah tanks*.

Some opposing Jewish denominations resisted and continue to oppose this type of celebration, which they believe, on the one hand, makes public a private celebration and, on the other, loses sight of the State-religion separation, mainly because renowned political figures frequently take part in the lighting of public *chanukiahs*.

In the U.S., opposition to public celebrations has reached the courts frequently, with Chabad Lubavitch arguing that the *chanukiah* is a universal symbol of freedom rather than a religious symbol. It is a strange turn of events for a group that proclaims religious observance and exemplifies the organization's political elasticity.

Apart from a few minor clashes in 1984 when they had to deal with municipal officials who did not dare to sign the authorizations, nothing of the sort happened in Argentina.

In the video that is being shown, the miracle of Chanukah is referred to as the miracle of liberation and, in passing, the oppression that the Jewish people had to suffer during the Soviet Union's years: "Like a shooting star in the night, the iron curtain falls, and tyranny gives way to democracy," the video shows while showing images of the falling of the Berlin Wall: "without firing a single shot, millions are liberated from oppression. With renewed vitality, Judaism re-emerges overnight throughout the former communist countries. A true Chanukah miracle." The video concludes with a sequence in which Russian President Vladimir Putin lights a *chanukiah*.

The announcer returns to the stage and insists that we complete the slips of paper and place them in the ballot box for the drawing. He announces the prize is a donated computer. He continues with a brief speech that compares globalization to the Maccabean feat. "The most difficult invasions to fight are not only in arms but also in culture and the mind," he says.

Below the stage, a Lubavitcher ties a messianic flag to the pipes supporting the structure.

"Keeping the Jewish identity is a miracle," says the announcer on the stage and gives way to Rabbi Shlomo Levy, who greets and says: "We have just come from an exciting moment. We went to Boca Juniors' stadium to light a *chanukiah* with Rabbi Yossi Baumgarten. It was a miracle that they won the game. And even more of a miracle is that Martín Palermo scored both goals. The miracle of Chanukah," he smiles, and the crowd applauds. "The Chanukah essence is the essence of the Jewish people: it is this flame that no one could ever extinguish and that no one will ever be able to extinguish."

According to the rabbi's speech, belonging means resisting. We, Jews, people in this square right now, the rabbi insists, are survivors of various massacres and attempts to erase our identity, as evidenced by the video. The rabbi then emphasizes that performing a *mitzvah* is a way of finding illumination in times of darkness.

I feel his word will appeal to people who can find comfort in the familiarity of the closed group. Through his skillful speech, people will feel cared for and connected to the other men and women here. It feels like an address a politician on a campaign trail would give. "*Mitzvah* is the only light we have. The only source of light we have is action; feelings are important, but action is what matters most."

What he says is consistent with how Chabad Lubavitch conducts itself: pragmatism in every sense to promote *mitzvot* fulfillment so that more and more people begin to do them daily. "That is the teaching of Chanukah. We all must see ourselves as a *Yehudi* close to Judaism and practice. When I meet with a *Yehudi* who tells me: 'I don't eat kosher,' I tell him: 'That's a lie. Because you eat rice, tomato, Coca-Cola, water, all that is kosher. So don't say you don't eat kosher. Maybe you must eat more, improve, but you already eat kosher,'" rabbi Levy continues.

This is it. This is the great punch line in the rabbi's speech. Telling people they are already fulfilling the *mitzvah* of eating kosher without ever realizing it. It also adheres to the Chabad manual's guidelines for making religious observances appear familiar and accessible when they are clearly not.

Rabbi Levy clarifies the *mitzvot* are not obligations but acts of love. "And why?" the rabbi asks: "Because *Mashiach* is coming. And how do we invite *Mashiach* to come? With acts of love and kindness."

The rabbi ends his speech with the phrase that has characterized Chabad Lubavitch for years "*Mashiach now!*"

People applaud. It sounds unreal to me to be in the third millennium standing in the middle of a public square in Buenos Aires City, listening to a speech that assures that the Messiah is on his way and will arrive at any moment. This aspect of Chabad theology appears to be an impossibility for me. It's something they'll never be able to persuade me of. I see it as nothing more than a medieval Sabbatean way of thinking. I'm still baffled about how they persuade so many people to believe in that aspect of their faith. If Judaism has always expected a savior Messiah to redeem the souls of its people, Lubavitch elevates that expectation to the apocalyptic imminence of what will happen at any moment.

The announcer calls out the names of men who should approach the crane next to the *chanukiah*. They will accompany Rabbi Shlomo Levy to the summit to light the candles. Then they give way to Rabbi Yossi Baumgarten, who explains some Chanukah customs, such as the meaning of the *guelt* and foods such as *sufganiyot*.

He finishes his speech, and Rabbi Shlomo Levy gets on the crane with a man and a boy. They go to light the *chanukiah* candles, while Rabbi Baumgarten recites the corresponding *berachot* (blessings) from the stage.

The crane goes up and down and loads the people mentioned earlier to participate in the lighting. The candles are lit from the top. The public celebrates and gathers to watch the event around the opaque golden-painted metal candelabra.

The lighting ends with applause, and the time for the celebration begins.

But first, some children are called on stage to read excerpts from the Torah. Rabbi Shlomo Levy says: "One thing the Rebbe emphasized a lot is that children are the soldiers of God. They are *Tzvios HaShem*. They are those who truly fight with their purity and joy. They will now teach us some verses, which we must repeat word for word with full force because this purity reaches the highest and deepest levels. This is what we must do now."

He asks the boy to his side what his name is. "Ariel," responds the child and starts shouting word for word in Hebrew, hoping the audience will repeat along with him.

A few men pass by and repeat the procedure, and when they are finished, the announcer says that the pop band *Kef* is up next.

They make festive music in Hebrew, with some messianic invocations, as in their song "Waiting for Mashiach" from their second album, *Extra Kef*. The song is a mash-up of a classic reggae song by the local band *Los Pericos* with Hebrew lyrics and Hasidic joy.

Everyone wants to join in the party. The first rows of chairs are moved, and the Chabadniks dance in circles, weaving hats and black sacks into braids around themselves.

Some parents dance with their children on their shoulders. Others watch from outside, sitting in chairs and listening to the music while singing *Hava Nagila*, the tune "we all know," when it plays.

I move away from the center and toward the background monument, where a few scattered people have been watching the whole thing without participating. Almost nobody wears a yarmulke here. One might think that there are neither Lubavitchers nor Jews in this area.

A couple smokes a joint not too far away.

During *Kef*'s set, which lasts about 45 minutes, the Lubavitchers don't stop dancing and partying.

When the mini-show is over, Rabbi Tzvi Grunblatt is announced. I take my place in the first row of an audience that is once again calm and ready to see what happens on stage with the magnetic presence of Chabad Lubavitch Argentina's CEO.

"The message of Chanukah is that in the face of physical force, even if it is many and powerful, when there is faith in *HaShem*, strength, and fidelity to our roots, to our traditions, no one can break us and the few can overcome the many," he says, eliciting applause from the audience.

His words appeal simultaneously to Judaism as a tradition and to religious faith. He weaves it carefully. The approach to the Torah and faith in God is present, but the dose may be low when one considers the specific weight of the man who pronounces them. His speech continues. He appeals to Zionist sentiment by stating that the cost of all Israel's armaments is in vain if even one Jew abandons his people. He says, "Every boy who receives Torah education is a battle won. Every home that is added is a light that is lit."

The next event is the drawing for the grand prize, a computer and some plush toys. A woman from the booth selling Jewish trinkets wins it.

Fireworks go off, and the announcer announces that the party for the young people continues at the Beit Chabad El Lazo with a Chanukah *Techno Party*.

For my part, I'm done for the day. I'm heading home.

Securing the future generations

"A child is like a tree. It will grow healthy and strong by nurturing from a very young age with true knowledge, deep values, and teachings that make its soul flourish. It will have deep roots to stand on. A strong trunk to support its development. It will bear fruit and produce the seed from which new trees of the same species will be born. The continuity of the Jewish people depends on our children, and they depend on us. This book is to watch them grow, learning the story of Pesach as they play."

From the back cover of *Camino a la Libertad* [Road to Freedom], didactic material used at Gal After School courses

Chabad Lubavitch has Judaic education programs geared specifically for children under the age of *Bar* and *Bat Mitzvah*.

On the one hand, the local version of the *Tzivos HaShem* ("Soldiers of the Lord") program created by the Rebbe in 1981, coordinated in its local branch by Rabbi Israel Kapeluschnik, is being developed.

The group is set up as a kind of army game, where the boys get points for the fulfillment of *mitzvot*, which allows them access to different "ranks."

This military language to refer to Jewish education was first introduced by the Rebbe, who used these terms for the first time when he spoke of a "spiritual struggle" against secular forces, atheism, materialism, and all the other contemporary ideologies that alienate young Jews from tradition. On the other hand, there is no military training in these programs. The only weapons the boys and the Lubavitchers have in the battle for Jewish souls are persuasion and a set of attractive activities they offer to the community. The "enemy" is what they consider an "evil inclination" within each human being.

The language of military ranks, prizes, and benefits are central to these Chabad programs aimed at attracting young Jews. And, assuming that an extracurricular Jewish study program is insufficient to entice this demographic, they become required to achieve their objectives.

Rabbi Kapeluschnik says: "The idea is to congregate every Jewish child, whether from observant or non-observant homes and to reinforce their Judaism from a very young age, from the very base. That is the fundamental concept. How do we do it? Through the ten campaigns that the Rebbe launched, based on the twelve verses that the Rebbe asked every Jewish child to know by heart. Twelve sage verses or sayings, so every child's mind constantly thinks about Jewish issues. It aims to convert every room where a child is into a space where he is surrounded by Jewish topics, such as Jewish books, and having a piggy bank for charity. The idea is not to wait for the child to grow up but to train them from a very young age. This is an entire campaign, with prizes and ranks in which the children grow up and are trained to be Israel's future leaders. We have people working here today in Chabad who were influenced by the campaigns we ran when they were kids."

Tzivos HaShem holds weekly meetings on Saturday nights and organizes winter and summer camps. At these encounters, educational and fun activities are done, but the most important thing is that Jewish values are taught. This is a substitute for Jewish education, which is no longer provided in many secular Jewish homes. "We take them ice skating or bowling," Kapeluschnik points out, "and we teach them verses. We organize special activities for the holidays: for Pesach, we invite the kids to a *matzah* factory. We provide them with an apron, a hat, and a stick. Then, they assemble, knead, and bake their own *matzah*. For Rosh Hashanah, we build a *shofar* factory. We bring half-raw horns and work them in front of the kids. For Sukkot, we go with the *Sukkah Mobile* to their school or central places for the children to take part. It is an open plan for all the community's children."

Rabbi Kapeluschnik's wife, Miriam, oversees, among other things, the Gal After School program.

The original project, then named Morashá, arose in 2001 and was the product of a union between Chabad Lubavitch and two other Jewish institutions: *Sucat David* and the *Asociación Comunidad Israelita Sefaradí de Buenos Aires* [Israeli Sephardic Community Association from Buenos Aires.] Argentina went through a time of economic and social crisis after its economy crashed in December 2001. Many private Jewish schools and colleges went bankrupt during this time and had to close their doors. Also, many families stopped sending their kids to the schools that stayed open because they, too, had to cut their costs. The concern of these institutions to preserve in Judaism those children who were being left out of the Jewish school network coincided with the emergence of two significant donors (an Argentinean and a donor from abroad) who wanted to contribute to avoid this situation. Rabbi Tzvi Grunblatt then devised a plan for a network of institutes for informal Jewish education outside school hours. Today, the program reaches about two hundred children.

The program is based on three main teaching axes: Hebrew, Jewish history, and tradition. The activities developed by Gal After School under these premises are varied and include recreation, like *rikudim* workshops (folkloric Jewish dances), soccer, and chess games. During the holidays, the program is articulated with a summer camp, which is also organized by Miriam Kapeluschnik's husband, rabbi Israel.

The teachers of each center under the program are provided by their coordinators with didactic material specially designed by Miriam Kapeluschnik and her small group of assistants. This type of material bears the Chabad Lubavitch branding for bringing the religious field to a broad public. They comprise biblical character figurine albums and, among other materials, a booklet titled "Googling HaShem in Everything," which imitates the typography and appearance of the famous search engine, with activities that mix recreation with the specificity of religious education. The booklet contains stories and parables with Old Testament characters, great sages, and rabbis. The importance of Jewish marriages is also taught in its pages, alongside God's presence as the ultimate determiner of human life.

Other didactic materials printed by Chabad Lubavitch's publishing house, *Kehot*, include books like *Camino a la libertad: Shorashim (Raíces) 2* [Road to Freedom: Shorashim (Roots) 2.] This book teases "the story of Pesach with stories and games" and has a colorful cover with child-oriented drawings that illustrate scenes from the Biblical Exodus. The book also includes brain teasers, word searches, sentence completion exercises, code-breaking, other games, biblical glosses, commentaries, and activities that teach the rules and history of the Pesach holiday. Along the same lines, the booklet Alef-Bet: mis primeros pasos con las letras hebreas [Alef-Bet: My First Steps with Hebrew Letters] presents the Hebrew letters with a hollow background for coloring. The entire Hebrew alphabet is taught with examples of words associated with *mitzvot*: *tefillin*, for example, is used to express the pronunciation of the Hebrew letter *Feit*. A glossary of Jewish terms such as *Shabbat, Mashiach*, and *mitzvah* is included at the end of the book.

Miriam Kapeluschnik says that a few years ago, they even organized a literary contest for science fiction and detective stories based on Torah themes, and the winner won a computer. "We try to offer them something they don't get at school," she says.

To keep reaching the children who "graduated" from the Morashá program at age 17, a new one called Morashá Universitarios was started. As seen before, Morashá *Universitarios* was later renamed ISEJ, and Morashá was renamed Gal After School as part of a rebranding effort.

After nearly ten years of free and uninterrupted operation, the local Jewish community has assumed that Morashá is a program aimed at children coming from poor families. Kapeluschnik laments this: "Many people put it that way. In reality, the program is for kids who are poor in Jewish knowledge. It could be a kid attending a private school and paying a lot of money but who is poor in Jewish knowledge. We have suffered because of not charging for the program. It hurts us because getting funds and fulfilling our obligations to our creditors is becoming increasingly difficult. It is a serious matter because it is not being valued for what it is. Normally when someone says to you: 'How much do I owe you?' and you say: 'No, it is nothing,' you take it as: 'Oh, it is a gift, it must not be so important. It shouldn't be worth that much.' So, we want to reverse this a little bit. We know what it costs us. We will not charge the program's operating costs, but from now on, we want people to contribute something so that they will be more committed. That is why we also changed the name. So that parents can see that this is 'after school.' It is not school. It is instead an opportunity for their children to have a good time and be part of the community after school."

With this new positioning, Chabad Lubavitch reverses its previous stand regarding youth: to offer something material for time spent studying Judaism.

Miriam continues to bet with all her strength on the program because she understands it is the only way for hundreds of Jewish children to learn about Jewish issues, which is the primary Chabad Lubavitch's mission.

She categorically states: "Our whole idea is: 'This is your inheritance. This is yours. It's not ours. It's yours. Do what you want with it, but get to know it.' You can reject something when you know it and say, 'This is not for me,' but not before you can access it. We aim to get these children to know Judaism through cool, attractive things. I am convinced that if people have the opportunity to get to know Judaism, they will not leave it because it is beautiful. Because it is something extraordinary. But logically, they first need to allow themselves to discover it."

Chapter Five

God's Salesmen: Chabad's Communication Machine

> "Some denominations see themselves as God's policemen. We see ourselves as God's salesmen."
> Efraim Mintz, director of placement services and adult education at the Chabad movement's Shlichim Office in Crown Heights.
> in Sue Fishkoff, *The Rebbe's Army*

Miriam Kapeluschnik oversees more than just Chabad's educational programs. As she speaks, she attends to unfinished business, directs her assistant, greets her husband, who casually comes into her office while we are talking, and instructs him to repair Rabbi Tzvi Grunblatt's computer.

The first basement of Chabad Lubavitch Argentina Headquarters, on Agüero Street, resembles a bunker and is a permanent anthill through which the institution's main rabbis, those in charge of the most essential global affairs for all Chabad in the country, pass.

She is no different. The room is far too small for her. She walks back and forth, looking for folders, materials, and old magazines. She answers hundreds of emails from people who write from the official Chabad website while planning vacations and giving herself time to tell me what she does.

She is in charge of Chabad's website, edits the Chabad Magazine and the *Weekly Teaching*, a booklet printed and distributed in every Beit Chabad in the country and other Jewish institutions, and is also sent by email. The *Weekly Teaching* includes Torah readings for each week and some Hasidic stories. So, she and Rabbi Ioshua Birman, who ran a web video portal for the institution and produced a Chabad TV show that ran for years on cable TV, are in charge of the institution's communications.

The Chabad TV show started in 1995 on the Argentine public TV channel ATC. It was called *Ventana al Judaísmo* [Window to Judaism] before being moved to the cable TV *Alef* channel.

In an interview published in the Chabad Magazine issue 118 (Fall 2009), Shaul Hochberger, host of the broadcasts, said: "From the long and interesting conversations I had with Rabbi Tzvi Grunblatt about life's themes and problems, as seen and analyzed from a Jewish point of view, we saw that the so-called 'dummy box' or 'electronic pacifier' can also be a great way to teach."

In 1999, the show was renamed *Un Pueblo* [One People] and aired on Channel 7 before moving to Sunday mornings on América TV. In December 2008, Radio Jai and MGM started to distribute it to the rest of Latin America.

On Sunday, April 26, 2009, the program's first broadcast was on cable TV C5N channel, which had already broadcast the Chabad Chanukah public holiday in 2008.

Near the end of 2009, the Jabad.tv website was launched, and several internal channels replaced the on-air show. It also made archive materials accessible and continued producing new ones, in a modernization that intends, according to internal comments, to put Chabad at the forefront of Jewish communication.

These conceptions and handling of modern technologies are striking, coming from an Orthodox Jewish religious group with many families in their community who do not even have a TV screen in their home, let alone an Internet connection.

Rabbi Tzvi Grunblatt dispels any doubts that a casual bystander might have about this apparent contradiction by discussing the ideas of the Seventh Lubavitch Rebbe: "It is based on a Jewish principle: 'Everything that God created in the world is to exalt the name of God.' To use technology positively is to exalt God's name. People believe that Orthodox Jews live in the Middle Ages. They live in the Middle Ages in terms of moral principles because they are the same as they were in ancient times, because 'do not steal, do not kill, and do not commit adultery' are timeless moral principles."

Miriam Kapeluschnik points in the same direction: "We have to use all the tools," she says with conviction, "that is what the Rebbe taught us. When he first asked his Hasidim to use tools like radio to transmit Torah and everything else, or even satellite or television transmissions of Hasidic meetings, Orthodox Jews became very upset. The Rebbe taught us that all these things are neither kosher nor non-kosher. There have always been waves. They are neither good nor bad. They are neutral, they are *parve*. It all depends on how they are used. So, if we use these tools to spread Judaism, television, radio, and the Internet are no longer tools that can cause harm."

The Rebbe's message was clear, and Chabad Lubavitch pioneered using the Internet to spread its message in the Jewish camp. This technological savvy has manifested itself in the sophisticated network of interconnected sites it has created, as well as its instant response capability, which allows them to create new pages to respond to specific events. Take, for example, the Haiti tsunami in 2010. Just a few hours after it happened, a Chabad webpage was already up and running to bring together relief efforts worldwide.

Not only that, but Chabad Lubavitch has specific websites for almost everything: for each holiday, for Shabbat, for internal news of the Crown Heights community, to honor the life and work of its Rebbe, and to educate anyone who wants to explore the site about Judaism, with many of these pages available in several languages. One needs only to explore their main web portal (http://www.chabad.org) to see how drop-down menus open up and lead to hundreds of specific contents, many of which are produced in-house and some of which are geared to a particular audience. For example, the "Kids" button redirects us to a portal specially designed for children, where multiple didactic contents are offered. *The Itche Kadoozy Show*, a puppet show that explains Torah to children, is among the varied contents. *Kabbala Toons* cartoons and comic strips are also available for children. In addition, the website provides video and audio commentaries on Jewish topics, as well as a Gregorian-Hebrew calendar converter. The Rebbe has his own website where you can watch hundreds of videos of him and his speeches. The options are dizzying.

With more modest resources but with the same spirit of teaching Judaism to those who enter the site, Jabad.org.ar has existed since around 1998 at the request of Rabbi Natán Grunblatt. The brother of Chabad Lubavitch Argentina CEO is in charge of the local branch of the Kehot, Chabad Lubavitch's local publishing house, which is dedicated to publishing the fundamental books of Chabad Hasidism and others on Jewish topics.

Miriam Kapeluschnik remembers when she took over the website's administration: "Nine years ago, or maybe ten, Rabbi Tzvi Grunblatt asked me to take charge of the project. The site was in its early stages and needed to be improved. We could see at the time that the Internet was rapidly expanding, and that we needed to devote ourselves to it. We worked hard with a colleague until we got the format we wanted."

The Jabad.org.ar format is an authentic local creation. Many of the Chabad houses in Argentina also have a web presence. Still, as Kapeluschnik clarifies, these are templates preassembled and distributed worldwide by Crown Heights.

Chabad Lubavitch aims to communicate, sell God, and reach as many Jews as possible. There has been a thorough understanding of the power of modern technology to accomplish this goal since the leadership of its last Rebbe.

The reach of the site, Miriam points out, is enormous: "We say that it is the Beit Chabad that receives the most people of all of them. Three hundred and sixty-five days a year. It is open twenty-four hours a day. That is why we say that it is a Beit Chabad by itself. It mainly receives inquiries from Spanish-speaking people worldwide, with most of its traffic coming from Argentina and other neighboring countries."

In a world where other branches of Orthodox Judaism dislike technological progress because they see it as a step toward secularisation, Chabad Lubavitch sees how it can bring Jews back to religious observance.

Miriam Kapeluschnik tells a story about a man in his fifties who was having a hard time and needed to talk to a rabbi. He looked online and found Chabad's website. He sent an email from there, which Miriam received and then forwarded to her husband.

Rabbi Kapeluschnik then set up a time for the man to meet with him, comforted him, and invited him to join the morning prayer service at the Agüero Street synagogue every day. The man started attending and was later invited to study Torah. Little by little, he overcame his personal crisis. He started a new business and got better in life. He was then hired by a large supermarket chain. He still attends the prayer service. "And all this thanks to the web page," ends the story Miriam with a smile. "Our site is not only a study site," she continues. "What you are going to find on the page is Jewish content. Our job is to relate the biblical part to things that have to do with the normal life of every Jew. We hope that by using this tool, every Jew will incorporate Jewish knowledge and experiences into his daily routine."

With an average of 25,000 monthly visits, the site holds a privileged position within the institution's communicational apparatus. It also serves as a testing ground for new proposals. Miriam seems to understand the site's importance within the institution's communicational framework as a battle space: "We live in a time in which the average Jew lacks information and Jewish education. Chabad is an institution dedicated to combatting this. Our mission is to spread Judaism. For that, we use different tools. A Jew can reach us through the real Beit Chabad, but they also have the option of a virtual Beit Chabad. Some people will never get close to the real one, but they suddenly put a piece of information in Google and find what they are looking for."

Glossy brochures play another critical role in Chabad's communication strategy: they are handed out during *tefillin* campaigns that students in their *yeshiva* carry out on Fridays. They are also passed out in the Batei Chabad whenever a new holiday occurs. They have detailed instructions on how to perform the accompanying festivity rituals. The Chabad Magazine, a quarterly publication published by the institution, stands out among its printed materials.

In 1990, issue number 1 of Chabad Magazine came out, dedicated to Menachem Mendel Schneerson's forty years of leadership, with a color photo of him in the foreground.

Kapeluschnik took over the project in 2000 and refreshed its brand, making it a more attractive format for a broad public.

The magazine is distributed free of charge to its twelve thousand subscribers by hand and another five thousand by mail, as well as through Batei Chabad, festivities, and campaigns. Its pages are filled with a majority of in-house produced content. It is the "lightest" publication regarding the religious load of all who come from Chabad Lubavitch's communication machine. This does not mean that it is not dominated by religious concepts. Still, they are presented in a modern and didactic form for a broad audience, which is not required to have much previous knowledge about Judaism. The four annual editions coincide with the most important holidays in Judaism: Pesach, Shavuot, Rosh Hashanah, and Chanukah. There are mixed editions when the dates coincide with other holidays, such as Purim.

The magazine serves as a good part of Chabad Lubavitch Argentina's imprint on these dates. From its covers, they announce and draw attention to the festivity. On the inside pages, advice is given on the best way to comply with the precepts to be observed during the holiday. Then there are other types of contents, such as stories and parables, which, contrary to Chabad custom, rarely include Hasidic tales but miracles through the Rebbe's intermediation. Also included are some personal anecdotes and experiences of people touched by Chabad's work, framed in a design dominated by color photos and text boxes with many blank spaces that lighten the reading experience.

The magazine is another tool within Chabad Lubavitch's external border. Without technical sophistication for connoisseurs, it is designed for readers looking to pass the time and become educated on introductory holiday rites.

Kapeluschnik maintains that the four annual issues are put together by her and a small group of collaborators and that one thing she enjoys most about this project is the possibility of receiving feedback from the community, which, while limited, is satisfactory when it appears: "I recently interviewed a person, a girl who came from the north of the country for a job interview. She had a non-Jewish father and a Jewish mother and was very interested in studying Judaism. That's why she came here. I asked her: 'How did you get in touch with Judaism?' She answered: 'My first contact with Judaism was with Chabad Magazine.' She didn't even know who I was or what I did or didn't do. She craved the magazine."

Miriam is silent for a few seconds, reflecting on what she has just said and remembering with satisfaction.

She will only pause for a few seconds before continuing at her usual frantic pace.

Chapter Six

Reborn from the Ashes: Chabad's Revived Synagogues

Lubavitch Neighborhood

"It was them, the people who were in charge at that moment, who offered me the position as chief Rabbi for this synagogue," says Rabbi Mordechai Birman in his office at the Beit Chabad Villa Crespo, on 69 Serrano Street, headquarters of synagogue Ahavat Israel, popularly known as "the Poles temple."

"Villa Kreplach" is also called, in a play on words, the Villa Crespo neighborhood. It is a neighborhood also known for its dense Jewish population. It is seen in many Jewish schools and synagogues of various currents scattered throughout a few blocks.: 649-661 Murillo Street synagogue (Comunidad Dor Jadash), 870 Camargo Street (Asociación Comunidad Israelita Sefaradí de Buenos Aires), 145 Antezana Street (Templo Berith Abraham) and also the Scholem Aleijem school (elementary, mid and high school), of Zionist socialist origins.

When Rabbi Birman first moved to the area in 1986, the synagogue was only open on Saturday mornings: "There were five families who kept it open," he says.

But then the rabbi arrived, and with him, Chabad. Today, after almost twenty-five years of work, the synagogue receives an average of two hundred people per week and functions as Beit Chabad, which is open every day; it offers courses, space for prayer and is the headquarters of one of the social assistance offices of the Chabad Foundation.

Ahavat Israel is not the only synagogue Chabad Lubavitch took over when the former administrators could no longer keep them open.

Secularization, the explosion of Zionism, and Jewish social clubs and community centers during the twentieth century diminished the Orthodox imprint in the local Jewish community.

Located in the middle of the Abasto neighborhood, another Chabad nerve center with several synagogues and institutions nearby, the Beit Chabad Almagro/Abasto was, before being recovered and refurbished by the Lubavitch, the Asociación Israelita de Culto y Beneficencia "Baron Hirsch." It was a community life center and synagogue in ruins, almost abandoned. That was until they were brought back to life by Chabad Lubavitch after they arrived in 1994.

The second floor currently houses the *Gan Jaia*, a kindergarten for sixty children. The Beit Chabad has a community dining room that feeds hundreds of needy people who come every day and organizes the CHAT youth group, among other activities.

Synagogue Iarjo Chabad Lavalle opened in 1993 under the command of Rabbi Rafael Lapidus. It also used to be a bankrupt synagogue until it was economically saved and reopened by the Lubavitch, who turned it into a center to house and encourage Jews to reconnect with their roots.

The massive return to a spiritual quest that Chabad Lubavitch has so well capitalized on has placed them in the center of a scene in which many boards of directors of synagogues and bankrupted Jewish institutions accept to entrust them with the administration of their synagogues and community centers as the only way to avoid closure.

Sociologist Damian Setton analyzes the situation: "What I believe is that Chabad has an image of efficiency when this is a powerful value. We went through neoliberalism, and the world went through a stage in which the philosophy on which social relations were organized was based on efficiency. Therefore, it is logical that an institution that seems to guarantee efficiency should be well regarded. I do not mean by this that Chabad is neoliberal. But suppose I was on a board of directors of a failing Jewish synagogue and wanted it instead to flourish and agreed with Orthodox Judaism. In that case, I would call Chabad to take over."

The myth benefits Chabad, and, like all reducing reality myths, it fails to mention that the alleged efficiency or lack thereof of each Beit Chabad depends on the rabbi in charge and his ability to raise funds to make it work.

Rabbi Birman himself started, before arriving at the current headquarters of his Beit Chabad, at Temple Etz Hajaim, which for the past five years he has also maintained as an annex of his center and which is currently under the control of another Chabad rabbi. "When I started at Temple Etz Hajaim, it had some worshippers. Maybe they were ten or twelve little old men. It was challenging because we didn't know anyone in the neighborhood. We were the oddballs. It was difficult when we wanted to start something, and we didn't know if we would get a call."

Five years ago, he assigned Rabbi Iejiel Frenkel to work in that synagogue, which is now an annex of his Beit Chabad: "He is a boy from the neighborhood who later went to study at the *yeshiva*," explains Birman: "He graduated as a rabbi there, came back, got married, started a family and worked here with me until I told him to take the synagogue under his belt. He took over a synagogue that was down, and closed. Today, on a Saturday, there will be about eighty people on Shabbat in the morning. He also organizes a very nice Kabalat Shabbat. There is also a *Morasha center* there. I think they serve around seventy children all week in it."

Under Rabbi Birman's direction, the Beit Chabad Villa Crespo was established in 1986, the fourth in the country (after Beit Chabad Tucumán, Beit Chabad Concordia, and Beit Chabad Bahía Blanca) and the first in the country's capital city.

The work done by rabbis who revive synagogues begs the question: Why could they do what earlier communities, who were also Orthodox, could not?

The rabbis do not offer earthly answers. They limit themselves to commenting on anecdotes that illustrate what they consider was and is their divine mission: "I remember the first year I started a kindergarten knowing no one in the neighborhood. I was going to be the *madrich*. My wife was going to help me. We had made some pamphlets and stuck them around the neighborhood, but we did not know any children. When we left my house on Saturday afternoon, on the way to the synagogue, we bet on how many children would attend. The most we expected was three or four. But when we arrived, there were twelve children at the door. That kindergarten was very successful because it was the base to meet many families. During our peak, we had nearly forty-five children. Those kids gave us a wide knowledge of many families with whom we began to work, bringing others closer to us."

Chabad rabbis must work one-on-one with Jewish community members to gain their trust. "It is difficult," Birman reflects, "but I think that no one who sees us today in the [bustling] corner of Scalabrini Ortiz Avenue and Corrientes Avenue doesn't know us. Moreover, the Chabad Central *yeshiva* guys come every Friday to convince Jews passing by to put on *tefillin* and hand out pamphlets. I live halfway down the block, and when the *yeshiva* guys come, they ring my doorbell to ask me for the *Weekly Teaching* brochures.

People from the area wait eagerly for Friday to come so they can get the booklet. Thank God I walk through the neighborhood today, and half of Villa Crespo greets me. Anyway, I am not satisfied because I feel we should do much more, that much more can be done, and, God willing, we will do it."

Chabad Bulldozer

Rabbi Aharon Stawski welcomes me into his office on the second floor of the Litvishe Shul - Beit Chabad Once and offers me a glass of water on a sticky, hot day in early January 2010.

The centennial congregation we are in is at 348 Uriburu Street, just in the center of another heavily Jewish-populated neighborhood in Buenos Aires. Surrounded by businesses whose owners belong to the Jewish community, three blocks away is the house of Rabbi Dov Ber Baumgarten, son of Chabad's first emissary in Argentina. Just around the corner from the headquarters of the Sociedad Hebraica Argentina [Hebrew Society of Argentina] and in a perimeter of only five blocks around are the headquarters of the AMIA [Argentinian Association of Israelites Mutuals] along with the synagogues Anschei Galitzia (234 Uriburu Street) and Jevre Mishnaiot (2186 Tucumán Street.)

In fact, due to a long-standing agreement, the three synagogues share a weekly prayer service that takes place in the evenings, from Monday to Thursday in this Litvishe Shul, and on Sundays and holidays in the Galician synagogue.

There is something unique about being in a Lithuanian synagogue today that has been administered since 1996 by Chabad Lubavitch.

For starters, "Lithuanian" is a nickname given not only to those from the country but also to those who, when the Baal Shem Tov's Hasidism emerged, became their most vocal opponents, adopting the name *Mitnagdim*.

The second reason it is surprising to be here today is that before becoming a Chabad Beit, this very Litvishe Shul was literally falling apart. The furnishing was rotting, and the neglect was total. The few worshippers who continued to attend were on the verge of closing it down due to a lack of funds and attendants.

Rabbi Stawski says: "This synagogue is one of the most important for Orthodoxy in this country because the great rabbis of the community used to come here. When the Jewish population moved to other neighborhoods, mostly to the north of the city, the public that used to attend here began to attend other, more prestigious places. Thus, many synagogues emptied. Some older people kept coming here, but their children moved away. But, just as many great synagogues changed to entice people to return, this synagogue decided not to change and instead to remain Orthodox. It got to where it was tough to keep up. After much back and forth, when they had no choice and were about to close, they accepted us, Chabad, taking command. They accepted it because we were the only ones to guarantee that the synagogueremained Orthodox."

The structure is deteriorating, that is clear, but I'm not sure if it's because of the age of the building or because some workers in the entrance hall have not stopped hammering the frames of the internal doors with monotonous and regular constancy, gradually turning the historic walls into little more than dust since I arrived here today.

"We are always making improvements and trying new things. We built a new room upstairs; we're finishing a men's *mikveh*; we're fixing up the entrance," Rabbi Stawski says happily.

He will later clarify that his work of destruction and reconstruction began four weeks ago, one week after the death of the last old guard attendant, Daniel Rubinstein, a devout follower of this synagogue since childhood, eventually decided that the only way to keep it open and Orthodox was to enlist the help of Chabad Lubavitch.

"He was a wonderful man, but obviously, he disagreed with all the physical changes made to the synagogue because he wanted to remember it as it was when he came as a little boy. Now that he passed away, I tore it all down. But I had to wait about seven years. We are not technocrats who come to demolish everything and don't care about anything."

The congregation needed repair, as evidenced by some closed wooden doors from the outside, giving the impression of a closed, abandoned place with no one inside. When Rabbi Stawski turns on the synagogue's renovated lights and the library, the shiny prayer books published by Chabad's Kehot publishing press come into view. Walking along the polished and refurbished pews, I notice a sense of new life in this massive structure with an uncovered stone front resembling a cave.

The rabbi points to the benches and tells me: "When I arrived, after two or three years, these benches were recycled. They were the typical benches, big, solid synagogue benches. The carpenter took everything out, and they were polished again. Some sides had rods in them. He took out the rods and found that on two or three benches, there were chiseled swastikas. The carpenters of the time when the synagogue was first built, or someone else, had put the swastikas and covered them up with the rods, but as if to say: the swastikas are there. Of course, the synagogue was built in 1945 or 1946."

The Litvishe Shul was established in 1898. The property was purchased in 1920, and it included a stable that still rented animals for traction, a simple house in front, and a shed. The synagogue operated in the tiny house until 1945 when all the buildings were demolished and construction of the current structure, which includes the current synagogue, began. The reinauguration was in 1947. The swastikas engraved on the pews' sides coincide perfectly with when they were manufactured and placed in the synagogue. It seems a story of old hauntings, fascinating and perverse, during the sixty-year history of one of Buenos Aires' most important orthodox synagogues. In silence, the sign of hatred mocked the faithful.

The upstairs now has a modern hall for lectures, screenings, and activities and is equipped with a kitchen, two bathrooms, and what the rabbi points out as the most important thing: a grill on the terrace. "This was the first thing we did," says Stawski, proudly showing off the work. "Mr. Rubinstein didn't see it. I think he came up once and never again."

The room is decorated in soft pastel tones; it is spacious, and even though it is empty now, it is easy to imagine it in full with about one-hundred-fifty people, which is what the rabbi estimates they gather during the holidays: Sukkot, Purim, Chanukah, Pesach, and Rosh Hashanah.

I ask him if the arrival of such a prominent Hasidic group as Chabad Lubavitch did not result in conflicts with the Lithuanian community to which the synagogue belonged. He flatly denies it: "No, that historical confrontation should be over now. And, in fact, it was finished until the seventies, when a Lithuanian rabbi in Israel generated some commotion again, reviving the hatred and generating a lot of trouble. This synagogue had nothing to do with those things. It was created by the Lithuanian immigrants who arrived in Buenos Aires at the beginning of the last century. They had no place in the conflict."

It's worth noting what Rabbi Stawski says about Chabad Lubavitch's image in the community as effective administrators, resuscitators of institutions on the verge of closing, or wealthy individuals capable of saving centers of Jewish community life: "The reason Chabad came here was to resurrect something that could no longer exist. Chabad did not just come and put money. A rabbi arrived and began working independently, raising funds like every Beit Chabad. Not that a global corporation came here and invested money. That is just a fantasy. Rabbi Shaul Moshe Elituv was the first to arrive. From 1996 to 2001, he was in charge of this space."

However, when I ask him how much money he has invested as a representative of Chabad Lubavitch in this synagogue since taking over, he gives an evasive answer that avoids any numerical precision.

With Chabad Lubavitch at the helm, the synagogue was clearly reborn. It benefited from building renovations and new books in the library. It became a welcoming place for secular Jews to rekindle their interest in Jewish religious life.

"What changed was the people coming here," Rabbi Stawski says as he leads me into the ritual bath (the *mikveh*) that is nearly finished, showers, and a men's locker room. The well opens into the ground over sixty meters. It has a complicated piping mechanism that guarantees that the ritual bath is kosher. "This synagogue is very particular. It is in the Once neighborhood, which has the city's largest religious community. A Beit Chabad in a more distant neighborhood needs a kindergarten, a social aid foundation, and activities for young people and children. It has to have everything. Our work is oriented toward adult education. We also had a period when we worked with single men and women from thirty to fifty years old. We work all the holidays, and we have a rabbi who works with businesses in the area. He visits them, introduces himself, puts up posters, leaves brochures, looks at the needs of the Jews who work in this area, whatever. No young people live in this area. We have already done a market study. The Jewish people who are left in this neighborhood are older."

The synagogue fulfills a very executive function: a place of passage for Jews working in the area to satisfy their spiritual needs and stimulate, as in all Beit Chabad, the study of the Torah.

One of the rabbi's plans is a Torah Lunch with Businessmen project: "Everybody has to have lunch, right? A businessman must have lunch. He doesn't stay all day at the cash register invoicing. So, I invite them to have lunch with me. They come here three times a week. Once a week, I go to a notary's office, and we have Torah Lunch. We study Torah and eat *kasher*. We order from the delivery or cook here. Those who can contribute do so. Those who cannot, do not, and it is fine."

Rabbi Aharon Stawski was born in Uruguay and, like most Chabad rabbis, grew up in a non-religious household. His grandfather was a communist. Rabbi Stawski started attending synagogue service at an advanced age. "As my grandfather started getting older, he also started attending the *shul* like every Jew. When the chips are down… Better late than never."

During that time and at that synagogue, rabbi Aharon Stawski first came into contact with Rabbi Eliezer Shemtov, the Rebbe's emissary to Uruguay.

It was 1986, and Stawski had just returned from Israel, where he had discovered his spiritual vocation to return to his Jewish sources: "I looked in many places, and thank God, I didn't have to do anything weird or join any cults. I was doing a lot of intellectual research. I attended college but couldn't find what I was looking for. I studied philosophy at the Hebrew University, but it appeared to be a lie. I was looking for something true, and the Torah was the only place I could find it. I started in my twenties in Israel. I did not meet Chabad there. I met it in Uruguay."

After returning to Montevideo and getting to know Chabad Lubavitch, the rabbi traveled to the institution's central *yeshiva* in New York. He studied to become a rabbi, got married, and returned to study for another five years. Until 1998 when Rabbi Tzvi Grunblatt brought him to Buenos Aires as an emissary. He worked at the headquarters of Chabad Lubavtich Argentina until 2002, when he took over as director of this Beit Chabad.: "When I first arrived in Buenos Aires in 1998, I wanted to do something no one had done before. I investigated the situation and discovered no one looked after Jewish singles. So, I got to work. You must do what needs to be done, not just what you like."

We are back in the synagogue with the lights on. It has a striking presence.

I am about to leave, and he asks me if I put on the *tefillin* this morning. I tell him no, and he proposes to help me put them. I accept, and when I finish the prayers, he makes me repeat to him in English: "*We, Want, Mashiach, Now!*"

"Do you know English?"

"Yes," I answer.

"Well, then you understood," he says and smiles, adding nothing else. Before I leave, he adds: "I'll tell you something. I was in Israel when my father called to tell me my grandfather had passed away. He asked my brother and me if we could pray for him at the *Kotel*. We went there and noticed a small Chabad booth for putting on *tefillin*. I was already familiar with how to put them on. I had done my *bar mitzvah*. I approached the booth, although I was not yet in Chabad. I informed them I intended to put them on. They asked if I needed help, and I said no, but when I tried, I realized I had forgotten how to do it... so they assisted me. I woke up the next day knowing I didn't want to go another day without putting them on. I started putting them on every day. Since I didn't have my own, I would go to my brother's every morning and put them on at his place. It was a big effort. That was until I could get my own. I was not religious at the time. I always tell a friend: 'You will not become religious by doing a *mitzvah*. Put on the *tefillin*, and, if you want me, I'll write you a certificate stating that you are not religiously observant.'"

I find the story mildly sympathetic. The rabbi walks me to the exit.

I had forgotten it was a very sunny and hot day while I was inside the synagogue.

"Can I come here for some Kabbalat Shabbat?" I ask him.

"With that face of yours, of course," he says sardonically. "It's just that many *goyim* here want to come. They get in. They want to pray. We have to tell them this is a place only for Jews. At the Chanukah party, I was lighting the fire over there. I have all the cans with kerosene — points to a golden can against the entrance gate — and a Korean came, or he was Chinese, I don't know. He was impeccably dressed. The party was announced at eight o'clock and was ten to eight. So, the guy came, and I said: 'Hello, how are you?' and he said: 'I am here for the Chanukah party,' speaking good Spanish but with a bit of an accent. Then I told him: 'Look, don't take this the wrong way, but it is for Jews only.' Then he said: 'Are you discriminating against me?' and I said: 'No, I am not discriminating against you. This is a Jewish synagogue, and our festivities are only for Jews. Discriminating would be if I didn't let you in because of your race, but this is for Jews only.' He turned and walked away. The *goyim* want to come in. They're interested. They want to see what this is. Other Jewish people invite non-Jews because they are interested. Some goyim send their children to Jewish schools, so they want to attend our festivities. A lady sends her children to the *Nathan Gesang* school because the kids' father is Jewish, but she is a *goy*. She came once or twice. I first thought she was Sephardi, but later, I discovered she was not Jewish. So, I told my wife to talk to her. She talked to her, and the lady insisted on coming because she felt Jewish. I had to tell her that while what she felt was very noble, this place was only for Jews. And she was not a Jew. It is paradoxical; those who are not Jewish are interested, and many are Jewish and do not want to know anything about their Judaism."

Chapter Seven
Educating in Torah

> "That's how we were taught. When we were kids, we were taught to be stubborn."
> Rabbi Rafael Tawil

The first thing I sense when I enter the *Menachem M. Tabacinic Jewish Education Center - Wolfsohn School* is the pleasant smell of *gefilte fish*, the stuffed fish we eat at my grandmother's when the Pesach holiday comes around. It's around noon, and the dining room is getting ready to feed about two hundred thirty students today.

It is striking that the *Wolfsohn School* (as it was known until 2004), one of the most traditional Jewish schools in the upscale Belgrano neighborhood, with a history dating back to 1963 and belonging to a community that has its roots much earlier, in 1906, is open and renovated, with the corridors full of Jewish children trying to squeeze the last minutes of class recess.

My own maternal grandmother, Diana Rubel, had a career around these same walls that are now remodeled. It was a completely different time. She joined in March 1970 as a teacher. In 1978, she was promoted to vice-principal; in 1979, she was appointed principal until she left in 1982.

The first thing that would catch the eye of a person like my grandmother upon re-entering the building after so many years would be the photo of Menachem Mendel Schneerson, the Rebbe, at the end of the corridor, to whose example of life and inspiration the rebuilt institution was dedicated. And I think this would surprise her because this has always been a Conservative Jewish congregation. To think that an Orthodox Hasidic group would ever place their Rebbe's picture anywhere in this school was unthinkable just a few years ago.

We speak of miracles because, in addition, the school was saved from inevitable closure and demolition. The Argentinian economic crisis of 2001 left many other Jewish schools with no choice but to close their doors.

But that did not happen to this one.

Gustavo Dvoskin (a computer scientist and Education specialist) is the new general director of the Wolfsohn School since Chabad took over, and he receives me in his office, going up several floors through the central ramps.

He does not belong to Chabad Lubavitch and, in fact, confesses that before being summoned, he did not even know anything about them.

"I had never spoken with a Chabad rabbi before joining the school. I did not know their work in Argentina, the world, or their ideological position. Just nothing," he comments. One night, he got a phone call. The person on the other end of the line spoke with a Yiddish accent. It stated that he was speaking with Rabbi Tzvi Grunblatt and asked if he recognized him and would be willing to be interviewed for an educational project. The computer scientist confessed to his interlocutor that he did not know of him but would be happy to hold the interview.

It was the beginning of what would end with Dvoskin sitting in this comfortable office. In an Orthodox-run school, the headmaster is indistinguishable from any other secular Jew or not necessarily Jewish man: he doesn't wear a yarmulke nor a hat, is not dressed in a black overcoat, and has a close-shaven beard. He is not a Hasid and states that his position imposes no religious obligations on him: "It does not demand from me anything beyond the school schedule and within the parameters of the school, to respect and enforce the very clear school rules. But it does not oblige me to have any personal commitment in my private life. Even this is written into the contract and proposed by them. They were the ones who inserted the clause about my personal commitment. Obviously, I try not to offend or stir up controversy. For example, if I suspect something that might cause discomfort, I try to avoid it, but I never force myself to do things I don't want or not do things I want. I am not subject to any kind of imposition," he clarifies.

The faint hum of the air conditioning is barely interrupted by the occasional shout of children playing through the window overlooking the inner courtyard of the building. It is mid-November 2009. It has been five years since Chabad Lubavitch took over this school. In mid-2004, the rabbi in charge of the school addressed the community's parents and informed them that the institution would have to close because of a lack of funds. In exchange, he offered the parents the opportunity for their children to continue their education at another conservative school he also managed.

Then, contact was made with Rabbi Shlomo Kiesel of Beit Chabad Belgrano, with over twenty years of presence in the neighborhood. The relationship with Kiesel was already established: on a previous occasion, he had rented a school hall to celebrate the High Holidays because his own Beit Chabad was growing out of space.

Chabad Lubavitch considered taking over the school and accepted the proposal. The Orthodox were most interested in not leaving the children of one hundred and fifty families without a Jewish education rather than the building itself.

Not only did the school not close, as the parents who turned to Chabad for assistance desired, but the Lubavitch invested approximately one million dollars in refurbishing the infrastructure by renovating the two buildings that comprise the school.

The money investment can be observed in the corridors with bright paint and modern design that contrasts with some areas of more traditional architecture, which are part of the building's heritage.

Aside from the initial investment, the Chabad Lubavitch Argentina headquarters contributes approximately thirty to forty thousand dollars monthly to cover the school's current deficit. "The school has a budget of one hundred thousand dollars per month, with which, if Chabad gives me thirty-five or forty thousand dollars, the other sixty-five or sixty thousand dollars are genuine school resources. The idea is to reach a balance, and then Chabad will withdraw from its contribution to support this school. If not for Chabad, this school would not be open today," explains Dvoskin.

The change of hands of the school, from Conservative Judaism to Chabad Orthodoxy, did not come up well with the entire community: many families stopped sending their children as soon as the change of hands took place. They did not accept the new proposal or meet with the new general director.

Dvoskin maintains that this results from accumulating prejudices and fears about Chabad. Still, he is happy to show that, just as many families left when the school changed management, many other families arrived and trusted in the project when it was nothing more than promises and reconstruction work had not begun.

However, the changes were not only at the building level, and Chabad's presence, although moderate, is easy to perceive because there is no intention of hiding it. Dvoskin says: "Everything related to Jewish education was changed from the beginning because there is now an Orthodox imprint. It is a school where the philosophy is Orthodox, but no behavior is expected from students in their personal lives. There is an internal regulation that does not affect the student's private lives. Obviously, this is a different type of Orthodox school. It is a school for non-Orthodox families comfortable with an Orthodox education. There are no pressures, no impositions. Each family lives as they want."

Education at Wolfsohn is under an Orthodox imprint, but it is carefully dosed. There is no gender separation; boys are not required to wear a yarmulke (though it is required during Jewish education hours.) Girls are not required to wear long skirts.

Children are taught courses that follow the required contents by the Government of the City of Buenos Aires to all the city's schools during the morning hours. The Jewish contents are developed in the afternoon: "The afternoon comprises twenty teaching hours, at a rate of four hours per day. Of those twenty hours, there are eight hours of English and eight or nine of Jewish education. The rest is divided into activities such as computers, art, and music... which are sometimes oriented toward religion and sometimes towards language. The computer class, for example, has a connotation of an English class. In Art, they do things related to the holidays, *mezuzot*, candelabras," says Dvoskin. In the morning, the children also perform a prayer when they arrive at the school, make the blessings before and after lunch, and do a new prayer when the afternoon begins. According to Dvoskin, the school model is unprecedented because he understands that the Wolsohn "is a school with an Orthodox imprint for non-Orthodox families. There are Chabad schools and other Hassidic or Orthodox schools that are much more closed. We don't get involved in things that are outside of school hours. We do not interfere with the food at home or with the intimacy of our students. We do not judge the behavior of the families and their commitment outside what the school demands. No one here questions someone else for working on a Saturday. If anyone believes this is a problem for them, we invite them to consider whether there is a school closer to their way of life."

The school is thus inserted within the Chabad institutions that seem to be on the outer border: the line of welcome to Jews who, because of history, have stopped practicing their religion and become secular. This non-intrusive way of doing things, this light Orthodoxy that welcomes all Jews and shows them the way, is undoubtedly one of the most characteristic things about Chabad Lubavitch.

"It's not a school for Chabad kids," Dvoskin maintains sharply: "Rabbi Grunblatt makes fun of me, he says, 'I would never send my children to your school,' and I reply, 'And I wouldn't send mine to yours, either. They have their school for their children."

Rabbi Damian Karo, a connoisseur of Chabad Lubavitch's outreach strategies (*keruv*), is suspicious: "What is the purpose of the open Chabad schools? For the kids to take a little step further. The system of thought behind it is: 'During the time they are in school, they will eat kosher. They will learn genuine Judaism. Over the years, this will intensify. Those kids won't all become religious observant like us, but some will. With the others who will not, we will ensure they will not discriminate against us. They will even accept us. We will probably prevent them from marrying a non-Jew. The elementary school will later open a high school, and many of those kids will eventually join our *yeshiva*.' That's how it works".

Where there is strong Orthodox control within the Wolfsohn is in the food. The *gefilte fish* that was cooking when I arrived is part of the strictly kosher menu that is served every day and is overseen by Rabbi Feigelstock, Rabbi Tzvi Grunblatt, and a third rabbi who supervises the school's daily activities. Dvoskin clarifies that this is not only for preserving the *kashrut* but also for what they consider fundamental in their school project: good nutrition. "We stopped allowing students to bring food to school in November 2007. Since then, the children's nutritional status has improved."

Regarding the contents that are being taught in this school, it is common for differences to arise between their positions and the programs designed by the Government of the City of Buenos Aires. Topics such as the Theory of Evolution or the Earth as a part of the Universe rather than its center are taught following State-approved curricula. Still, they are contrasted with Torah knowledge, and the teacher teaching these contents usually makes it clear which of these versions he prefers. Another delicate issue is the school's position regarding the State of Israel. Like most Hassidic currents, Chabad Lubavitch is ideologically opposed to the existence of the State of Israel if not founded by the Messiah. Although, unlike other positions, theirs is not an extremist position. Dvoskin clarifies that the Wolfsohn "is not a Zionist school. In fact, Chabad does not define itself as such. But in the general director's office, we have the Israeli flag. We received the Israeli ambassador less than two months ago. He honored us with his visit. There is no Zionist parent who sends his children to this school who can claim that we do not have a pro-Israel position, even if it is the bare minimum. We have Orthodox and Zionist teachers who are not Chabadniks. They are religious people. Some might be Sephardi. People that are not Lubavitch but are still religious Jews."

The balance seems delicate: How to run an Orthodox school that can also attract non-Orthodox people?

"In this school, we are not guided by absolute truths," says Dvoskin. "I mean, for example, we don't say 'eating pork is wrong,' as it's not well seen to say it like that. Instead, we say, 'eating pork is wrong for me.' The same thing happened during Israel's war. Which side are we on? In opposition to the war. The school is pro-peace, and we pray for the Israeli soldiers' health and well-being."

It is in this ambiguity that the school thrives. For example, although non-Jewish children already enrolled in the school could stay when the new administration took over, the school now only accepts Jewish children. This means children of Jewish wombs, with children of mixed marriages admitted only if the mother is Jewish.

The doorbell rings. It's time for lunch. I can only imagine all the fish stew that will be served in a few moments as I step out into the spring morning sunshine.

A Conversation with the Wolfsohn's Rabbi

I return to the Wolfsohn a week later to meet with the school's rabbi, Shmuel Kiesel. He is in his thirties and also serves as the Wolfsohn School's community director. He is the son of Shlomo Kiesel, the rabbi in charge of Beit Chabad Belgrano, and president of the society of this new Wolfsohn reborn thanks to Chabad Lubavitch. Shmuel greets me in the rabbinate's office at the school. He makes me sit down and offers me a glass of water while he finishes typing an e-mail.

He is not wearing a hat or an overcoat. Instead, he is wearing a yarmulke with a colorful design of a butterfly and some flowers on it.

He'll tell me he doesn't usually wear an overcoat because he suffers from the heat. He wears it on Shabbat, along with a hat, but he tries not to wear it daily.

A pair of yarmulkes is in one corner of the desk; on the other corner is a picture frame with a picture of the rabbi with his wife and two daughters.

A picture of the Rebbe wearing his tallit is on the wall before me. It seems a more relaxed image than the ubiquitous photo of him in a black hat.

A gleaming black cabinet houses books, prayer books, and a candleless candelabra. A twenty-nine-inch television with a PlayStation 2 completes the office.

I ask him how they treat children in school who come from socially risky situations. He tells me: "Those who need support have *morot* (teachers) who give them more specific follow-ups. Attention is given to those who need it. They are given a lot of love here. There is a lot of affection. Each one is not just one more. Each one is a universe."

Rabbi Shmuel Kiesel is the son of a *baal teshuvah*. I am intrigued by how he lives the experience of being a first-generation Chabadnik.

"I don't really pay attention to being the son of a *baal teshuvah* or having been the son of someone who was already Chabad. It's indeed different because you have relatives who are not religious. Somehow, you have a more open field of vision. It's not that I only interact with Chabad people. As a child, I always spent more time with non-Orthodox people. I grew up differently in another environment, which enriched me. For example, all my cousins or my grandparents are not religious."

I'm curious if he plays with the PlayStation 2 or has it to soften up kids, get closer when they talk to him, and become more familiar. The boundaries between Orthodoxy and secular life are vast. Rabbi Shmuel seems to move between them easily, as if it doesn't make a big difference to him. "If my friends get together to eat at a restaurant, I don't go. However, about ninety percent of my relationships are with non-observant people. With religious people, I have a minimal relationship," he says. I find it difficult to understand that someone can make sacrifices such as not going out to eat with his friends because of religious convictions.

Chabad's discourse is powerful and compelling for anyone who wants to hear it.

He asks me if I speak English, I answer yes, and he tells me: "Ah, then you have to go to the Internet to watch videos of the Rebbe. Write: chabad.org", and he enters his PC to Chabad's webpage, looks for the section "Video", then "The Rebbe" and in there, he enters "Living Torah" where there are videos of the Rebbe. He goes halfway through one, but it is very long, so he plays another one from November 1989, where the Rebbe is seen talking to a Knesset (Israeli Parliament) member. The politician asks him how he can make his country more secure. The Rebbe answers he must teach "the people of the Land of Israel" that they have to live there not only from a physical and geographical perspective but also spiritually. The MP doesn't seem convinced and repeats the question, so the Rebbe again insists on the same advice.

Then, the rabbi puts another video. In this one, I can see the Rebbe singing and clapping, along with the accompaniment of hundreds of other Lubavitchers in one of the famous Hassidic meetings he used to hold.

The video ends, and he tells me spontaneously that there are good people and bad people in Chabad. That it is not exclusive to Chabad.

"The human being is the way he is everywhere. He is not perfect; he can make mistakes. One tries to do everything to the best of one's ability. But there may be some people who, in their fallibility, don't do things right. Then later, they point at them and say, 'All Chabad is like that.' That's not right. It's like when they say, 'All Jews are hustlers.' Sure, there are some Jewish hustlers, but you can't generalize."

This is the first time a Lubavitcher has told me I don't have to trust all Jews just because they are Jewish. It seems a sort of unspoken rule: "If he's Jewish, he's a good one," a communal advertising phrase would say. It doesn't tell me that there can be "bad Jews," but it tells me that Jews are just human beings and can make mistakes. This strikes me as a rather euphemistic way of forewarning me about the possibility of meeting a rotten apple inside Chabad Lubavitch. In fact, his advice appears to contradict everything I've heard from Lubavitchers thus far, which I could summarize as follows: "It makes no difference whether he is good or bad as long as he fulfills the *mitzvot*."

He says something like this when he tells me: "Many start doing *teshuvah* in Chabad and then go to other places. They start in Chabad, grow, and then go to other communities with other approaches. But, *Baruch HaShem*, because as long as people are with the Torah, it doesn't matter if they are here or there. What matters is that there is more *mitzvah* in the world. The purpose is to prepare the world for the coming of the *Mashiach*, in the sense that by doing *mitzvot*, we bring the *shekhinah* to this world. The more that is done, the more the arrival [of *Mashiach*] is sped up."

As we have seen, the level of Orthodox observance at the Wolfsohn is not as great as in other Chabad-managed schools.

Kiesel attended a Chabad elementary school and then took some exams to validate his knowledge in a State-controlled school. This was because the Argentinian State does not recognize Lubavitch boys' schools in the country as they do not teach the mandatory essential contents approved by the National Ministry of Education. Commonly, the most liberal Lubavitchers send their children to study in their community schools and then make them take the validation exams. Shmuel Kiesel attended Toratenu for his high school, an Orthodox but officially recognized school. At the same time, he attended another Sephardic school after hours. He completed his studies with two years of study abroad in the United States and one in Australia.

Until I say the name of Kfar Chabad, a town founded by Chabad Lubavitch, he doesn't say anything about Israel. Then he tells me something about the rabbi who started the town, and then he tells me he knows it and spent a couple of hours there. According to him, the people who live there are Hassidim, who have developed a higher level of spirituality.

He then tells me he and his wife lived six months in Safed, a town considered the birthplace of the Kabbalah and of the kabbalist Isaac Luria, one of the fundamental precedents of Hasidism. Safed is also regarded as one of the most religious areas in Israel, with residents frequently throwing stones at tourists who, unnoticed, violate the strict rules of required modesty by wearing inappropriate clothing.

I was in that town in 2008 when I traveled to Israel with TAGLIT. It seemed like a pre-modern enclave in the middle of the mountain, a small town with narrow streets and intact synagogues painted light blue. This is because of the local belief that the demons that fly over the area confuse this painting's tone with the sky and, thus, do not come down to enter the houses.

"How do you see other branches of Judaism, both more and less Orthodox, from Chabad?" I ask Rabbi Shmuel.

"There are various approaches to understanding the Torah. Sometimes, some people fit better in one movement and others in another. Within Orthodoxy, some need a more rigid, harder style, and others need the approach of Hasidism. That is a way of serving God motivated by love rather than fear of punishment. Knowing the greatness of *HaShem*, the greatness of the Universe, one naturally desires to approach Him through Torah and *mitzvot*. Others may like the attitude, 'Look, if you don't do this, God will punish you' more."

Kiesel is undoubtedly at ease within Chabad Hassidim, which he reaffirms when he comments: "Yesterday I was visiting a father from school, who told me he and his family went to China. Once there, in a small town in the middle of nowhere, he found a Beit Chabad that had opened just six months ago. They went there and were able to eat kosher food. They could pray. He told me: 'Chabad is a machine for making *mitzvot*.'"

We talk a little about the Sociedad Hebraica Argentina [Hebrew Society of Argentina] where I work as a librarian, and he tells me that a few weeks ago, he attended a Krav Maga course in its facilities. I imagine him, a Hasidic rabbi, making some moves of one of the world's most violent martial arts developed by the Zionist Israeli Defense Army, nonetheless.

He checks the time on a much more modern cell phone than the one I have and tells me he will go to put tefillin on a boy who is hospitalized a few blocks away from the school. Alan is from the western province of Mendoza. He was involved in a car accident, and after doctors told him he had no chance of survival, he awoke from his coma and is showing neuronal improvements.

The rabbi of Chabad Mendoza interceded for Alan's family and himself to be received by the Chabad people in the country's Capital.

We go out to the street. A few drops of rain fall, and Shmuel asks me if I mind getting a little wet. I tell him no, and he suggests we go by car, but we are already halfway there. It's not worth it.

He tells me that Alan's family is having lunch at Wolfsohn's during these days to help them with the financial burden of having to live in Buenos Aires for the duration of Alan's hospital stay.

"Does Wolfsohn have an open dining room for the community?"

"No. It's just on Tuesdays. But this family is a special case, a special arrangement."

We arrive at the ULME rehabilitation clinic, a modern health center with a garden in the back and a balance of light that makes it comfortable. Rabbi Kiesel seems to be used to coming. He takes me directly up the stairs to the second floor, room 113. Alan's grandmother, mother, sister, and father greet us inside. Alan is in a wheelchair and is semi-conscious.

Recovery has been slow but prodigious, considering the medical diagnosis. Alan can already express affirmation or denial by shaking his head. Later, as we descend the stairs to leave, Rabbi Kiesel will tell me, "All of this is because of the sister. She refused to give up. She insisted. With a diagnosis like Alan's, there were only two options: despair and acceptance that he would die or fighting day and night to help him recover. That's exactly what she did."

The family welcomes the rabbi joyfully and never asks who I am and what I am doing there.

We put on antiseptic protective clothing. Alan's sister's collar has a gold charm with the Hebrew letter Chai, which means "life."

While the rabbi prepares the phylacteries, the mother comments that Eduardo Elsztain, one of the country's wealthiest men, called to inquire about the boy's health.

"His secretary called us on his cell phone. I don't know how she got our number," she says.

The sister says joyfully, "It was *HaShem*," and Shmuel adds it was undoubtedly *HaShem*'s work.

Alan's neurologist recommended that he be transferred to another healthcare clinic, where he can have rehabilitation more in line with his needs.

"They don't want Alan to do his rehabilitation here with the rest of the people because of something they say about the bug," says the sister. I ask her what "bug" Alan has. "One that eighty percent of the population possesses. You and I are both likely to have it. They don't want him infecting people with weak immune systems," she says.

"Do you want gloves?" Alan's mother asks me.

"No, it is unnecessary," I answer.

"If you're going to touch Alan, you will need gloves," she says.

"I'm not going to touch him," I tell the mother.

The family leaves. We are left alone with Alan and his sister.

The rabbi encourages him: "Hi, champ! How are you today? It's raining! It's a beautiful day!" Looking at me, he tells me that Alan loves cloudy days. He puts a yarmulke on his head and pulls the leather straps over his arm as he prays in Hebrew. Alan has his eyes half closed, his head thrown back, and a neck pillow. His arms are crossed. "Come on, Alan, help the rabbi!" his sister says. Shmuel finishes putting the tefillin around him and prays aloud in Hebrew.

"The neurologist was astonished yesterday," the sister tells me as the rabbi finishes the ceremony. "He asked Alan if he knew how to play *truco*[1]. He said yes with his head. We did that. He couldn't do it before. And then she asked him if he remembered the card values. Alan winked when he asked about the ace of clubs. That's very important. It means Alan hasn't lost his memory. The knowledge of the game of *truco* must be something he remembers; it can't be a new knowledge he gained now."

I see Alan in the wheelchair, a little white tube sticking up his nose and taped to his forehead, high stockings covering his legs almost to his knees. Behind him is an older man in a wheelchair, his eyes closed, making sounds.

"Alan is lazy today," his sister says to the rabbi for the little cooperation he has given so far, "and they got him up late."

---

1. A popular card game in Argentina and Uruguay. It is played with a Spanish deck of cards.

We say goodbye, and Alan's sister tells rabbi Shmuel that she will see him later today or tomorrow. This afternoon is the beginning of Shabbat.

As soon as we leave the room, I ask the rabbi if he invites them to dinner at his house to spend Kabbalat Shabbat with him and his family. He tells me they usually attend the synagogue on Saturdays. We walk down the hall to the waiting room, greeting the family before heading downstairs.

Outside, it is raining harder than it was a while ago.

"It doesn't matter," Rabbi Kiesel tells me. "The rain is a *berakhah*, a blessing."

We walk back to the Wolfsohn, and I ask him if Eduardo Elsztain is collaborating financially with Alan.

"No, no, he only asked about him. Anyway, the treatment is covered by health insurance."

"Do you come every day to put tefillin on him? Do you help other children?"

"Not every day. Unfortunately, there are many more cases like this one. There were some kids at school… for example, a little boy who was found with a tumor. Now *Baruch HaShem* is doing fine. He had surgery. We supported him and his family while he was undergoing this situation."

It seems dark even though it is just before noon, and the falling rain is light but insistent.

"Rabbi, what do you mean by rain being a *berakhah*?"

"Water nourishes everything, gives life, and is everywhere to nourish. And it is not controlled by man. It is controlled by *HaShem*. He is wise and knows how to send it when it is needed. That is why one has to ask for rain on the right measure. Not more because it causes floods, and not less because it generates droughts."

We arrived at the school gate and said goodbye with a handshake.

Trotsky, Freud, and Jewish Orthodoxy: The Story of Diana M.

The Wolfsohn School experience represents one of Chabad Lubavitch's most ambitious bets within its philosophy of "bringing Jews closer to Judaism." However, it is not the only school in which Chabad puts together an educational proposal that arises from Orthodoxy and is aimed at secular Jewish families.

Diana M. has a degree in psychology, and for over twenty years, she was in charge of the private progressive elementary school, *Instituto Acuario* [Aquarius Institute.] I have a personal relationship with her because I attended that school as a child, and my mother later became the vice-principal of its kindergarten. "It was a haven of free thought in the dictatorship's time," she says. We're sitting at a table in a café on the busy intersection of Corrientes and Medrano streets.

After a traumatic departure from *Acuario*, Diana M. landed a job in Chabad Lubavitch, where she worked for over a decade. First, she started working within Chabad's Social Assistance organization until she was offered her current position as director of the Hillel School, a kindergarten and elementary school set up by Rabbi David Stoler.

Diana M. observes that, based on what she has heard, the rabbi would have spiritually assisted the owner of the building where the school now stands during a long illness, causing him to donate the space on the condition that it be reused as a school.

Rabbi Stoler set up the synagogue and opened a kindergarten with eight students.

"Today, the school has one hundred and twenty children in kindergarten and eighty in elementary school, which didn't exist when rabbi Stoler opened it," says Diana M. "In addition, the kindergarten was mainly attended by children from social programs; kids who had to be given scholarships; children from Jewish families in a state of absolute social vulnerability, living in slums. With the Chabad slogan, which this rabbi makes his own, that 'no Jewish child should be left without a Jewish education,' the kindergarten was set up."

The project began in 2004. It was when Diana M. was called by the rabbi for a personal interview.

"They didn't know yet that they wanted to assemble the elementary school. We had an interview, and the rabbi said, 'Look, I want to know what you think about behaviorism?' I said: 'What are you asking me? I adhere to psychoanalysis and Piaget, not behaviorism.' Then he said: 'Let's see, tell me about it.' I explained to him; I almost gave him a class. Then he said, 'Well, I would like you to assemble the elementary school project. Would you like to?' And then everything came to me. Putting together a school project... He told me he would introduce me to a person he had already been talking to who would be responsible for Jewish education and that I would be in charge of the official education aspect of the school. I asked him about his requirements, and he replied: 'Fly, dream, it doesn't matter.' So I began meeting once a week for four months with the girl who organized the Jewish area, with whom we quickly connected, and with the rabbi. We worked on the project's objectives, organized an outline, and presented it to the kindergarten parents."

Thus, the kindergarten was set up, and, soon after, the elementary school, too. Twelve of the first thirteen children who finished preschool enrolled in first grade.

Diana M. has mixed memories of her time as the elementary school principal at *Instituto Acuario*. That project was forged in progressive and left-leaning idealism, carried out with love and will until it collapsed in the 1990s neoliberal frenzy in Argentina, leaving a profound mark on her. That's why, when Rabbi Stoler suggested she take over as principal of the elementary school she'd helped to build, her first response was a resounding no. "For me, the job was over. I was going to go on with my thing. That's when the rabbi insisted he wanted me to be the principal. I didn't want anything with that. He insisted on me a lot, with that characteristic Chabad insistence. They look for you, they look for you, insist, give you arguments, and convince you."

Despite the rabbi's arguments, she did not want to assume the responsibility of being an elementary school principal again. She looked for her own arguments to refute the rabbi, to make him uncomfortable with her free-thinking, Trotskyist sympathies, and non-observant Judaism. None of that worked. The rabbi kept insisting until he achieved his goal. How did he do it? Diana M. explains that a mixture of situations, intertwined feelings, and insistence changed her mind. "The rabbi couldn't persuade me, and I was determined not to give in, but the ground was shifting with each step. Evidently, I had the desire to be the principal of a school once again. I wanted to make up for my painful experience in Acuario, to recover the story with another ending. I began looking into where my grandparents had lived before immigrating to Argentina, assuming that their hometown was very close to, precisely, Lubavitch. Why did I look at the subject? Because, like Chabad's Rebbe, my father's name in Yiddish was Menachem Mendel. I found that my grandparents and great-grandparents lived in Russia, very close to where the Rebbe was born. 'Who knows if my great-grandfather wasn't religious?' I reasoned. He was known as Menachem Mendel, and later, my father was known as Menachem Mendel as well. I saw similarities between the Rebbe and my father. A similar look. So, what did rabbi Stoler do? When the Rebbe was alive, people wrote him letters for advice. Now, they still write to him and send them to him at the *ohel*, his tomb, by fax and by e-mail. Other people write him letters and put them randomly on some pages of the Rebbe's correspondence, which has been entirely published. The rabbi went to his library and took out a book. He asked me, 'What's your name in Hebrew?' I told him, 'Dina'; 'What's your mother's name?' I told him, 'Betie.' Then the guy closed his eyes, said 'Dina Ben Betie,' and randomly opened the Rebbe's correspondence book. He looked, smiled, and said, 'Do you know Hebrew?'; 'Yes, of course,' I said and read. It was a letter that said many things but ended by saying: 'And you will educate the new generations.' He told me, 'Here is the answer.' And I accepted. I believed the Rebbe. Of course, later, my husband told me: 'He knew which tome to take and which page to open it too! He had it marked.' What can I say? They may have fooled me. Imagine that if I, with all my political, secular, and well-founded criticism, can be moved by the words of the Rebbe, this rabbi, and this illusion, why can't the rest of the people?"

So, in 2005, the Trotskyist, atheist, and Freudian psychologist took over the formal education part of an Orthodox Jewish institution's elementary school.

Like the Wolfsohn, the Hillel School keeps the structure of any non-Orthodox Jewish school in the community: mixed classrooms for boys and girls and the morning obligation for the boys to recite a prayer.

S. is a former Hilel School kindergarten teacher who preferred to remain anonymous for professional reasons. She worked for two years at the school and says she finds recognizing any positive aspects of her experience difficult.

Although she remarks the classrooms were always well equipped, that she had state-of-the-art teaching materials, and that her fellow teachers were all qualified, she complains about two aspects in particular: on the one hand, the informality of hiring: "We were a group of about fifty teachers, forty of whom were paid under the table. The second year I was there, we were able to push for a change in that situation partly thanks to a lot of complaining. But even then, I worked eight hours daily, and they still paid me three hours under the table. The salaries were paid with donations. Then, if there was a contextual issue, such as a donation not arriving or the donor ceasing to give, they would stop paying us. So, it happened once that we didn't get paid for two months. The rabbi told us that *HaShem* was going to help us. However, during that time, *HaShem* didn't provide me with food; *HaShem* didn't pay my bills or rent; *HaShem* didn't solve any of my problems. That was something the rabbi couldn't understand. And then, when Pesach or any other holiday on the Jewish calendar arrived, the synagogue would transform into this crazy thing filled with food. They spend a lot of money on the holidays. So that's when I told myself: 'This is no longer an administrative issue. This has nothing to do with them not having money. This is a problem they have with me. Because I do my job and comply, and yet I am not being paid for my job.' Then they wouldn't stop bragging about how much money they would spend during the holidays. It was all to show off."

S. also complains about what she considers excesses in the Orthodox way of educating children. The teacher says: "Once they gave us a substantial donation of toys. They were games with buttons and drawings of animals. They forced us to hide the images of little pigs. So, the piggy isn't an animal? Aren't Jewish kids supposed to go to the zoo and see pigs? It is fine with me if parents don't want to talk to their children about pigs at home. However, if we have to teach about animals in school, it seems obvious to me we have to teach about the dog, the cow, the horse, and the pig. They put religion so much in the foreground that they leave aside many other things that are part of childhood and infancy. I don't think it's right for a child to reach the age of five or six without knowing that there is such a thing as pigs. I think it's fine if he doesn't eat pork, but he should know that the animal exists." She clarifies that this is her personal position and one reason for leaving her post at the school. However, according to her, most other teachers who worked there had the same complaints. One situation finally confirmed to her that Orthodox Judaism is not what she chooses for her life. S. says, "We collected money for charity with the children for a year. Nothing was needed in the classroom; classes were ending, and a teacher volunteered in a non-Jewish soup kitchen. We proposed to buy toys to donate to that soup kitchen. The rabbi kicked us out. He literally said to us: 'But how? If they are not Jewish?'"

All of these events added to S.'s overall dissatisfaction with the school and its administration. She observes she knows many parents who enrolled their children in the school because of a scholarship but were not interested in providing their children with an Orthodox Jewish education.

The celebration of Kabbalat Shabbat is one of the first forms of Jewish education given to the children at the school. S. says, "Starting in the third grade, they have Hebrew. In the second grade, it is a brief introduction to what Kabbalat Shabbat is. They put on a yarmulke and sit down to sing. Because Shabbat is approaching, the girls wear their headbands and look cute. Everything is explained to them through songs, such as the fact that they must walk that day and that there is no car, keys, or anything else because it is a holiday. The candles are lit, and the *challot*, which is the bread, is blessed. I think it's terrible that they take away a child's right to play or do anything else for one hour a week for all that."

For her part, Diana M. laughingly recounts her surprise when she had to convince some parents why it wasn't wrong for the school to require their children to perform daily religious services. "One time, a parent came to me and said, 'Don't come here and bust my balls. I don't want my son to do the *tefillah*, and he doesn't want either. So don't force him to do it.' Then I answered him: 'Excuse me, but why does it bother you that your son thanks every morning for being healthy? To ensure he has friends, family, and enough food to eat? Does that take anything away from your son?' And he said 'no.' He then asked me if I prayed, and I said I didn't. 'But this is the school your son attends,' I said. 'If you don't want your son to pray every morning, make him attend some other school. Don't try to change the rules.' And that's how I convinced him to let his son do the daily prayers."

Despite their apparent openness to the outside world, both the Hillel School and the Wolfsohn School face challenges when it comes to teaching specific subjects.

Diana M. explains, "For example, when we have to teach sex education, or the subject of the world's creation, the planets, the Universe, and all that. The rabbi said, 'You have to teach them how it is: *HaShem* created…,' and I looked at him and said, 'But rabbi…. the kids go to the Planetarium… Can't we find a way to say that when the Torah says it was all Chaos, that was the Big Bang?' His answer was a flat no. But we negotiated and agreed that the kids would read what they had to read, and then he would explain to them what his position is according to the Torah."

The Hillel School and the Wolfsohn share a joint base and have the same function on a general level: to colonize secular Jewish spaces and contribute to orienting those spaces towards greater religious observance. However, Diana M. clarifies that the Wolfsohn school is more liberal than the Hillel school. Although Wolfsohn is a little more progressive, it is a project under the direct control of Rabbi Tzvi Grunblatt. "Everything the executive director does has Grunblatt's endorsement," explains Diana M. "They need to be more progressive because the Wolfsohn population wanted to keep a certain profile for the kids already attending the school before Chabad's takeover. They had to convince those who stayed that they would not turn them religious. That's why certain religious activities are optional."

"On the other hand, the school where I am was built from scratch. In the Wolfoshn School, for example, they continue to celebrate *Yom Hatzmaaut* (Israel's Independence Day); the Israeli flag is still present in the school. We don't celebrate *Yom Hatzmaaut* nor have an Israeli flag on display. They take part in sports tournaments we don't. The Lubavitch adapts and colonizes little by little. Very little by little. That is how it works. It is evangelization."

The conflict between her free-thinking ideals and the religious ideas that provoke her rejection is a daily work matter for Diana M.

"It's a constant negotiation," she says, "I learned to negotiate. I say to myself that it is as if I had done a 'doctorate in negotiation.' Something I always had a hard time with. And, above all, with religion. I had nothing to negotiate with religion."

"Do you feel they have tried to make you more religious?" I ask her.

"All the time. They're always asking for a little more. With the children, with the parents, it is always, 'Well, what if now you light the candles?'; 'What if you fast on *Yom Kippur*?'; 'What if you celebrate Shabbat?' The first time I attended one of their Kabbalat Shabbat, I liked it. I had a good time. They sang songs that brought back memories of my childhood. To neutralize them, you must have very clear ideas. If you are a little weak, you will fall to them."

"And how do you experience the contradictions of working for an institution that represents, to a large extent, the opposite of the education you had and your life experience?"

"I try to be consistent with who I am. I take it as my job and try to have fun with some things. I dance and laugh my ass off when they get into this *Mashiach* thing. At some point, I dream of a *Mashiach* coming and saving us all. Who knows? Maybe this kid I have in school now who wants to be a Rebbe someday will be the *Mashiach*."

Chapter Eight
Chabad is Everywhere

> "Chabad is bigger than Coca-Cola because Coca-Cola may not be available in every country, but Chabad is."
> A popular saying among Chabad's Hasidim

And you will spread out to the West and to the East and to the North and to the South

If they say that where there is a need, there is a business opportunity, it could be argued that where there is a Jew, there will be Chabad Lubavitch.

Territorial expansion, which can also be understood as a network of Jewish services started during the life of Rabbi Menachem Mendel Schneerson, became an essential characteristic of the movement, and today is part of its work strategy: to open Chabad branches (Beit Chabad and other institutions) in as many places as possible. Even so, it's worth noting that in many cases, previously established Jewish communities invite them to occupy their spaces as their populations decline and congregations disband.

Thus, Chabad Lubavitch reaches out to communities that could not adapt to modernization while maintaining their Orthodoxy and occupies spaces that have gradually become vacant.

Just looking at the provinces in Argentina, they have established a presence in big cities like Bahía Blanca, Bariloche, Córdoba, La Plata, Rosario, Salta, Tucumán, Mendoza, and Santa Fe, without counting their twenty locations in Buenos Aires City.

Miriam Kapeluschnik says, "Why do a young man and his wife go to live abroad? To assist a Jew who needs something from him."

She and her husband established in December 1982 the Beit Chabad Concordia in the province of Entre Ríos, which was the second "Chabad House" in one of the Argentinian provinces, after the one in Tucumán, opened by Rabbi Daniel Levy in July of that same year.

"I was very young," recalls Miriam, who moved there when she was twenty-three, her husband twenty-seven, and they already had three children under their arms, "I was a spoiled child; I didn't know how to do anything, and there I learned to do everything. Because there was almost nothing to do with traditional Jewish life in Concordia. There was a synagogue and a Hebrew school. But the biggest challenge was that we differed totally from everybody else. It was a community where no Jewish observant person had ever lived before. It took a lot of work to get rid of people's prejudices, making ourselves known little by little and bringing them the message of Judaism, the Torah, the Hasidic vision of Judaism (Hasidut), and the Rebbe. The work of an emissary is impressive. Even more so in a place where there was nothing. We created everything from the ground up."

In that environment, her husband, Rabbi Israel Kapeluschnik, had to not only ensure the stability of his observant life in a desolate environment, but he also had to sell that lifestyle, customs, and traditions while also taking on the rabbinical tasks that the community required. The rabbi says: "I had my obligations in the community, to take care of all the questions related to the religious activity, the cemetery, the synagouge. But also, fundamentally, to approach the Jewish families living there."

Face-to-face work has been a critical method in Chabad Lubavitch's operations since Rabbi Dov Ber Baumgarten arrived in the country (see more in the Appendix: *Chabad Lubavitch in Argentina*.) Chabad's trademark style of combining pragmatism and strict adherence to precepts in one's personal life creates a commotion in the areas where the institution settles.

The Rabbi recalls: "On Wednesday nights, at the Bialik Center, a recreational center, the community boys used to play a game of soccer and after that have a barbecue. The barbecue was not kosher, but soccer was. So, I went every Wednesday to play soccer with them. That impacted people. It forged a very close relationship between them and me. I remember there were two opinions: those who thought it was great that a rabbi would play soccer with them and those who rumored whether I had nothing better to do as a rabbi than to play with them. I would invite the players to my house as soon as the game was over. That brought many people closer. Until then, most of them had the idea that a religious person is far from what they do. I showed to them that as a rabbi, I was a normal person, like any other, who enjoys playing soccer but also has a strong moral compass."

The Kapeluschniks worked as a team. They started getting involved with the local Jewish congregation (*kehillah*.) Soon after, Miriam also started teaching courses at the Hebrew school: "It's not the same thing for someone to teach you something as it is for that person to teach that thing and act on it," says the rabbi about the work his wife did: "For example, if I teach you about Passover because I am a *moreh* and I teach you all the laws, everything you have to do, but then in my personal life, I am not as strict about following those laws, you are likely not to comply either. However, you will feel more compelled to follow my example if I act on what I preach. This creates a revolution in the child. And it also shakes their parents."

Chabad Lubavitch's greatest capital lives in its emissaries, who travel to remote areas and, through educational programs, inventiveness, imagination, and strict Jewish observance, become not only educators who spread a message from person to person but also role models for the rest of a community.

Wherever there is an opportunity to open a new movement branch, Chabad proceeds similarly. First, they will try to make a space for themselves in the already instituted local Jewish community. This is generally achieved by taking over some pre-existing Jewish institutions. The makeover begins with community outreach activities to appease local non-Orthodox Jews while adhering strictly to rabbinical Judaism's rules. However, leading a life of strict observance in a location far from the comforts of the great metropolises or centers of Jewish life implies challenges that the emissaries must overcome.

Rabbi Kapeluschnik says it was partly because of this that he earned the nickname "butcher": "My oldest son was in kindergarten, and they were seeing what everyone's parents did for a living. Then one would say: 'My dad is a doctor,' another, 'My dad is a lawyer,' and so on. My son was asked: 'What does your father do for a living?' he answered: 'He is a butcher.' Because he didn't think of being a rabbi as a job, it was just something I was. And so why a butcher? Because I was in charge of bringing kosher meat from Buenos Aires. I would collect the meat from the freight, transport it to Concordia, and distribute it to local Jews who desired kosher meat."

There was no problem with non-animal products (fruits, vegetables, and canned goods) since they are already considered kosher. For the rest, the family had to resort to a huge freezer that was filled every two weeks. Raising so many small children was a significant complication in this sense; the rabbi remembers when extended shelf-life milk appeared on the market as a milestone in his task as Chabad emissary in Concordia: "That was a blessing, because we brought twenty boxes at a time, and we already had enough for a few days."

After some time officiating as the rabbi of the community and having earned a certain place of respect and acceptance, the Kapeluschniks were able to open a Beit Chabad of their own. Opening a Beit Chabad is the second milestone of every Chabad emissary after settling into a previously existing Jewish congregation.

"Our goal was not to compete with the community," says Rabbi Kapeluschnik, "but to carry out activities we couldn't do in the community. While we tried to make the programs as strict as possible at school, suddenly, deeper issues were not studied at school. So, we would invite kids from other families to come and study at the Beit Chabad with our children, who were already growing up. We would emphasize Hebrew reading a lot, especially related to prayers."

After the center was set up, they built a *mikveh*, or ritual bath. This is another thing that every Chabad emissary is supposed to do as soon as he arrives, but that is usually put off because of how much it costs to build. However, the difficulties entailed with not having an available *mikveh* are among the most significant challenges Chabad emissaries face. Jewish women are supposed to go through it once a month to purify themselves after their menstrual period.

"My wife had to make a significant sacrifice at the time when we still did not have the *mikveh*," says Rabbi Kapeluschnik. "She had to travel every month to Buenos Aires City. Although sometimes there was a plane, and the commute would only take her an hour, there were other times when the plane did not arrive. Other times, the roads were flooded. She had to take a detour, turning a five-hour trip into a twelve or fourteen-hour journey because she had to pass through Rosario, Santa Fe, and Paraná, then cross the sub-fluvial tunnel just to get to Buenos Aires City."

After much thought, the Kapeluschnik family returned to Buenos Aires City in 2000.

Miriam explains: "It was a hard decision because we traveled to Concordia with the Rebbe's consent, and when we returned to Buenos Aires, he was no longer in this physical world. Our return was motivated primarily by the professional aspects of our work. We wanted to expand it even further, and because Concordia is a small community, we felt we had a lot more to offer after all these years. We had plenty of time. It was like when a person grows and reaches a ceiling that does not allow him to continue growing. That happened to us. We discussed it extensively and decided it would be better for us to move to another location to continue contributing and growing while supporting the Concordia community."

The family then left what they had built. In their place, another Chabad couple took over, a rabbi from Buenos Aires and his Israeli wife with their children.

Despite everything, the Kapeluschniks never lost contact with the Jewish community of Concordia; Miriam comments: "We still have an excellent relationship with the people over there, especially with children and young people. My husband still gets requests to perform marriages from them. Boys of marriageable age who do not hesitate to ask 'their' rabbi to marry them. Boys whose circumcision or *bar mitzvah* were also performed by him. We continue exchanging phone calls and e-mails with the Jewish community there. We keep in touch. We take part in their joys and, sometimes, also in their misfortunes. For us, it was not just a job. It was something powerful. We spent eighteen years of our lives in that community."

One of the significant concerns in Chabad Lubavitch's mission to bring Jews closer to observance and tradition is to curb assimilation and secularization. Intermarriage, the marriage between a Jew and a non-Jew, is seen by them as the vanguard of this process and, therefore, the hardest battle to fight. This is a detail that this movement understands as the greatest tragedy, and that can already be seen even in the stories of the Jewish-Argentinian classic literary short story collection, *Los gauchos judíos* [The Jewish Gauchos] by Jewish immigrant Alberto Gerchunoff. In his 1910 book, it is possible to see how Jewish immigrants from Russia established themselves in those same Entre Ros communities, such as Concordia, bringing all of their Orthodox customs, and how their children born in the new country began to marry non-Jewish locals, gradually abandoning religious observance and traditions.

"Concordia is quite a traditionalist city," says rabbi Kapeluschnik. "When we arrived, we found they celebrated the holidays their own way. They tried to keep the synagogue quite Orthodox. The cemetery was pretty well managed. On the other hand, I had the chance to see firsthand how assimilation is in the country. The number of mixed couples I saw there was significant."

In its fight against secularization, Chabad Lubavitch understands only one way: "The only antidote," says Rabbi Kapeluschnik, "to fight it is to maintain a Judaism of the roots, a Judaism of the Torah, not a low-calorie Judaism. We need a Judaism that is seriously fattening. An authentic Judaism. Where Shabbat means Shabbat. Where *kashrut* means *kashrut*; *tefillin* means *tefillin*, and *bar mitzvah* means *bar mitzvah*. There is no other way. You can preach nicely in the synagogue, but everything falls apart if you don't show by example. Suppose a family finds you in any environment and notices you acting like you do in the synagogue, school, or while preaching. In that case, it impacts them. That is also what inspires respect."

How to remain an Orthodox Jew in Argentina's most Catholic city?

I am thinking a little about preserving the taste of custom when I read — sitting on the plane that will take me to spend the Passover at Beit Chabad Salta in one of Argentina's northern provinces — an article in the *LAN* airline magazine. The article states that some speakeasies, like those of the Prohibition era, have recently become fashionable in New York.

I wonder if in a hyper-modernized world where people are losing touch with their traditions and safe places are disappearing, these proposals to resurrect lost customs are not comparable to that of a religion like Judaism. After all, with its strict rules and clothing, Orthodox Judaism recreates the imagination of an ancient, medieval time.

Salta is an eminently Catholic city. It is noticeable from the start by the metallic structure in the shape of a Christian cross of over thirty meters high that, placed in January 1901, greets the San Bernardo hill at whose feet the metropolis rises.

But Niv, the Jewish manager of *Metzadá*, the hostel where I'll be staying, says that at least two hundred Jewish families live here.

What seems visible to anyone is that in Salta, before anything else, there is no lack of religious fervor. The imposing Salta Cathedral, all pink, placed diagonally to the town hall and in front of the 9 de Julio square, which is the rectangle of park and green around which the central life of the city is organized, is an example. So is the San Francisco de Asís church, painted in a furious red, and appears to compete with the cathedral and the many other churches that sprout throughout the city.

Judaism also has a profusion of communities in this very religious province: two congregations (*kehillot*), one Sephardi and the other Ashkenazi, barely separated by two doors, on the same street. They share a wall at the back of both buildings and are internally communicated but ideologically separated.

The story I am told shows that the two community centers lived with their old tensions between the Sephardim, who were more attached to Orthodoxy, and the Ashkenazim, who developed a conservative Jewish stance.

The mixed marriages significantly diminished the Sephardi parish, as anyone who got married outside Judaism got expelled from it. Also, younger people began to gravitate toward the Ashkenazi congregation, drawn not so much by belonging to one of the community's branches as by affinities of a different kind. The Sephardi congregation shrank, and when its last parishioners died off, it closed its doors.

Around 2005, an important businessman in the city was interested in donating to the community. He contacted Rabbi Daniel Levy, in the bordering province of Tucumán, who was the Chabad envoy of Argentina's northwest region.

Levy spoke with the Sephardi community's president and instructed him to request a rabbi as a donation.

The businessman agreed to pay half the costs of keeping a rabbi for the congregation. The name of Rabbi Raphael Tawil, then twenty-four years old and living in Israel's West Bank with his wife and newborn daughter, to take the post, also came up through Levy.

Rabbi Tawil comes from one of the first Chabad families in Argentina. He is the great-nephew of Aharon Tawil, the first Argentinian sent to study at the Chabad *yeshiva* in New York. Rabbi Rafael studied all his life in Chabad and emigrated to Israel with his family at seventeen. For two years, he studied in Jerusalem. Then, he traveled to the United States and completed his training in the Chabad *yeshiva* in New York. From there, he returned to Argentina, then to Israel, where he met his wife. A year and a half after marriage, they settled in Salta as Chabad emissaries.

During his years of study in New York, he snuck into one of the famous annual meetings of emissaries that Chabad Lubavitch organizes in that city and decided to become a Chabad emissary.

Tawil says: "Seeing thousands of people dancing together, everyone from somewhere else, forgetting all the problems they were dragging around, left me impressed. Suddenly, people had forgotten everything and were just floating in the air. That day, I decided I had to become an emissary."

He claims that when he met his future wife, he made it a requirement that she be open to his life plan of becoming an emissary. There was a coincidence: she also longed to go out into the world.

After reflecting and consulting with friends about Levy's proposal, he took on the great responsibility of returning to Argentina to settle in this Catholic and bring the bankrupted congregation back to life.

"I told the plan to my wife. We talked about it. We looked at a lot of information on the Internet," the Rabbi recalls. "We asked some friends who had been here… I had been here in 1999 on a tour that we, *yeshiva* students, had made. I had traveled from San Luis to Jujuy. I didn't remember much more than a Shabbat I had spent here and two or three families who would be my contact people. Then we talked to my friends. One was the one who gave me the definitive push to come. He had been offered and had said no. I asked him why he had rejected the proposal, and he said: 'I don't see myself educating my children in a place where there is no Jewish school. Salta is a delightful city if you and your wife think you can make it.' And I thought we could make it. So we made up our minds and came here."

The rabbi, his wife, who did not speak a word of Spanish upon arrival, and their little daughter got into Salta shortly before the Rosh Hashanah celebration, which falls every year during September when the Salta province celebrates the Catholic Feast of the Miracle. The newcomers organized a Rosh Hashanah celebration from scratch, having to get the food imported from Buenos Aires City. They invited a few local families for dinner in their newly rented apartment in the heart of a city clogged with hundreds of thousands of Catholic pilgrims for the Feast of the Miracle.

Despite everything, they appeared to have succeeded until they received a phone call: some Israeli tourists in town had heard about a Chabad rabbi and wanted to spend the holiday with him. "I don't even know how they got our phone. We had just moved. I had barely any space to receive people at home. I didn't even have a table. I had nothing! We had to bring some planks from the Beit Chabad to my house, and we couldn't get through because all the streets downtown were blocked off, full of people because of the Feast of the Miracle. In the end, I asked a friend for some help. He had to go all the way around the city, engage in discussion with some policemen and many people, and finally arrive just before Rosh Hashanah so we could spend it with the Israelis. It was very nice".

The Beit Chabad Salta, like many other Chabad "houses" in remote parts of the world, serves as a refuge for Israeli tourists. After their mandatory military service is completed, it is customary for Israeli youth to travel as backpackers for years, investing the savings from their years of service.

Chabad Lubavitch knows this, which is also why it has branches in distant cities, perhaps without large Jewish populations, but with a unique attraction for Israeli tourists.

Throughout the year, these Batei Chabad organize public festivities in which Israeli tourists are honored guests, ensuring they can have a Jewish celebration wherever they are in the world.

The first night of this year's Pesach celebration is on a Monday, and Rabbi Tawil has organized a community dinner for the Israeli tourists in the city.

Argentina has a strange privilege regarding these kinds of celebrations: the Beit Chabad Bariloche boasts of hosting the world's second-largest Passover dinner (the record would have been set in Kathmandu, Nepal, with a thousand young Jews seated at the table.)

I don't know how many Israelis there will be tonight. In the hostel room, I am alone, with two other empty beds. However, I encountered some guys talking in Hebrew in the kitchen and on the shared computer as soon as I arrived.

When I ask Niv, he says that not as many Israelis appear to have arrived this year, at least in the last few days.

The sky is cloudy in the city, and I'm afraid a storm will just roll during the few days I'll be staying in the city.

Niv tells me that today and tomorrow night are the Chabad dinners and that following Monday, the Ashkenazi *kehillah* will have its own; he is volunteering a little with both congregations. From what he tells me, there is a strong sense of Jewish militancy: there are few Jews, and they all work to ensure that those who are do not diminish, disperse, or assimilate.

For example, he will be at the Beit Chabad door tonight, ensuring that the Israelis entering are on a list and have passed a personal interview conducted a few days ago.

"It's going to be full of Israelis. You need to take some precautions. You can't let just anyone in," tells me Niv.

He then remarks that, while things are now fine between the local Sephardic and Ashkenazi congregations, there were some conflicts in the past and that there was recently some commotion when Rabbi Tawil opened a kindergarten. As a small community, some did not understand the need for two Hebrew schools. But that seems part of an old story because he insists again that things are calm nowadays.

I ask for what kind of kosher foods are available in the city:

"It is all packaged products. Rafi (Rabbi Tawil) brings the meat from Buenos Aires."

I ask him for some directions to get around the city. He excuses himself for not having a map to give me. "They are about to arrive," he says as he shows me two routes: one through downtown and its pedestrian areas and the other that borders the side of the hill and ends in a shopping mall.

Niv tells me that the shopping mall belongs to Eduardo Elztain, our Jewish "Scrooge McDuck," as he calls him and that it has a lot of *mezuzot* on its doors, which causes locals to stop more than once without knowing what they are or what they are for.

***

I go for a walk through Salta's downtown. The streets are bustling with people, but they appear to live at a slower pace than in Buenos Aires. Café tables can be found on the cobblestone pedestrian streets surrounding 9 de Julio square and its colonial buildings. I sit at a Café and order toasts with sour cream and strawberry jam. It's almost five o'clock in the afternoon, the perfect time for the typical "merienda" or the Latino snack before dinner.

I go back to the hostel and talk some more with Niv, who tells me that "before Chabad arrived in the city, not much was going on in the Sephardic *kehillah*. Since then, prayers and other activities have happened there every day."

"Do you think there will be many people tonight?" I ask him.

"On these holidays, it is always full because of the Israelis. You can put a Beit Chabad wherever you want, and it will be full because there are always Israelis everywhere."

"But, for example, how many people attend the local synagogues on any given Shabbat?"

"On Shabbat, I would estimate about fifteen people attend each of the two *kehillot*. On Yom Kippur, however, they always get much more people."

"How was the reaction of Salta's Jewish youth when Rabbi Tawil first arrived in the city?"

"First, he became friends with those who attended the Sephardic *kehillah*," he explains, "then he became friends with the rest, and we all began to attend his activities. We grew closer gradually, but we became friends right away. We started going to his house to play soccer. He arrived in Salta when there was little support for Jewish youth."

"Was he able to provide that kind of support?"

"Before his arrival, we had never had a rabbi here. Everyone was looking for him at some point. Many children in Salta had little connection to their Jewish background. One of Rafi's merits is that these kids began reconnecting with their roots because of his presence here. They became very involved in the local Jewish community. Some of them have even joined the Ashkenazi *kehillah*. Rafi and Chabad are responsible for that. He provided a lot of help to the young people who needed it. His home is much more than a Shabbat dinner; it is a gathering place for the community's children."

I return to my room and pack my bags while I make time until eight o'clock at night.

At about six, I descend again to the downtown, which is now overflowing with people, primarily children and teenagers, who are out of school for the day and fill the public space. There are also a lot of cars that seem to have appeared from nowhere. They crowd a city where there aren't many traffic lights, and crossing the street on foot becomes a risky task.

I try to buy something at the supermarket, but it is overflowing with people up from their siesta.

I walk calmly back to the hostel as the sky darkens and the rain catches me just as I'm about to arrive.

***

Niv is not here, and I needed him to give me the last directions on how to get to the Beit Chabad, but his girlfriend explains it to me clearly. It's close about twelve blocks in an almost straight line, in a city designed in a strict Spanish checkerboard pattern. She asks me if I want her to order me a taxi.

"I'm going to take a shower, and when I come out, I'll see if it's still raining and if you need to call me a cab."

I take a refreshing bath, change, and walk the few blocks. The rain has almost completely stopped.

I walk and arrive at the Beit Chabad, which I can guess by the many people at the entrance.

It is the facade of an old, horizontal building with no sign that it is a Beit Chabad or even a Sephardic *kehillah*.

I spot the door of the Catholic school Colegio de la Divina Misericordia [Divine Mercy School] across the street and an evangelist temple just a block away.

Niv sees me at the door, in the middle of all the people and noise. He tells me to go straight in and tells the guy guarding the entrance that I may enter, even though I didn't do an admission interview. The man moves aside to let me in.

It is hot in here. People are everywhere, sitting on chairs, on the floor, on an armchair, and standing. There is a half-open door leading to the synagogue. I see the rabbi praying in Hebrew with some boys there. It is necessary to wear a yarmulke to enter that section of the *kehillah*. I forgot to bring one; no more are available for free use. Several boys have found an imaginative solution to the problem, tied the ends of paper napkins, and wrapped them around their heads.

I flip through a copy of an essential Chabad philosophy book, leaning against a frame, when a tall guy calls my name. I turn around, and he says,

"Could you come with me for a moment, please?"

I follow him to a side room with a window overlooking the entrance lobby where Niv and his colleagues were just greeting people. The man asks me to take a seat and asks me to explain who I am and what I am doing there.

I explain it to him, and after consulting with Niv through the window, he apologizes and lets me go, asking me not to record anything or take pictures.

"I hope you understand... it's just that with so many Israelis together, we must take extreme precautions," he finishes.

I wander around for a while, unsure where to sit or if anyone speaks a language other than Hebrew. I don't understand a word about it. I sit down on a chair that is vacated, and a girl in her thirties asks me a question, to which I answer:

"*Ani lo medaber ivrit*" is all I know how to say in Hebrew, and it means, "I don't speak Hebrew."

"I was just asking you if you speak English," she tells me.

We start speaking in English.

Her name is Ela. She is Israeli but has been living in London for years. Besides that, she will be my interpreter the whole evening, the only person who will translate for me and comment on what the rabbi will say in Hebrew.

I tell her about visiting London and how I liked the city. We speak some more about travel until I tell her about my time in Israel. When I tell her about my TAGLIT experience, she understands I am experiencing a sort of reconciliation with my Jewish roots and Zionism.

"It's what they want. That's why they take you to Israel. They just show you the pretty part."

The prayers end, and the people leave and head straight for the hall.

Previously, community marriages were celebrated here, but as Rabbi Tawil pointed out, "In Salta, the last marriage that took place was so long ago that last year we did their daughter's *bat mitzvah*. That is to say, it was done fourteen years ago." It is also necessary to say that the hall no longer fulfills that function and looks abandoned, with dirty and deteriorated white walls. Otherwise, it is a beautiful space with a kitchen at the back and a window overlooking a large garden.

But tonight, it is set up for the occasion, with three rows of long tables and a headboard that joins them, cutting them perpendicularly. Each place is marked with a little plastic cup and a *Haggadah* (a book of instructions for the Pesach feast) in Spanish and Hebrew, so we can all follow the ceremony. However, I presume I am the only one who does not read Hebrew at this dinner.

At a glance, I estimate that about two hundred people are already taking their seats.

Ela looks around for some French friends she came with who, she tells me, don't speak Hebrew either and depend on her to understand anything tonight. By the time she sees them, they are already seated elsewhere. Now we must hurry to grab two seats together, as I don't want to be left without an interpreter for the night.

Men and women sit together, breaking the Orthodox sex divide. Some boys wear a yarmulke, while others wear a napkin with knotted ends that dangle from their heads.

There is joy, singing, fist-pumping on tables, as if this were a concert. A small group takes the lead and sings a song in Hebrew, spreading the melody to the rest of the group.

When I ask Ela what they're singing, she tells me it's an Israeli patriotic song.

It is nine twenty-five at night. Rabbi Tawil is leaning out from the head of the table. He is easy to spot in his black clothes and hat, standing straight and asking for silence. The people listen to him. The rabbi has admirable control over two hundred boys and girls fresh out of military service and on a joyride.

Volunteers pass by the tables, leaving little plastic trays with the six components of the Pesach table: *beitzah* (a peeled hard-boiled egg), *chazeret* (a piece of lettuce and some celery), *charoset* (shredded apple mixed with cinnamon), *karpas* (raw onion rings) and *zeroah* (chicken thigh bone.) The presentation is not showy. It makes me sad because my family has done nothing even remotely Jewish. I feel like I'm missing out on seeing how the Jewish liberation holiday is celebrated "for real."

The rabbi explains the ceremony that we must perform with the ingredients that were given to us.

Some prayers begin, and the yarmulke-napkins return to rest on some heads.

Tawil invokes the people present and asks those of us from Argentina to stand up. Three people stand up, me and two others at the other end of the table. He continues making people from France, Switzerland, and Germany stand up. They are few, and the rest applaud, and when he finishes with the Western world, he mentions cities and towns of Israel, and more and more people stand up in small groups.

It is now ten minutes to ten. The rabbi says it is time to eat the herbs: lettuce and onion dipped in salt water. Those near the multiple centerpieces do so. There is not enough for the number of people filling the room. I barely fish out an onion ring that I chew dismissively because I'm starving.

The recitation of a text from the *Haggadah* begins. I read and flip forward in the booklet to see how long this will last.

It looks like it's going to be a long one.

The rabbi goes around the tables urging different boys and girls to read excerpts in Hebrew aloud for the entire audience.

I ask Ela if they are going to read the whole thing. It's very long, and I'm hungry.

She looks at me with a raised eyebrow.

"You Jews from Argentina sure have it easy, don't you?" she says.

The ceremony continues. A girl stands up to read and is greeted with whistles and applause that do not frighten her. The rabbi comes and goes, lecturing one and all, making people stand up to read.

The French women stand up and read in good Spanish. Then it's the turn of some blonde triplets to do their thing. It is now half past ten at night, and we have yet to have dinner. Then, a group of volunteers passes through the middle of the tables, asking for plastic plates. I'm guessing they're bringing them back full of food.

The reading continues and is interlaced with joyful songs in Hebrew.

At twenty to eleven at night, the volunteers arrive with some salad pots and others with a mixture I can't quite identify. Still, they appear to be eggplants or something similar.

Soon after, others appear carrying plates of fish.

Now, *matzah* is being passed around as well. Still, it is common, which disappoints me because I was expecting to taste *matzah shmurah*. While they are both *matzah*, the *shmurah* is cooked by hand under obsessive production standards and imported from

Israel. As a result, it is much more expensive and is only consumed by some Orthodox Jews, including Chabadniks.

On the rabbi's table, he is seated with his family, surrounded by the elements of the Pesach seder arranged in the traditional orthodox way: the plate with the six elements, the *matzah* under the plate, and glasses with kosher wine.

"The rabbi just said that they're going to give us grape juice instead of wine because they gave wine once in Bolivia, and as a result, everyone got drunk," Ela translates from Hebrew to English.

I have already heard that story. According to what I was told, during a Beit Chabad La Paz celebration, they served wine instead of grape juice, as stated in Chabad's "procedures manual." All of this is said to have culminated in a hundred drunken Israelis having sex on the table while the rabbi attempted to lead the prayers.

Pragmatism is understandable and can justify minor rule changes. After all, these ceremonies are designed to facilitate the immersion of approximately 200 secular Jews into Orthodox Judaism practices at a time. That is why things differ from what Chabad Orthodox prescribes: instead of *matzah shmurah*, they serve the common one, which is much cheaper, especially given the size of these crowds. Instead of the potentially disastrous ceremonial wine, they serve inoffensive grape juice.

It is an image that encapsulates how Chabad Lubavitch operates on all levels. While those of us who are being seduced into religious observance are tolerated for not celebrating exactly as we should, tradition is observed down to the smallest detail at the rabbi's table.

The rabbi asks us not to eat *matzah* yet; in exchange for that little abstinence, he will tell us a good story. Then he shows us how to make a sandwich with *matzah* and lettuce leaves previously dipped in the *charoseth*, a sauce made of apple, walnuts, cinnamon, and wine. Some make it, and the rest eat it as it comes.

Some volunteers dressed in Lubavitch custom pass by, leaving more lettuce where it is missing, and others bring more fish with *chrein* (chopped and seasoned radish and beets.)

They pass us a Hebrew songbook and a group sings with effusion, stimulated by an Orthodox boy who may be the same age as them. Hugging each other, they raise their arms and sing at the top of their lungs. The rabbi sits at the head table with his sons and watches the party unfold.

Ela tells me she has spent Jewish holidays in India and Honduras. Chabad has no headquarters there but sends *yeshiva* students to organize the corresponding celebrations with the Jews in the area during those dates.

"I always go to Chabad parties when I'm not with my family," she says.

We finally start eating the *gefilte fish* and the *matzah*.

Ela talks with an Israeli guy sitting before us, and I feel isolated.

At half-past eleven at night, plates of meat with sauce, boiled potatoes, and carrots are brought to our table. People eat and sign, and I feel like watching a soccer game.

The meat is tender and soft, so I use two plastic forks to pull it apart. By the time the knives come, I've already eaten all of my serving, and some people have already left.

At ten to twelve, the room empties, but meat plates keep coming to the table.

I walk around and stand in line until I get one more ration.

The rabbi appears much more relaxed now as he dines with his family at the head table. The guests converse among themselves and begin an exodus that has left the entire hall depopulated at five minutes past midnight. Tables full of garbage are left behind, which volunteers remove by putting everything in black trash bags.

Ela tells me she and her French friends are going out for ice cream downtown. She asks if I want to go with them; I thank her and tell her I'll stay until the ceremony ends.

I am tired. The rabbi's table becomes the new center of the meeting. It contains the remnants of the celebration as he finishes the rites. Just over ten of us are left beside his family, and almost all of them are Israelis, so I barely understand anything they talk about. The volunteers are now stacking the chairs, and the rabbi's eldest daughter plays with her siblings to climb on the stacks and hide.

The rabbi is speaking with a large, bald, bearded man. He's a local who assisted the rabbi in planning today's seder and the details for tomorrow's more intimate celebration. Later, Rabbi Tawil will tell me that the man who is assisting him tonight, who also macerated and cooked the beef neck meat we've eaten for hours to tenderize and flavor it, was one of the first opponents to Chabad Lubavitch when he and his family arrived to settle in. And now he is one of his most loyal collaborators.

The rabbi and his family appear tired but happy. They do the math to figure out how many people came. The rabbi bets on about two hundred thirty guests, so my estimate wasn't too far off.

They bring grapes, and then Rabbi Tawill brings out the *afikoman*, a piece of *matzah* taken from the table at the start of the ceremony. It is meant to be the last thing eaten on this special night.

Now I realize the ceremony is finally over. I say my goodbyes to the rabbi and walk alone through Salta's silent colonial-style sidewalks.

***

I awoke earlier than I would have liked the next day. I had breakfast in a downtown bar before returning to the hostel.

I asked Niv where I could find Rafi before dinner.

"Look for him at his house. It's nearby," he said and gave me directions. "If he's not there, you'll surely find him at the Beit Chabad."

No one answered the doorbell at the rabbi's house, so now I am knocking on the Beit Chabad's door.

I ask for the rabbi, and he tells me he is doing the morning prayer.

"Will it take long? Because I can go for a walk and…"

"No, I don't think it will be much longer."

It's now noon.

The boy unlocks the door and welcomes me inside. I rush inside the synagogue and put on a yarmulke I found in a public-use basket. Four or five Israelis are praying, a boy from the local community, three volunteers, Chabad *yeshiva* students from Buenos Aires, and other parts of the world. Rafi is praying with his back to me and his head covered by a *tallit*.

I take out a prayer book and try to follow some prayers.

Some time passes until the rabbi walks through the synagogue, still praying and at an impressive speed. He points to my watch; I show him it is now two o'clock in the afternoon, and he ends the service.

I say hello and tell him I'd like to talk briefly. He then invites me to lunch with him, his family, and others.

We leave the synagogue and walk in the sun. I'm expecting people to stare because Rafi is dressed all in black, and I'm walking to his side through the streets of such a Catholic city, but nothing happens. No one seems to notice or care for us.

"How do you live Judaism in such a predominantly Catholic city?" I ask him.

"There is a lot of respect," he says as we walk up Caseros Street. "They respect the religious precisely because it is a very religious city. At the very least, I am not experiencing anti-Semitism or discrimination. On the contrary, they hold high regard for me. Aside from that, many people seek a spirituality they do not always find in Catholicism. They talk to me because they want to learn," he smiles.

It never really amazes me to hear that. Salta is a city with a colonial-Catholic heritage that can be seen in every brick and every facade of its houses, which appear frozen in time as we pass in front of them.

"People see we go against the flow," Tawil says, "that we come, we work, often for free. And some of them think we do it for the money," he says of his perception of the prejudices that Chabad arouses and the difficulties he encountered when settling in this community. "Someone once said that I charged everyone who came to my Shabbat dinner. I almost cried when they told me that because I had just taken out loans to keep working here." The Israeli boys and the other people going to the rabbi's house are just a few steps behind us. "Since then, I've tried to keep my books in order. I show all the balance sheets when I go to Buenos Aires," he says.

The rabbi looks comfortable as he walks, with absolute control of his body, absorbed in our conversation.

"Chabad indeed has relations with economic and political powers," he continues, "but this speaks of the reliability of Chabad's projects. Consider Eduardo Elsztain, who earns millions for a single consulting assignment. He is not someone who is easily duped. He meets with Rabbi Grunblatt every month to review the balance sheets."

However, life as an Orthodox Jew is difficult here. Because the community does not yet have a *mikveh*, the rabbi's wife travels eight hours (four each way) to neighboring Tucumán City every month to take the ritual bath.

"We are looking at building one," he says when I ask him. "Actually, the Rebbe asked that the first thing you should do when you get to a place is to build a *mikveh*. But, well, things didn't work out for us just yet."

He tells me that the Beit Chabad develops diverse activities: visits to families, talks, personal attention in private to those who need it, and inaugurations of stores. With such a small Jewish community, I can't imagine how Orthodox and Conservative Jews coexist.

"How do the Orthodox and Conservative Jewish communities, whose congregations are only separated by a wall, get along?" I ask him.

"The relationship is wonderful, fortunately. The issue between the two communities goes beyond Chabad. The *kehillot* never got along very well before Chabad arrived. Some very unpleasant situations arose when I first arrived. It was challenging. They even wrote a letter to express their displeasure with us as soon as we arrived. Sometimes, I felt I was completely alone. I had no support from anyone, not even from my community. Everyone loves you, but when it comes time to take a chance on you, you find yourself alone. — his face hardens. — That hurt me a lot, but it was only the first year, a year and a half. After that, I realized things I hadn't before, which strengthened me and caused me to look at things differently. People who came to my community from the other were not allowed to attend mine. They would tell them, 'You are here or there.' People were afraid to attend my congregation. But then I got closer to them. They changed their board of directors, and the relationship improved. The treasurer of the new Ashkenazi *kehillah* board of directors now visits our synagogue, and the president sends his daughter to our summer camp. He was going to send her to our little school as well, but he didn't because he couldn't, as president of the other community, send his daughter to ours and not to his. I have a relationship with the entire board of directors. I did the *bar mitzvah* for all their children. After five years, I knew how to stand up for certain things. Once, for example, I told your president: 'It cannot be that a member of your board of directors meets with the parents of my school's students to persuade them not to send their children to my school. That is not how I work. That's called dirt play. When people tell me they are going with you, I congratulate them and encourage them to continue.' I'm a nice person, but I'm not dumb."

We arrive at 9 de Julio Square and dodge tourists taking city tours under the shade of the trees that provide relief from the dry midday heat.

"Nowadays," he continues, "people may disagree with me on certain issues, but they all respect me. The two congregations collaborate on some activities. We celebrated Chanukah and Purim together. That prompted some to ask, 'But why not unite?'; 'Why not tear down the wall that divides the congregations?' The answer is that between Orthodox and Conservatives, we have fundamental differences. Particularly in prayer, and that is something that can never be united. But who said that we have to unite in prayer? That is sufficient as long as we are united in our activities. I hope people see the situation as two options the Salta Jewish community has for people who want Orthodoxy and conservatism. They are not required to take it as one against the other. The important thing is that activities that can be done together are done so."

Besides carrying the work that his community role entails, Rabbi Tawil is committed to developing a very close relationship with all of Salta's Jews. He also has a straightforward relationship with the local Jewish youth, as seen in his relationship with Niv.

"Ask the guys in the local community who their guide is, and they will tell you, Rafi," he says. "I think there are two ways to relate to the community, from respect or from friendship. They don't usually go together. With the young people, I decided on the side of friendship. I am their friend. The respect that perhaps one has with a rabbi, they do not have with me. But they have a lot of affection for me, and I love them very much. That's how we get closer: playing soccer together and sharing. Once, they called me one Saturday night and told me: 'Hey, Rafi, all of us lazy asses got together for a beer here. Would you like to come? I said: 'Yeah, let's go.' I asked my wife. She told me to go, and that's how it was. I am part of 'the lazy asses' now. Do you understand? That means the conversation and dialogue I have with them are different. The relationship is unique. I talk to them as friends, and they will listen to me. Okay, I lost a little of their respect. But I think friendship is better than respect. It's not that they don't respect me. But I'll give you an example: people here are used to being rough with each other. That is their way of being. Once they got the nerves of one that was older than the rest. They got into a fight with him, which turned into a big mess in the end. So, I grabbed one of the 'lazy asses' and talked to him. 'Hey, don't make him mad,' I told him. 'Why do you keep messing with him when you know he gets mad? If you're so brave, give it to me.' A few days later, my phone rang at three o'clock in the morning. I responded. They began speaking to me in Hebrew. They were the kids. I recognized them almost immediately. 'Hey, you told us to take it on you!' they said."

"Is this relationship you have with the boys a way to get things done?" I ask him.

"That is the Rebbe's teaching. He said that just one person is worth everything you can do. And it is written in the Talmud: 'He who saves one soul of the people of Israel saves the entire world.' For us, one person is as important as a multitude, as a hundred people. If you save just one Jew, he will be followed by generations and generations of Jews. He, his children, and the children of his children could add up to millions of Jews many years from now. I learned about how important each one is."

"I'm at ease here," I tell him. "Perhaps there is an overabundance in Buenos Aires... and you are here alone. Salta instills tranquillity in me by combining big city and small town vibes."

"The atmosphere, people, and everything here allows you to work calmly," he says, opening his arms as if to embrace the people walking through the narrow streets, "and it gives you certain freedom in the sense that you can live a calmer life. We often can't get certain things here, which makes our work harder. For example, now, for the Pesach *sedarim*. Everything has to be brought from Buenos Aires. There is nothing here. Think of the fish, the meat, the wine, the *matzah*. Everything is brought from the Capital city. I remember that once, for Pesach, I needed to do all the shopping. I called a store in Buenos Aires to place an order, and they told me: 'No, we can't deliver to you. We already have many deliveries here in Buenos Aires,' and I told them: 'But I'm sixteen hundred kilometers away from Buenos Aires! It's not like I can take from the shelves myself. I am asking you please to deliver to me. I am paying you.' Sometimes, very few people will help in situations like that. It feels like you're on the wrong side of the tracks on those occasions. You notice everyone is going one way, and you want to go the other way but can't. You cannot hire a caterer to handle everything. It entails being in the kitchen, overseeing the menu, purchasing the vegetables, purchasing the disposable items, and ensuring everything run smoothly. At the same time, you need to register the children who will come to the dinner. There comes a time when your head gets saturated. Luckily, it's only on specific holidays. The rest of the year is quiet. And besides, it's nice. You meet people, and you make friends. Israelis or people who attended the festival the previous year often write to us, telling us that their Pesach was unforgettable and that they still remember it. Things like that make you feel like all of your efforts were worthwhile. It's okay. You don't work to be congratulated. But it's like saying: 'If people liked it, if they had a good time, it's because things were done well,' and that's comforting."

"And your children? How do you educate them in a society like this?"

"That is the toughest challenge a *shaliach* must face. Without a doubt. Above and beyond anything else. Because one is always saying, 'I am here. I'm willing to pay the price. My wife can also pay the price,' but when we have to force our children to pay the price... that is the most difficult thing."

"You may also hear things from the kids that are satisfying and others that are not. For example, once, with my oldest daughter, I experienced great satisfaction. She was two or three years old. She was a beautiful girl. She was walking with her nanny, and they entered a candy store. Then the cashier said: 'Oh, what a pretty girl, here. I'll give you a chocolate,' and my daughter answered: 'No, I can't. This chocolate is not kosher. I can't eat it. I have chocolate at home.' That gave me a lot of satisfaction."

"But another time, on another occasion, we were in the car with my children, talking about the pride of being Jewish, giving them that support for being different here in Salta. And she, the oldest, told me: 'I don't know if it's so nice. Because I would like to eat whatever I want, and I can't.' And I was like: 'Now what do I do?' An answer came to me. *HaShem* enlightened me. She was just learning about the car, about gasoline and that stuff, so I asked her: 'What kind of gasoline does my car use?'; 'Premium'; 'That is right, premium. Okay, well, you know there is premium and regular gasoline. Some cars use super gasoline, and cars use regular gasoline. Some cars use premium gasoline and can also use regular gasoline, and nothing happens to them. But there are cars the manufacturer said must use premium gas, and if you put regular gas in them, they will be ruined. *HaShem* created many people in the world. Some could eat regular, which is everything, and to others, *HaShem* said: 'You must eat premium. That is called kosher.' I told her that God knows kosher is good for us, so we must eat kosher and not regular. The one who eats regular can eat premium too because he can eat everything. But we, *Yehudim*, who have a divine soul, a soul that is not physical but something God created, and thus he is the only one who knows how to care for it. We must care for it with kosher food. So, when we eat kosher, we do what God commands and care for our souls. So, she liked the answer and told me: 'Ah, then yes, I am happy to be a Jew.'"

"However, education is an entire issue. For example, she is starting first grade, and we don't know what to do. We are debating whether to send her to a regular school because we are concerned about the influence other children may have on her. We consulted various rabbis, including my rabbi in Buenos Aires. Then we decided to enroll her in a private school run by a well-known Jewish family."

"She started going there. She goes for a few hours every day. The rest, my wife and I teach her, and then we have the little community school, the Beit Chabad. There we are the teachers, the *morot*. We are the *morot* at school and Mom and Dad at home," he finishes. We halt in front of the only building on the block, meters away from restaurants that offer special regional food, such as fish empanadas, from their windows during Easter.

We wait there until the rest of the guys who were accompanying us arrive.

We all go up a few flights of stairs once we're all together. A neighbor runs into Rafi and remarks about a rabbi we both know, causing him to think aloud. The rabbi mentioned to him was apparently the Chabad envoy in another province of Argentina, who had to move to Chile because he could no longer support himself there. Tawil is surprised and says he can't believe it until we enter his house through the service door and cross the laundry room.

Because the kitchen walls, oven, and stove are all covered in aluminum foil, entering the house through the kitchen gives the impression of stepping into a spaceship. In the context of *chametz* cleansing before the start of Pesach, it is customary in certain Orthodox interpretations to cover certain kitchen areas with aluminum foil. This is done to prevent *chametz* from being spread around.

At the back, we enter a comfortable living room with a large balcony. The table will receive many people, and the rabbi's children are walking around everywhere.

The wall facing the kitchen has a bookshelf filled with Judaic books; the walls have pictures of some of the seven Lubavitch rebbes, with one showing five rebbes in a forest watching a dancing Menachem Mendel Schneerson as a child in pajamas in a painting based on a well-known photo of his childhood.

I sit between the rabbi's wife and his eldest daughter. In front of me, a boy from the Salta community and the rest are Israelis.

When we are all seated, the rabbi invites us to the sink for the ritual hand washing, where a young volunteer instructs us on the prayer to be said.

After the ritual, we return to the table, and the rabbi's wife hands out small bags of *matzah*, instructing us to eat it over the table to avoid crumbs all over the place.

The rabbi's daughter shows me some books in Hebrew with illustrations for children.

"But this one is from Chanukah!" I tell her, understanding only from the drawings of the Maccabees fighting against the Romans and the recurrence of the candlestick drawing.

She is a chatty young lady who tells me several stories. When the rabbi dances with an Israeli in the middle of the living room and exchanges his hat for the boy's in the middle of the dance, she says to me:

"Dad got everything mixed up! It's Pesach, not Purim," she says, noting his father's "disguised appearance" now that he wears the secular Israeli hat.

Educate Lubavitch children, and they will leave with reflections on the Jewish holidays.

"I lost a tooth," she says.

"Really?"

"Yes, and I saw the Tooth Fairy! She left me a coin under the pillow, and I saw her. She was tiny."

I am amazed at how each Lubavitcher approaches the boundary between their religious beliefs and the secular world. While some Lubavitchers are very strict, others may allow their children to relate to ideas outside their belief system. Take, for example, the Tooth Fairy.

The rabbi sits down again, and the maid brings salads and bowls of boiled fish from the kitchen.

We eat the fish and the *matzah*. On my side of the table, I can only hear the rabbi's daughter and a local community boy, but that soon fades as the Israelis pound the table and sing, *We want / We want / Mashiach! / Mashiach!* to the beat of Queen's *We Will, Rock You.*

Rabbi Tawil plays along by beating his fist on the table.

This is a party. It's about third thirty in the afternoon, and we're just starting lunch.

***

Rabbi Tawil is putting on a second Pesach *seder* for people in the area who couldn't have one with their families. He has already told me it will be a much smaller dinner and that I will probably feel more comfortable there because I will understand everything said.

I get to the Beit Chabad a few minutes after eight-thirty in the afternoon, which is when it was supposed to start, and six or seven people are sitting in the hall. The rabbi is talking to a man who is telling him a sad story about his family. At one point, the man tells the rabbi that his grandmother or great aunt, I can't quite make out which, cursed her own granddaughter because she mistreated her. Soon after the death of the old lady, her granddaughter also died. He asks the rabbi if Jewish tradition considers such supernatural acts, and Tawil responds words are extremely dangerous and must be cautiously handled.

The discussion continues until they inform the rabbi that it is already late and he has not completed the *tefillah*, the prayer before the Pesach *seder*. We go to the synagogue and perform a brief service.

The room overflowing with two hundred people and several rows of long tables last night is now a wasteland, with only two tables joined horizontally in the middle.

"You will not start eating before finishing the reading of the *Haggadah*," Rabbi Tawil tells us when we sit down, "because last night it was impossible for the Israelis to wait."

Just thinking about reading that endless text again before dinner is served makes me feel a pit in my stomach.

The table is divided into two sections, one religious and one for the local community: a woman from Tucumán who lives in Salta, the man I sat within the synagogue, another girl in front of me, a man from the Córdoba province at the other end, a boy, and the Beit Chabad volunteer who was in charge of the kitchen last night.

I sat on the border between the two tables, trying to take notes away from the gaze of the Hassid on my left because recording or taking notes during the first two days of Pesach is forbidden. Until now, I could go unnoticed because the crowd of Israelis was so big, but now I have to make an extra effort.

The prohibitions create a problem for the rabbi, who cannot talk on the phone with his wife and one of his sons, who was sick during the afternoon. He sends another son to see if everything is okay. When that son returns and says that the boy is still sick, which is why neither he nor the rabbi's wife will come, he discusses taking the boy to the emergency room with his collaborators. The rabbi isn't sure if he should go through with the ceremony or cancel it. When he hears what his wife said, he realizes it's not a big deal, so he starts the ceremony by reading the *Haggadah*. He says he will do it quickly this time, because he notices we are hungry and impatient and started the service too late.

The *matzah* is separated first to save a piece for the *afikoman*, the last thing we will eat tonight. The rabbi wraps the piece in a little bag and sits it beside the table. He continues reciting the text until he reaches the part where the plagues that fell on Egypt are described. He pours his cup of wine, saying: *Detsakh, Adash, Beachav*. I do not know what those words mean.

Once the rite is completed, he tells us that the spilled wine represents the plagues and has power when thrown against our enemies.

"When I was a kid," he tells us, "we lived with my family in a building in Once, and we had a neighbor who was anti-Semitic. A truly Judeophobe. Then my mom grabbed the wine spilled during Pesach with a syringe and threw it at her door. Soon after, the woman moved out. So, it worked," he concludes, and people celebrate the anecdote.

"Later," he continues, "that same woman moved back into our building, and then my mother did the same thing. She threw the spilled wine at her door once more. We emigrated to Israel at the time," he says, smiling.

Now, the rabbi tells us that the Hebrew word for "Egypt" is the same as for "limits." So, Pesach is a holiday where we can think about breaking out of the limits that society has put on us.

"Every generation must feel that it is coming out of Egypt," he concludes.

They bring meat and salads, and the man from Córdoba tells some Jewish jokes.

I hear the end of one that says, "Is it free? Give me two!" I try to imagine the rest.

Another joke he tells goes: "How do we know Jesus was a Jew for sure? Because only a Jew can think that his mother is a virgin; only a Jew can have a mother who thinks that her son is God, and because only a Jew could have started a business that has been going on for two thousand years!"

We all laugh, and a couple more jokes are told until Niv and some friends, fresh from playing soccer, enter the room. Rabbi Tawil affectionately reproaches them for choosing sports instead of coming to the *seder*.

The group gathers around the table and sings Sephardic songs about returning to Israel that I have never heard before.

Tonight's and last night's big and small celebrations erase the diaspora and the over 12,350 kilometers that separate this dry, hot land from the dry, hot land of Israel. The surrounding people continue celebrating as if that distance didn't exist.

Chapter Nine

No Jew Left Out: Chabad's Social Assistance

"We are not desk rabbis. People often say, 'I called you; you were never around.' And well, we are where the people are. Our goal is to be where the people are."
Rabbi Israel Kapeluschnik

"What happens today to most Jews who have no community or don't belong to something? Who takes care of them? That is what the Rebbe encourages us to do. To get close to every brother, wherever he is, to hold him, to help him, to see him, to know that they have a belonging, that they have something, they have a part of God."
Rabbi Moshe Blumenfeld

One of the most vivid memories rabbi Mordechai Birman has of his time helping to establish the Chabad Foundation is of Jews living in slums. That an Argentine Jew could be poor was taboo in the local Jewish community. It was not within the parameters of what was expected. "In those early years of searching, we found Jews in the San Martín slum, in Villa Mitre, behind Villa Lynch, and in other places. I remember, for example, that I had gone to look for someone. I didn't know the address, and a guy there saw me, came up, looked at me, and said: 'Jew.' I thought he had insulted me. Without getting out of the car, I called him and asked him: 'Why do you call me a Jew?' and he answered: 'I am a Jew too.' Then he told me who he was, and that's how we discovered that Jewish family living in the slum," the rabbi recounts.

The experience profoundly impacted him and those who worked with him then. According to Diego Melamed, the Chabad social aid foundation would have started the day a Chabad donor told rabbi Tzvi Grunblatt that a Jew was asking for milk at the steps of a Catholic church. The person in charge of starting the project was Rabbi Birman, who in 1988 took charge of this new Chabad Lubavitch project: "Because of the need of many people who came to ask us for help," the rabbi tells me, "With the help of some people we put together some files; we hired a social worker, and we began to look for people who needed our help. At first, it was by word of mouth. Following that, we began to refer to Jewish schools. We asked for the last names of the people who had received scholarships and the socioeconomic status of these families. They told us, so we called these people and offered them our assistance."

Tzedakah, or social justice implemented through charity, is one of the most important precepts that a Jew must follow, and Chabad Lubavitch was establishing a network to channel those social-helping impulses to a growing public.

That first family they found living in the shantytown was not the last, and it paved the way for Chabad Lubavitch Argentina's approach to social assistance. "They had a house where a woman lived alone with four children and two of her brothers," recalls the rabbi of that first family that triggered the work of the Chabad Foundation. "Everyone, including the lady with the children, slept in the kitchen because the other rooms had no roof. They had no drinking water, and the toilet was disconnected from the sewage system. We made renovation. We installed roofs, heating, a water tank, and a sewage system, and eventually, we wanted to get them out of there. We were in contact with them for many years."

Birman stepped down from the foundation's management in 1994 but had already laid the foundations for its operation. Among the proposals made in those early years, before the great Argentine economic crisis of 2001, were soft loans to pay for minor repairs in beneficiaries' homes or small projects, assistance for surgery abroad, international trips, rent payments, and grocery rebates.

In 1999, Chabad Lubavitch reached an agreement with the *Fundación Tzedaká* [Tzedakah Foundation], another Jewish charity, and both institutions set up their first social aid center. The 2001 crisis sped up Chabad's charitable efforts, prompting the establishment of nine additional food banks.

In 2002, Chabad entered an agreement with the American Jewish Joint Distribution Committee or *Joint* to co-finance some actions and establish the Community Social Aid Network, which included both institutions, AMIA and the *Fundación Tzedaká*.

Diana M., whom we have already met, became involved with Chabad Lubavitch after working at the *Joint* office in La Plata. Because the institutions were linked, she was promoted to work in the network's Chabad center when a position opened up. She remembers those early days: "I can't forget the first event that took place at the San Martin Theater, where the wife of President Toledo of Peru was present. She had been invited because she was Jewish. Peru's Minister of Social Development was also there. She began her speech by saying: 'Welcome to the Third World.'" Those words were a harsh reality check for Argentina's proud Jewish population, mainly composed of middle and high-class professionals.

The community assistance network was built on the foundation of these four powerful institutions: Chabad Lubavitch, AMIA, and the Fundación Tzedaká, all receiving direct funds from the *Joint*.

Diana M. explains: "Tzedaká operates decentralized and collaborates with Jewish institutions. Among those partners, there was Chabad. They had an office on Azcuénaga Street. Chabad gave them a place to meet and helped pay for some of the social programs and the salaries of the professionals who worked there. In addition, Chabad donated food to the food bank. They usually provided kosher meat and chicken."

Marcela Schilman, a graduate in social work, has been the director of the Chabad Foundation since 2000 and explains: "The rabbis lend us an office, telephone, electricity, and so on. They also lend us rooms for our activities. Because rabbis are involved in many centers, the coordinator meets with them regularly to discuss programs and actions. Many rabbis contribute financially; some even provide coffee and snacks for our workshops. It helps us a lot."

Rabbi Israel Kapeluschnik explained his role in providing spiritual assistance to some of the foundation's program beneficiaries in an interview published in Chabad Magazine, issue 118 (Fall 2009): "When I approach the beneficiaries, I do so not simply to provide a service, but to make them feel like they are a part of the great Jewish family."

The Chabad Foundation assists over three thousand eight hundred people, representing approximately one thousand four hundred families. It has ten social assistance centers, twelve in-charge professionals, and five programs that guide its operations: home-based social care; *Javaia*, for the elderly; *Iedid nefesh*, self-reflection workshops; *Maon Tapuli*, a therapeutic space for people with mental illnesses, and an employment office that functions as a job center. The network is interconnected to the various community social institutions to maximize resource efficiency.

Although Ms. Schilman ultimately directs all Chabad Foundation centers, each one is coordinated by a professional who may be a social worker or psychology graduate. This person in charge works with the various family referents who come to the center and defines, after a technical evaluation, the type of help to be provided: food benefits, free medicines, individual treatment, whatever is required, to be as comprehensive as possible in a context of great need.

As a result of the 2001 crisis, which destroyed the economic foundations of many Jewish homes, the Jewish social network was fundamental to keep families afloat. Schilman highlights the lasting effect of the devastating psychological impact on many Jews and how the Chabad Foundation contributes what it can to help them: "The emotional consequences of the crisis were so strong that even today we have people who have been beneficiaries since 2002. So, it was not only a question of economic readjustment but also of family readjustment. The family's head may have become physically ill, died, or become depressed and unable to get out of bed, forcing the wife, who had not worked in twenty years, to return to work. It also implied a readjustment in thinking about what we could do with those untrained women over forty years old in a perverse labor market as we have in Argentina. So, we invented training programs. We went out to talk to our donors to see if they could lend us a hand. It is challenging, but we have made some progress."

"And it is still today that people arrive asking for assistance, people who should have asked for assistance back in 2002. However, during all these years, they tried in every way they could to get ahead without asking for help. They were too ashamed to ask for that. We have, for example, people that we meet outside our regular business hours so that we can keep their privacy. The Argentine Jewish community might be big, but we all know each other. We are all half relatives. Many people come to our clothing banks when they are closed to the public. We open them just for them so that the rest of the public doesn't see them. Or they come to one of our three community food banks at three o'clock in the afternoon or eleven o'clock in the morning to avoid crossing paths with other people. Sometimes, we deliver the food directly to their homes. Since many of these people can't keep paying for their health insurance, we also try to help them attend public hospitals and health centers. We get them their appointments."

The Chabad Foundation provides immediate material assistance and attempts to create a network of social relationships for its beneficiaries to reintegrate them into the Jewish community through various activities. In addition, anyone who walks into a Chabad social assistance center will be inserted into their congregational space. After all, every Chabad institution adheres to Lubavitch's political and ideological guidelines.

However, the Chabad Lubavitch Foundation is not the only source of social assistance coming from Chabad. The institution also has two other significant legs in Argentina: *Ieladeinu* and *Leoded*, each focused on a different type of assistance. Many of the cases that arrive are gathered by the Chabad Foundation and then by these other two institutions.

Rabbi Tzvi Grunblatt recalls, behind his vast desk full of papers, books, and ornaments, the origin of *Ieladeinu*: "It is a care and rescue program for Jewish children who have experienced abuse, violence, and neglect. It began in 1999 with the separation of two Jewish children from their mother's care. On that occasion, we offered the Jewish community's care of these children."

"After a Judge ruled to separate the boys from their mother, he summoned me and said, 'I know, rabbi, that I can trust you with the boys, and I know because my counselor had dinner at your house last Friday night.' It was the only time that woman was in my house. It was the hand of God. Then, the following dialogue with the Judge occurred: 'I know I can trust you with the boys. What are you going to do with them?' I answered, 'We will hire a social worker to assist the mother in her home so that even if the woman cannot care for her home and children, the social worker will provide her with all necessary assistance so the children can continue living at home.' The Judge told me, 'The house is destroyed. The kids can't live there anymore.' And I said, 'We're going to repair the house. We'll replace the floor, paint it, repair it, and thoroughly clean it.' The Judge ruled and gave me the care of the boys. After a few weeks, he called me again and said: 'There is no one who can care for Jewish children in crisis situations.' I answered, 'What do you expect from me?'; 'Rabbi, may I place more Jewish children under your care?' he asked. 'Other religions have institutions to care for their own, but you Jews do not.' I told him to send me children in need. I was expecting two or three per year. They sent me a list of all the children who needed assistance. There were two hundred children in total. That is when Karina Pincever, a professional lawyer, and a group of her colleagues came together to form what is now *Ieladeinu*."

At the time, Ms. Pincever, a child abuse specialist, worked with Grunblatt's wife at the Chabad school, *Oholei Jinuj*. She was *Ieladeinu's* general director for over ten years until

2009, when she stepped down and left Javier Fajn, a graduate in administration, as interim director.

The institution has a complex structure that attends to the needs of 257 children and has a budget for 2010 estimated at US$ 2,176,000, financed primarily by private donations and a small proportion of contributions from the federal government and the City of Buenos Aires. The institution is divided into directorates that handle child admission to accomplish its mission. *Ieladeinu* has day centers where children in need can get help after school, "family programs" where community members offer to sponsor them for a time, and two boarding homes, one for boys and one for girls, for more severe cases.

Valeria Marckiewicz, director of the institution's admissions, explains that home placements are an exceptional instance where particular cases are assigned: "In general, the children who are institutionalized are all children whose lives were at risk or who were victims of a sexual crime."

She tries to shed light on what she considers an unfair myth against the institution: Chabad, through *Ieladeinu*, is "kidnapping" children to raise them in the Jewish orthodoxy. The professional says: "Many parents say or have said that *Ieladeinu* takes their kids away to make them religious, that Chabad kidnaps these kids and puts them in the care of religious families. These things happen because of the parents. Sometimes the work is enjoyable because the parents accept the intervention and times when they don't. Ninety-seven percent of parents do not want assistance from *Ieladeinu*. Most cases were referred by someone else. That is precisely the definition of child abuse: it is within the family, secret, and not revealed. A parent seeking help from *Ieladeinu* assumes he or she is an abuser. If that were to happen, we would have completed half of the work."

Since *Ieladeinu*'s work, supported by UNICEF, is with children in danger, the decision to send a child to internment is made by the Juvenile Justice Board after a long, careful process. Marckiewicz clarifies that the institution's goal differs from teaching Orthodox Judaism to children: "*Ieladeinu* has a general goal that is the same for every system we set up: protection, treatment, which is the most important thing, and the return of rights. When a child is admitted to the program after living in a home where child abuse has been found, a therapeutic, all-around plan is made to help change the situation. Violent situations do not end immediately, but require a comprehensive approach that takes time and a lot of professional work."

The internment in *Ieladeinu's* homes is an exceptional case: at first, the Marckiewicz-directed area tries, after relevant evaluations, to work in the same family home to accompany a recovery in environments where children's rights have been violated. For this purpose, they have a large professional group of psychologists, educational psychologists, assistants, and social workers who manage each situation.

The director of Wolfsohn School, Gustavo Dvoskin, has children from the *Ieladeinu* program in the school's classrooms and emphasizes the value of the program: "It is a life-saving project for children. They live in specially purchased houses and day homes, where they are cared for, fed, and loved. We're talking about abandoned, abused children with the most bizarre life circumstances piled on top of them."

Each child has his or her own routine in an *Ieladeinu* home. The program tries to keep children in their previous school if they are well-integrated and have a well-developed network. A daily social routine is built for them with shared spaces, group meetings to work on coexistence, and what Marckiewicz defines as "the subjective constitution of a human being; many times, from scratch."

She clarifies the religious content: "Not in any of the shelters. There are indeed religious employees, but there are also secular employees. However, there is no spiritual assistance, no hour of prayer, all that does not exist. Of course, the *Ieladeinu* homes belong to a religious congregation. As a result, a picture of the Rebbe and *mezuzot* hang from the frames at the entrances. On Shabbat, all the children in the shelter homes are invited to spend time with community families. Attending these dinners is a cause for celebration for them. Do all the children take part in these kinds of activities? No. Approximately eighty-five percent of those invited attend. We focus a lot on what the children like and want."

After ten years of service, the *Ieladeinu* program is facing new challenges: the children who grew up in the program require a way out that will allow them to leave their past behind and achieve social insertion as adults.

Some of the renovating efforts of the institution's directors are focused on these challenges: "What networks are the children going to have when they leave?" asks Fajn. "That is exactly what we are working on. We're planning how we'll assist them in selecting tools for adulthood. Tools from the labor market, so they can one day grow outside *Ieladeinu*. We intend the institution to be just a step in their lives."

Support for job placement, procedures for those wishing to emigrate to or study in Israel, and training for social reintegration through group solidarity projects are among the services provided to children leaving the program.

The third leg of the social assistance conducted by Chabad is the *Leoded* (Encourage) center.

Rabbi Moshe Blumenfeld, the program's director, is fond of soccer and its metaphors. Behind his desk in the old house that serves as the institution's center of operations, he explains the meaning of the name: "Cheering for a team that may not have many stars or figures, but has a lot of encouragement and support, generates and awakens unknown forces within the players. Suddenly, the player realizes he can make a dribble, a pass, or a goal. We work with members of the Jewish community who are hospitalized or experiencing difficult life situations and any combination of problems that a person may be experiencing. We detect them in hospitals and rehabilitation centers. They are people who are in a state of vulnerability, who have no family, or who have reached the most marginal part of society."

At *Leoded*, as in the Chabad Foundation and also in *Ieladeinu*, Chabad's work is focused on creating and locating support networks for beneficiaries, based on what Blumenfeld refers to as a psychological principle that proposes rehabilitation in society: "We take advantage of the fact that a person belongs to a specific collective or group and try to reintegrate him or her into social life from that environment," says the rabbi. "For example, we go to the mental hospital and locate a person from the Jewish community who is there not because he is unbalanced but because he once had a mental breakdown. He is now stable but stayed there because he had nowhere else to go. Staying in the mental hospital exposes this person to any atrocity that may occur there, so we work to reintegrate him, make him a part of a community, and restore his Jewish identity. It is an extensive work of containment, of orientation, of spiritual awakening, as a former president would say: 'Today, we work for poor children who are hungry and for rich children who are sad.'"

The work of the various Chabad Lubavitch institutions for social assistance is articulated constantly. Diana M. recalls the case of a student she had at the Hillel School. They had met the mother because her husband had tried to burn her alive, and while she was hospitalized, a priest had gone to give her last rites when she said: "No, no, I am a Jew." The woman had never met her mother but knew her maternal grandmother was Jewish. Then *Leoded* stepped in.

According to Blumenfeld: "There is a part of the population that has been hurt by life and needs an outlet, a way to keep their feelings in check, or a word of comfort. So, connecting them to their Jewish identity is a very spiritual work. There may be a person who has been abandoned in a hospital, and to say to them, 'Look, God is going to help you. I have come to give you a blessing' gives them hope. I need to go there and help them, try to find someone to take care of them and get that person back on his feet. What I do encompasses many activities and is best summarized as spiritual support and guidance."

Leoded, like many Chabad Lubavitch institutions and community proposals, arose to fill a void: Rabbi Gabriel Setton, who is in charge of Beit Chabad Caballito, had heard from many people who were upset that only priests and pastors, but never rabbis, came to visit them in public hospitals. In 1999, he devised "Servicio Asistencial Rabínico Leoded" [Rabbinical Assistant Service Leoded], a program of visits by rabbis to Jewish patients in public hospitals. At that time, the program was based on a small office and was run from the start by Blumenfeld, who says: "I began working three to four hours per day to develop this. Initially, it was a rabbinical visit, similar to a priest visiting the sick and telling them: 'May God heal you; may God bless you.' But since I started working, I felt very dissatisfied because I would go to the mental hospital, visit the patients, help them put on *tefillin*, which is already a lot for a Jew, make him do a good deed, connect him with his Jewish identity. However, I could see that what I was doing wasn't enough because when I left, the person was still in the same miserable state of being alone."

One situation changed Blumenfeld's perspective: he met a man who spoke to him in fluent Hebrew on one of his visits to a psychiatric hospital. That unsettled him: "A surprise, we think those living under those conditions are crazy or people from the bottom of society. As a result, all hospitals are in areas where those who do not fit into the social framework are invisible. It is as if Buenos Aires was designed so that these people, the weak or the sick, could never be reintegrated or rehabilitated, become part of society, or be supported by society because they are different. Then, this man spoke to me in Hebrew; his speech was coherent. He wasn't talking about little green men or anything like that, but about everyday issues. Then we started talking, and he introduced me to another Jew and another Jew. It was a population of dozens."

The rabbi did some research and asked the hospital's doctors questions until he found out that many Jews were in the psychiatric ward not because they had a current mental disorder but because they had once had a mental breakdown and could not get back to the outside world because they had nowhere to go. No family or friends to help them.

Blumenfeld proposed to the doctors that the patients go on small outings to spend Shabbat with his congregation. He conducted his first experiment when he received approval: "They attended a Kabbalat Shabbat, prayed, and ate as everyone else did. They took part socially, and they felt included and integrated. Then I discovered that many Jewish doctors and professionals in the hospitals are waiting for someone from outside to help these patients escape this situation. So, I started some small programs to help them get better. I got them out to bring them back to the world. The pilot project gave us the idea for everything we built after that."

In 2005, Rabbi Setton bought a bigger building for his Beit Chabad and told Blumenfeld that he could no longer support the *Leoded* project. Blumenfeld then took complete control of it. He comments: "I turned what used to be the rabbinical help service into an action center bit by bit. Not only to work in hospitals but also to have a center where people can get help and have a safe place to unload their problems and talk about their pain. To find a Jewish view and a professional view that is honest."

Leoded offers social and health containment based on the idea of religious community: "What we work on is inspired by everything the Rebbe teaches us. We try to work from the Jewish soul, giving the Jew his identity back, helping him grow as a person, and connecting him to his identity and God. Medical science has shown that a person is more likely to get better if he or she is spiritually connected, has faith, believes in something, and is involved in the community."

The Abasto neighbor's old manor, which houses *Leoded's* offices, also houses a small synagogue where patients are encouraged to share prayers, read the Torah, celebrate holidays, and are invited to barbecues in the courtyard.

A group of supervised professionals work together with volunteers to develop the daily work of the program, which is well received in the hospitals: "In the hospitals, they are waiting for someone to show up. All the public hospitals are overloaded with work, with patients. When someone from the outside shows up out of the blue and says to one of these patients, 'Here I am,' it's like their *Mashiach* has come. It's important to them. They are glad to know that someone outside can help and care about them."

Thus, Chabad Lubavitch's work in social assistance is presented to bring joy and social support while restoring religious networks and the sense of belonging to Judaism.

Blumenfeld sums it up: "There are Jewish souls who have lived their whole lives in places that are hard to imagine. They are sparks, Jewish brothers. They are all brothers, but these are especially close."

Chapter Ten

Queen Esther's Heiresses: Women in Chabad

What is the place that Chabad Lubavitch reserves for its women? Could the Messiah, so long awaited and so called by the Lubavitchers, be, for example, a woman? The one who answers, bursting into laughter, is Jani Gorovitz: "Many women expect the Mashiach — she says jokingly — but no, the *Mashiach* is a man."

Jewish Orthodoxy keeps somewhat marginal spaces for women within its scheme of life: they may not become rabbis (something that Reform Judaism allows), they have restrictions for specific practices, and they must dress "modestly" so as not to seduce men who are not their husbands, among many other issues.

Jani Gorovitz is thirty-five years old, the oldest of thirteen siblings, and married to a man who is the oldest of twelve. Between them, they have nine children. For fifteen years, Jani has been the director of the *Majon Or Jaia* (Light of Life), a center she defines as a space for Jewish girls who want to learn more about Judaism or a kind of *yeshiva* for women.

Located a few blocks from Chabad's headquarters in Buenos Aires, the *Majon Or Jaia* is a striking building with mirrored walls and modern design, and if it were not for the giant sign on the door reading "Chabad Lubavitch Argentina," it would surely pass for a modern office building. Inside are classrooms, a living room, a library, a bar area, a residence for girls who come to study from the Provinces or other countries, and a large gala hall frequently used for meetings organized by Chabad Central for various purposes.

In her dark wood-paneled office, Gorovitz defends her position as a Lubavitch woman and tries to show the world how comfortable she is with that role: "I feel good enough about my role as a woman to accept that the *Mashiach* is a man or that the Rebbe is a man. What's the problem if a patient, for example, seeks treatment from a male doctor because she knows he's a good doctor?"

Not everything seems so simple or shiny if you look at it closely: the role of women in Orthodox Judaism is far from equal to that of men, and Chabad Lubavitch goes to great lengths to try not to let that show. And, if it is noticeable, it tries to make the women of the community feel comfortable with the role they have to play.

A first visible element of misogynist differentiation appears in men's morning prayers, in which they express gratitude for not being born women. Chabad theology has explanations for these aspects of their system of beliefs since it is possible to find in the sacred writings both explicitly sexist quotes and others that rescue and enhance the role of women. It's enough to look at what you want to see to find a way out, and the Chabad rabbis use this to their advantage when they are called sexist.

But this is not the only inequality that Jewish Orthodoxy proposes for men and women: Orthodox Jewish women share the 365 negative divine precepts and some of the 248 positive ones with men, except for those that require a specific time to be fulfilled. Women are exempt from these precepts because, in the Lubavitch explanation, God created women different from men, with other needs regarding the care of children, family, and home. For this reason, God does not obligate them to fulfill precepts that imply a certain temporality, except those related to Shabbat and the High Holidays.

Now, if following the precepts is a way of being close to God, does the fact that women don't have to do some of them mean they are less close to God than men? According to Chabad rabbis' interpretation of the Kabbalah, the root of a woman's soul is higher than that of a man's, so these exceptions in fulfilling certain *mitzvot* do not imply that they will not connect with God. Gorovitz maintains: "The role of the woman is to generate a climate in the home and a community so that there are people who want to fulfill the precepts and go to pray. The Torah releases her from the obligation of attending the synagogue, praying the *minyan*, putting on *tefillin*, and putting on *tzitzit* so that she can devote herself more to her crucial role, which is that of a transmitter, a generator of Jewish life. It is also a question of women having an affinity, a spontaneous connection with *HaShem*, according to the Kabbalah. Not that women are not apt, but on the contrary, we have a natural connection, so we do not need to take it to the material plane."

To respond to uncomfortable questions about sensitive subjects, Chabad Lubavitch employs several strategies, including the stylized modernization of its buildings and headquarters, an image of efficiency, and a variety of well-armed tools. All these factors allow them to experiment with shifting the public perception of the congregation's traditionalistic stances. This is how Gorovitz responds when I ask her why women in Chabad synagogues must attend separately from men, usually on a floor above where the prayer is held: "If we were not upstairs, men could not be downstairs. Some things are not noticed from the outside. Still, the basic precepts of Judaism, Shabbat, *kashrut*, the family unit, and purity are preserved by women. Perhaps from the outside, it is not very noticeable. Still, the daily Jewish experience is very much about the role of women. First, there is the issue of blood: even if your father is a rabbi, if your mother is not Jewish, you are not Jewish."

The ambiguity of women's roles in Jewish tradition is intriguing. There is a little-known biblical figure: Lilith, the actual first woman, whose background and implications are extensively explored in the *Zohar* and Jewish mysticism, from which Chabad Lubavitch emerged.

Lilith would have been created by God together with Adam and of the same material as him. Still, she would have abandoned him when she refused to be his servant. Other versions maintain Adam did not satisfy her sexually, and that is why she left him. According to Chabad's webpage, "Lilith was a woman of absolutes, intolerant of anything but perfection in her man and his relationship with her. Not a great recipe for a marriage. Chava (Eve) was ready to look the other way for the sake of the relationship, aware that things are never perfect, but love can make it work. She contained within her some of Adam and could feel his heart's rhythm within her own."

Jewish mythology and mystical beliefs have made Lilith a diabolical woman who allied herself with the forces of evil after leaving Adam's side. Lilith represents a free and egalitarian way of being a woman, which has no place in a religious congregation that keeps a strictly patriarchal imprint.

Jani Gorovitz believes that there are more interesting women to study in the Torah and sacred texts, so she dismisses the possibility that the *Majon* classes will discuss Lilith: "Rather than her, there are so many other women with such strong messages, so positive, so important."

According to Heilman and Friedman, women in Lubavitch have gained a much more prominent role in the last fifty years than in traditional Orthodox Judaism and even in Chabad before the beginning of its expansion around the world. The authors say: "Lubavitcher women have not taken a back seat to men in the missionary vocation. While elsewhere in the Hasidic and traditional Jewish world women were encouraged to find a husband who ideally would be a Torah scholar studying in the yeshiva and whom they would support in that effort, contemporary Lubavitcher women are expected to go out into the world as emissaries with their husbands. In practice, much of the work falls on their shoulders, including coordinating Sabbath or holiday meals for all sorts of guests — often invited on short notice — and acting as a nurturing guide for the Jewishly uninformed... Women in Lubavitch are not second class; they are full-fledged emissaries who have their own kinus [annual convention] and are encouraged no less than men in their mission." (6)

Chabad women are trained to serve in the home, supporting their husbands and caring for the children. Jani explains the matching process: "Most of the time, the parents know matchmakers in the community. When they hear about someone with an interesting profile, they talk to their son or daughter about it and try to schedule a date. Because men and women cannot have physical contact before marriage, outings comprise chatting and drinking coffee, and then more coffee, a soda, and more talking. A high success rate is seen in couples who meet in this way. There is a lot of emphasis on the intellectual, which a sentimental connection must always accompany. There is no such thing as 'I'll get married, and love will come later.' It is different with girls who are just beginning to explore Judaism. Some do not want to adopt this way of life so suddenly and prefer to meet boys wherever they go. In such cases, we advise them to meet Jewish men."

If the man and woman are in tune with each other, the couple is formed, and, with no courtship involved, they are ready to get married. The news soon spreads in the community, where everyone knows everyone else.

It is a model of a couple in which what is privileged is a sort of "working unit": a new family that will bring many children into the world and who will go in the same direction because they have common goals.

Contraception is not permitted in marriage, and the precepts require spouses to maintain sexual relations, so large families are typical in the Lubavitch community.

This is "the most natural thing in the world," according to Gorovitz. She uses a personal anecdote to make her point: "I recall going to see my mother when she was expecting my twelfth sister. I met the obstetrician, who was Jewish but not observant. 'Everyone in the delivery room thought she was a first-time mother,' he said. This is because each child is unique to us. Every child is desired, applauded, and loved. A mother's love is multiplied rather than divided among many children. We try to instill that in the girls who visit the *Majon Or Jaia*."

In exceptional cases, which include the possibility of the mother's life risk or physical exhaustion, specific contraceptive methods are permitted in consultation with the rabbi. To help support these families, the community offers spiritual support and couple therapy. The difference between the Lubavitch and other Western conceptions of love is illustrated on the pages of compiling and reformulating Rebbe's teachings. Jacobson glosses over the Rebbe: "True love bears little resemblance to the love we read about in novels and hear about in songs. True love is transcendence, linking our physical selves to G-d and, therefore, to everyone else around us. All too often we look at love selfishly, as something we want and need, but true love, because it is integral to our relationship with G-d, is selfless." (59)

The same book explains the institution of marriage as how two souls that were united in heaven before coming down to earth are reunited in this world: "Husband and wife need to invite G-d into their union by dedicating their lives to eternal values and connecting to a presence higher than their own, by acknowledging G-d who created them as two halves of one soul. This instills each spouse with a commitment to each other, to their families, to the world around them." (50)

The *ketubah*, the Jewish marriage contract, sets out the terms of the man's acquisition of the woman in return for which he agrees to provide her with three things: sustenance (food), shelter (from clothing to a house), and sexual fulfillment.

Orthodox Judaism also recognizes divorce (though only as a last resort), and one ground for a woman to seek it is that her husband cannot fulfill his obligation to satisfy her sexually.

Jewish Orthodoxy and the Lubavitch consider that menstruation makes a woman impure during the days it occurs and during the seven following days until she performs an immersion in the *mikveh*, a ritual bath. The restrictions on physical contact with an impure woman are absolute. During the time between her menstruation and ritual immersion, her husband may not share a bed with her.

The Lubavitch points out the "benefits" of the ritual bath in the *mikveh*, defining it as a "spa mixed with spiritual retreat." In the words of Gorovitz: "The *mikveh* precept is a very rich precept that takes special care to ensure that the woman is valued not only on the physical plane but also on the spiritual plane. Today's baths are modern and nice; the water is warm and clean, and it has all the cares that any pool would have to keep the water crystal clear and impeccable."

An atheist Jew who works in Lubavitch institutions and doesn't want to be named takes all the ornaments off this rule: "It is a bath associated with the prohibition of sexuality. It's more than just a bath. A man is not permitted to touch a woman while she is menstruating. That is why religious men do not shake hands with women other than their wives. It's because they don't know if she's menstruating or not. As a result, the woman has a permanent impurity. Every month, there is a week when the woman is menstruating, then a week of purification. Then she goes to the *mikveh* after those fifteen days. It is a precept from then on to have sexual relations, which always occur on the days of fertility when the woman ovulates. She is then likely to become pregnant again."

The same can be said of the modesty precept, which requires women to cover their heads not to stimulate men other than their husbands. While other branches of Jewish Orthodoxy require women to shave their heads and cover them with a headscarf, Chabad's fashion is to wear natural hair wigs. Still, they also require long skirts and long shirts that cover every inch of skin, as does all Orthodoxy.

Chabad Judaism is felt in the body: it involves a high burden of bodily discipline and control of sexuality.

Gorovitz points out the importance of teaching Jewish women who come to the *Machon Or Jaia* to observe the precepts regulating intimacy and sexual life: "An observant woman may avoid contact with other men. She can have the contact of an embrace or a kiss only with her children, in a limited way, with her parents, grandparents, and husband, without restrictions, but at the appropriate time."

Jacobson explains, "Healthy intimacy requires two ingredients: discipline and sanctification. We must exercise self-control, and we must also see sexuality as sacred. One must approach the sanctity of sexuality with awe, like entering into the Holy of Holies, where every action counts, where any blemish is intolerable. We must experience sexuality in a controlled environment with appropriate boundaries — not to dampen the expression of love, but to channel the powerful physical energies into a healthy passion. In modern society, sexuality often involves two people who are each interested only in satisfying their own needs. But sexuality is meant to be transcendent, not indulgent, allowing you to let another person inside your soul so you can build something greater together. Only by introducing G-d into the relationship can a man and woman overcome their individual desires, and marriage is the only perfect environment in which to do so. In all other environments, intimacy is unhealthy and harmful." (70)

The Rebbe's teachings, collected and adapted in this book, serve as a reference and reading material for the young girls who attend classes at the *Majon Or Jaia*.

According to Gorovitz, there are thirty to forty classes per week for an average of one hundred twenty students, with interns having a mandatory attendance regime and the rest attending classes based on their interests.

Aside from classes, special activities are planned, such as the *Shabbaton*, an all-night Shabbat celebration in which a family from the community is invited to spend the ceremony with the *Majon Or Jaia* inmates until the next day.

Despite all the above, in Chabad Lubavitch, as Heilman and Friedman pointed out, women have a more relevant role than in other expressions of Jewish Orthodoxy. They may exercise professions, study university careers, and work if this does not prevent them from taking care of their multiple children and taking care of the precepts of the home. But that is the external, visible face. On the internal frontier, things are not quite the same.

I ask Jani Gorovitz to explain why a Lubavitch woman could never become a rabbi. She answers me: "When I see a woman rabbi, what comes to my mind, without meaning to offend anyone, what did she miss as a Jewish woman that she needs to be something she is not? There's a table and a chair for your comfort," she points to where we are sitting. "The day the chair wants to stop being a chair because it's nicer to be a table, we're going to miss the chair, aren't we? I don't see the need for a woman to become a rabbi. What does being a rabbi imply? To live Judaism intensely? One can live it as a Jewish woman. Does it mean to transmit Judaism? Who else but the woman in the home and in the community to transmit Judaism? If it involves putting on *tefillin* and praying in the synagogue, that is not the way *HaShem* said in the Torah."

I say goodbye to her and look for the elevator. In the café area, some girls chat happily in the comfortable armchairs.

They are the future women of Chabad.

Chapter Eleven

The External Front: Chabad's Public Affairs

"The Lubavitchers are among the most militant of all Jewish groups in their desire to retain the territories. The ultra-Orthodox response to this issue is confusing and contradictory. Where some Hasidic groups, Satmar in particular, would like to see the State of Israel dismantled and the Jews allowed to live peacefully under United Nations or even Palestinian governance, there are others, such as Lubavitchers, who while not willing to call themselves Zionists, behave like them in the extreme. While they take pains to reject Israel as the resurrection of the Davidic kingdom that existed before the destruction of the Temple, they see the establishment of the State as a sign that the age of redemption is near."
Robert Eisenberg, *Boychiks in the hood*

"You can go dancing and study while still keeping Shabbat obligations."
Rabbi Shlomo Levy

Matisyahu: Chabad dances at the sound of reggae

The man wears black mourning clothes, a hat, a beard that has not been shaved for years, and *tzitzit* that reminds him of the precepts he must fulfill. Standing center stage in a television studio, he sings the hit song *King Without a Crown* from his first album, *Shake off the Dust... Arise.*

The words come out of his mouth as quickly as they would during a *tefillah*, but with a traditional reggae beat. *I Want Mashiach Now* repeats the chorus and then asks *HaShem* to bring the light that will come from the dark and shine from Crown Heights.

The video of Matisyahu's January 16th, 2006, visit to David Letterman's iconic late-night show now has millions of YouTube views.

Matisyahu was in his prime when he surprised the world and the music industry by revealing himself as an Orthodox Jew who made a fusion of reggae, hip-hop, and rock filtered through the sieve of Chabad Hasidism.

An enlarged image of that iconic moment in his early career appears on page one hundred and forty-three of the magazine celebrating the twentieth anniversary of Beit Chabad Belgrano, led by Rabbi Shlomo Kiesel.

Matisyahu is a *baal teshuvah*, which means he is a secular Jew who converted to Jewish Orthodoxy through Chabad. Once he did that, he overcame many obstacles to become a big reggae star worldwide.

But that man and the one who, four years later, is sitting in his dressing room at the Teatro Gran Rex in Buenos Aires, passing a door with a certificate stating that the catering is kosher, seem not to be the same.

He reluctantly answers my questions, as if he is tired of being that odd figure who draws the attention of an increasingly skeptical public.

Matisyahu complains, saying he left Chabad Lubavitch because he was tired of being their *de facto* representative: "I'm not affiliated with any movement. I decided at a certain point that it wasn't fair to them for me to represent them since I was only in Chabad for two years. From that, I was supposed to represent generations of people worldwide. So, I said to myself, 'I'm not going to represent any of them,' so I took a lot of things from different Hasidic traditions, and now I don't have one path."

Those are my principles, and if you don't like them... well, I have others

Matisyahu is an excellent example of how Chabad Lubavitch takes the notion of Judaism to previously unthinkable heights. The commonplace imagines the Orthodox as obscurantists who dedicate their days to studying sacred texts, prayer, and little else.

Even though some people in Chabad strictly adhere to this archetype, they are not the most common. This is one reason Lubavitchers must deal with other, more extreme forms of Hasidim daily, such as the Satmer Hassidic court, who mock them by claiming that the Lubavitch are not real Jews but just an excellent imitation of what it means to be Jewish.

Lubavitchers who are not engaged in Rabbinic life can opt for secular professions, such as, for example, being a reggae star.

Matisyahu's case is perhaps particular. He sees Judaism as a synthesis of what he likes best for each current. When I entered his dressing room with a photographer to interview him, he greeted her with a kiss and a hug, despite Jewish Orthodoxy's prohibition on contact between men and women.

Not long ago, he declared via his Twitter account that he had become vegan. I ask him if that choice has anything to do with Jewish dietary laws, which can become so extreme as to imply almost enforced vegetarianism: "I never became a full-fledged vegan. I stopped drinking milk because I couldn't find organic milk that was also kosher in the United States. But here in Argentina, we went insane at the pizzeria the other night. I want to be natural in my understanding of Judaism and my lifestyle. There are many Jews who eat kosher, but not because they are concerned about animal cruelty."

Authenticity or imposture? He says he still attends a Lubavitch synagogue and lives in Crown Heights, Brooklyn, steps away from Chabad Lubavitch International Headquarters.

I ask him how his time in Chabad Lubavitch influenced his music: "The song 'I Will Be Light' from my album *Light* expresses the idea that there is a small moment in life to shine. It is a universal concept. It isn't even a religious concept. The *Tanya*, the foundational book the First Lubavitch Rebbe wrote, provided the inspiration. In his teachings, he compares a person's soul to a dying star or a spark in the night, both of which are insignificant in the grand scheme of things. In my track 'Youth,' I also quote: 'Youth is the engine of the world,' which is from a book of the Lubavitch Rebbe's teachings."

Then I ask him about the Rebbe's place in his work since he no longer feels part of Chabad: "When I became religious, I started with rabbi Shlomo Carlebach. Then the next step was to go to Chabad. I then moved to Crown Heights, studied a lot of Chabad Hasidut and the *Tanya*, and I would take quotes from what I read to use as backing for many of my songs. For example: 'From the forest itself comes the hand for the ax,' from the track on my first album, *Shake off the Dust*. These are all universal ideas. I was in Chabad when I learned about them, but they are not from Chabad. They are mostly fundamental concepts about life, spirituality, and God. The Hasidic songs I listened to at the Crown Heights *yeshiva* were also Chabad *niggunim*. Some of those melodies appeared on my first album. As in the songs 'Short Nigum' and 'Aish Tamid,' which are Hasidut teachings."

A few weeks ago, rabbi Tawil of Chabad Lubavitch Salta pointed out to me that the Lubavitch community no longer felt the same affection for the artist as before: "Now he said that he is not so much with us... I don't know. Anyway, if he wants to come, we will welcome him as always".

Changing skins

Matisyahu's visit to Buenos Aires mobilizes a community that is always sensitive and waiting to be challenged. The show's promotional posters are displayed on *Scholem Aleijem*'s walls, a progressive Jewish high school where I teach literature and Spanish.

The concert's audience is diverse. The first to approach are some Rastafarians, the winners of a radio contest, and some older men who inquired at the box office what all this "Matisyahu" thing is about. Some men wear yarmulkes on their heads, and at least one orthodox woman stands out with her wig and long skirt.

Matisyahu appears to be approaching observant Judaism more calmly than in previous years. This is not uncommon in Chabad Lubavitch: many people begin their journey to become Orthodox Jews at full speed, only to hit the brakes in the middle of their journey.

Like many of his generation, the musician seems to take Judaism as a kind of market of spiritual goods where he buys the most convenient or satisfactory and discards the rest.

"Is it possible to feed on all the Hasidic tendencies while overcoming the differences that divide them?" I ask him.

"I don't believe there is much conflict between different Hasidic courts. I believe most Hasidic groups coexist, and then there's Chabad, you know?"

"You still live in Crown Heights, the world center of Chabad, though."

"Crown Heights is Chabad," he replies reluctantly. "But then there's Boro Park, another orthodox Brooklyn neighborhood, or Mea Shearim, in Israel. Hasidim from all over the world live together. Chabad is an entity unto itself. Because their understanding of Hasidism is not as religious in some ways as it is in other groups. They also have emissaries sent everywhere. That also distinguishes them from all other types of Jews. I don't believe there is any real tension between Chabad and other Hasidim as there might have been years ago. For example, when I'm not traveling, I go to Williamsburg to pray with the Satmer. They have no problem when I tell them I live in Crown Heights."

"How do you spend the Shabbat when you are not traveling?"

"When I'm at home, I go to the synagogue. I spend it with my kids."

"Which synagogue do you attend?"

"I live in Crown Heights. I can't travel during Shabbat."

"Then you attend 770, Chabad headquarters?"

"I don't attend 770. I usually go across the street. I go to 770 during the week for afternoon and evening prayers. Every night when I am at home, I walk there. When there are not too many people. I spend much time with the Chabad *shluchim* when I'm not at home. I've visited hundreds of Batei Chabad worldwide and continue to do so. One day, I am going to write a book about it."

Matisyahu's aesthetic shift in how he dresses and presents his albums coincided with a shift in his music. The messianic slogans became weaker, and the lines of songs extracted from sacred books dwindled until they became scarce in *Light*, his third album. Instead, his first record was so heavily influenced by the teachings he received at Chabad Lubavitch that it could be considered a continuation of prayers through other means. His second album, *Youth*, followed the same line, although lowering the ante a little. He still had a very pronounced passion, which now, in the album he came to Argentina to present, seems to have been softened a bit. The promotional photos already show him without black clothes, without "palpable" Orthodoxy, and with lyrics with a universalist innocence, making them appealing to a broader audience.

On stage, he will give a concert filled with energy and much more rock than the audience expected. Matisyahu is a talented artist and has something to offer.

But he's not the person he used to be, which shows in his words and performance.

"The slogan 'We want Messiah now!' appears prominently in your first album. Do you believe we are nearing the arrival of the Messiah?" I ask him.

"I'm not sure. I attempt to maintain the vision, hope, and dream in my mind and heart. Although it is not a realistic notion, I try to think about the possibility of his coming every day when I pray."

Most of the audience is over thirty-five years old, and they follow him with zeal, especially when he covers his eyes to sing the Shema Yisrael. Judging by how full the theatre is, it doesn't seem to matter to this crowd that the musician's relationship with Jewish Orthodoxy has changed. Those who came here to listen to reggae and may not be interested in Judaism also seem to enjoy the spectacle. The musician reflects: "Is it possible to draw a line between Judaism and the Rastafarian movement? Maybe. But that's not what interests me."

Matisyahu shakes his *payot*, the curls of hair that extend his sideburns that Orthodox Jews usually wear on stage. He makes them dance in the best style of *Twisted Sister* or any other hair metal band, those big-glam boys who made their long hair an extension of their body movements. He turns his songs back into rock music, cutting out as many messianic verses as possible.

"Hold on, Russian boy!" people in the stands shout now and then, and some boys unfurl a large Israeli flag in the upper stalls.

There don't seem to be many religious people in the crowd anymore. Rabbi Shlomo Kiesel is the only person who stands out. He is the same person who put together the book about his twenty years of work in the Belgrano neighborhood, which includes a photograph of the musician during his performance at Letterman's show. When I showed the musician the photo and told him where it came from, he looked at it with a crooked grimace and said: "Sure. You see? They put the photo from when I was still like them."

During the last song, a Jewish Orthodox boy appears on stage and begins dancing wildly, with the artist's approval. Then, a swarm of other boys also appear on stage, hugging and dancing in the Hasidic style, and the musician joins the crowd for a mosh pit on stage.

The recital ends after two hours with almost no interruptions.

Matisyahu looks like a reptile shedding its skin. He is still known by his old one, but he is trying to eliminate it without losing who he is and what he is about.

Politics and other public issues

Matisyahu is an example of Chabad Lubavitch's public relations: a young boy becomes baal teshuvah, studies for two years in Chabad's New York *yeshiva*, and then revolutionizes the image of Jewish Orthodoxy around the world. Chabad Lubavitch uses these situations to soften the congregation's image by demonstrating that its members are just regular people living ordinary lives, even though they must follow a set of rules and customs that most people do not.

But Matisyahu is not the only example of Chabad taking advantage of a public figure to show its openness to the secular Jewish world, even though his case is robust.

In truth, Chabad Lubavitch goes against the grain of other Orthodox Jewish currents in several aspects, which surpass this presumed insertion from the edges in the modern world.

Another good example is the relationship with the State of Israel. While many Hasidic groups are staunch opponents of Israel, believing that a Jewish state cannot be established in the Holy Land before the Messiah's return, Chabad takes a more cautious approach. While they do not recognize themselves as Zionists, they neither exercise an active and militant opposition like other groups.

In his book *A Threat from Within: A History of Jewish Opposition to Zionism*, Professor Yakov Rabkin deals with the various manifestations of Jewish opposition to Zionism, mentioning Chabad Lubavitch as a pillar of anti-Israeli thought. This characterization is taken from context, creating an inaccurate picture of Chabad's beliefs and practices today.

The Fifth Lubavitch Rebbe was indeed a staunch opponent of the State of Israel. Still, Rabkin overlooks the Seventh Rebbe, who maintained a similarly staunch defense of Israel's borders and launched his *tefillin* campaign, first implemented among Israeli soldiers stationed at the front during the Six-Day War.

This biased view of the place of the State of Israel within the cosmogony of Chabad Lubavitch is pointed out by Damian Setton:

"In the book *A Threat from Within: A History of Jewish Opposition to Zionism*, Yakov Rabkin proposes Chabad opposes the State of Israel." I say to him.

"Indeed, the Fifth Rebbe was against Zionism. He condemned Zionism. But it must be said that Rabkin's book is quite biased. He quotes what he wants and gives a wrong picture that Chabad is against Zionism. Obviously, Chabad adapted and changed. A Lubavitcher will never tell you it changed. He will say they always thought the same, but you must examine the context. I believe that Chabad changed. The previous Rebbe even founded the colony of Kfar Chabad in Israel."

"There were also Lubavitch settlers living there before the founding of the State of Israel," I add.

"Yes, but that is different. It can be said that there were settlements in Eretz Israel (The Land of Israel) long before the creation of the State and that it had nothing to do with the creation of a nation-state. In fact, when the Zionists arrived in Palestine, among their enemies were the Hasidim themselves, who had been living there since before and opposed the creation of the State. But remember that Jewish Orthodoxy was weakened after the Nazi Holocaust. It is not by chance that the previous Rebbe created Kfar Chabad in 1949. He created it after the founding of the State of Israel, not before. Once the State existed. And he created it in a context in which the ultra-Orthodoxy was already very discredited for not having removed the Jews from Europe, from Germany and Poland. What happened? After the Nazi Holocaust, the Zionists said: 'Did you see? If they had taken the Jews out of Europe to Palestine, what happened would not have happened.' Then another answer appeared, which is that of Satmer, who proposes the religious interpretation that the Holocaust is a divine punishment. Chabad disagrees with the interpretation that the Holocaust was a divine punishment. In terms of Zionism, I believe the shift is because of a general weakening of ultra-Orthodoxy in the face of what was the 'success of Zionism' in creating the State of Israel and the Orthodoxy that was accused of being indirectly responsible for the Holocaust. Chabad's current position is that occupied lands should not be returned because they are sacred."

According to Setton, the Sixth Rebbe encouraged settlement in Israel's newborn State by sending seventy-four Lubavitch families to establish the village of Kfar Chabad in the Lod Valley between Jerusalem and Tel Aviv in 1949. Time is spent on agriculture and Torah study in this Chabad model village.

In his doctoral dissertation, Setton also states: "However, this does not imply that the Lubavitchers consider themselves Israeli citizens, but that, as in other segments of the Jewish community, the destinies of Israel and the Jewish people are intertwined. Indeed, Israel's wars are not conceived as wars between Israelis and Arabs, but between the Jewish people and their enemies. Solidarity with this State is unquestionable, despite rejecting the possibility of a Jewish identity based on Israeli national belonging." (24)

Many Chabad rabbis study in Israel before completing their education at Chabad's New York *yeshiva*, a popular immigration destination for people from the Lubavitch community.

This is the chase of rabbi Shlomo Kiesel of Beit Chabad Belgrano. He claims that his stance on Israel represents that of Chabad: "There is no room for confusion. What the Chabad rebbes opposed was the idea of a Jewish State without a Torah ideology, without a spiritual presence. But they were never against Israel. On the contrary, they have always supported it. The current State of Israel is a Jewish state. Still, it is not managed, lacks laws, and does not conduct itself by what the Torah and religion command. This does not mean that we are against our own brothers. We try to assist and support them, particularly our soldiers who defend us and our borders. Israel is the Jewish people's homeland, and under that perspective, I would say that we are not Zionists but hyper-Zionists."

Lubavitch political positions on Israeli issues place them on the far right of the debate. They believe that neither Jews nor anyone else has the authority to divide or give away the land of Israel, which God has given to the Jewish people.

Using its pragmatic plasticity once more, Chabad Lubavitch as an institution is not opposed to the State of Israel, even if they disapprove it was built by secular human hands rather than the Messiah.

Alex and Clara Valansi are an Argentinean couple who have been living in Israel for over 25 years. When they first arrived in Israel, they went to live in a *kibbutz* before moving to the Mediterranean city of Haifa. They acknowledge Chabad's influence and ubiquitous presence everywhere: in universities, public spaces, and cities. Still, they also maintain that Israel is another location where they operate, not necessarily the primary one. Alex says: "This movement was born in the United States, so it is Disney and Chabad, Donald Duck and Moses. In the Diaspora, it has much more impact than in Israel. There is much more 'clientele' in other parts of the world. Just as Catholics go on mission, so do they."

As the parents of a son who served in the army and two daughters who will soon have to do the same, they know how Chabad works in tourist centers around the world, where young Israelis usually travel after finishing their conscription: "After three years in the army, many boys would take their backpacks and go to India to learn about Buddhism or to South America, where there is a lot of coca and a lot of drugs. Many of them got lost and never came back. They were looking to recover their spirituality because three or four years of military service is bullshit. So, on a spiritual level, these kids were 'grass for the sharks,' as they say in Yiddish. Chabad realized this and is now waiting for them. Everywhere you see Israelite backpackers worldwide, there is a Chabad institution. It's built like a well-oiled machine. They know exactly what to do. They provide shelter for the children while they are traveling. They provide them with a home and a hot meal and encourage them to remain faithful to Judaism and our traditions. They are powerful because these children are spiritually depleted, and they fill them up."

Regarding the political positioning of Chabad Lubavitch within Israel, Alex emphatically states what has been said: "They accept the State of Israel and are one hundred percent right-wing."

Chabad Magazine made the relationship between Lubavitch and Israel its cover theme for issue number 8 (November 1990), with the subtitle *Lubavitch in Israel: Then and Now*. The article was illustrated with an old photo of settlers and an aerial view of a large urban conglomerate and referred to the Chabad pioneers who went to settle the land of Israel sent by Shneur Zalman of Liady himself, the founder of the movement; in fact, Chabad's first Rebbe intended to settle himself in the Holy Land but had to return to lead his community in Lithuania. The article did not mention Israel's history in how it became a nation-state. Still, it mentioned the founding of Kfar Chabad. Also, it discussed Chabad Lubavitch's support and commitment to the Israeli armed forces. The article reads: "Chabad's activities in Israel have profoundly impacted the ranks of Israel's defense forces, soldiers, and their families. The victory of Israel in 1967 brought both joy and tragedy to hundreds of Israeli families and children whose parents gave their lives so that Israel could exist."

The Seventh Chabad Rebbe never set foot in the territory but founded a town in the name of Chabad, as the magazine describes: "1969. Nachalat Har Chabad, a Chabad town in Kiryat Malachi, is established on the Rebbe's orders. It was specifically designed to absorb the influx of Soviet Union immigrants. Soon after, schools, *yeshivot*, vocational schools, and other institutions were established, transforming it into another thriving center of Jewish life in Israel."

As an official account from Chabad Lubavitch in Argentina, the text clarifies the congregation's position on Israel-related issues. As it is then clear, Chabad understands that the State of Israel is where most Jews live and that, ultimately, it is the promised land, even though the Messiah has not yet arrived. That these Jews live there is already a sign of his impending arrival, and thus, the land must be defended.

Chabad Lubavitch does not intervene directly in local politics to impose its ideological agenda. While it is true that the institution has well-oiled relationships with people in positions of power, they rarely use institutional lobbying to push their agenda, but to get more donations and special favors.

Rabbi Daniel Levy, a Chabad emissary in the province of Tucumán, often refers to an anecdote that shows the institution's interest in making itself known among people in the highest spheres.

During the public celebrations of Argentina's Independence Day (July 9th) in Tucumán, during one of Carlos Menem's presidencies[1], Levy tried to approach him, who

---

1. The charismatic politician Carlos S. Menem (1930 - 2021) was Argentina's president from 1989-1994 and from 1995-1999. He was of Muslim faith but converted to Catholicism in his 40s.

was then accompanied by the presidents of Bolivia and Uruguay. When the rabbi arrived at the official stand, he introduced himself. He informed the former President he was a rabbi of Chabad Lubavitch, an institution the latter claimed he was unfamiliar with. Then, former Uruguayan President Luis Lacalle allegedly told Menem, "But how Carlos, you don't know Chabad?" and taking out his personal wallet, he showed he had a picture of the Rebbe and a dollar that he had given him.

The anecdote illustrates how they handle relations with power within Chabad Lubavitch.

An Argentine Chabad executive tells another anecdote illustrating how Chabad Lubavitch interacts with the powerful. One day, this person entered Tzvi Grunblatt's office and found the rabbi holding a phone conversation. Then, he was told by him in an alleged joke, "Wait a minute, I'm talking to George W. Bush." In reality, it was no laughing matter. Rabbi Grunblatt was really in direct contact with George W. Bush when he was still the President of the United States.

Lubavitchers manage powerful friendships and work to gain and maintain them. Still, they do not get directly involved in the political arena.

Rabbi Damian Karo comments on how political relations work within Chabad Lubavitch: "They hold a position of 'we have the Divine truth. Politicians' power is fleeting, whereas ours is eternal.' From a political language standpoint, this means, 'How long will these rulers of the day last? Four years? Eight years? Maybe twelve years? They're going to leave after that. We'll be here in five hundred years because we've been here since the beginning.' Understood at a pragmatic level, it means: 'We should not mess with these people too much, but we should not turn against them either. Everything they can give us that will help us is appreciated. That's all there is to it. They're up to something else. It is beneficial for them that the government donates a building in a high-priced area to build a Beit Chabad. That a government leader goes to light the *Chanukiah* is also good for them. They work for it, but not as hard as they do for other things."

Chabad Lubavitch takes advantage of the opportunities that high-level contacts can provide, where the benefit may not be solely economic but as favors and access to figures with greater power to spread their message.

Says Karo, "It's one thing to get a donor to put up a hundred thousand dollars and another thing for a guy to get you to pick up the phone and talk to the president."

Thus, Chabad Lubavitch politics is conducted as a chain of favors and is kept separate from daily political life.

Karo adds: "An important Jewish community leader once said that Chabad does 'high politics.' It does politics in ways that differ from how politics are usually done. That is what Chabad does: they take advantage of everything they can, giving nothing up."

"They are quite honest in a world of liars. As truthful as those convinced of a way of life can be. Chabad is more concerned with spiritual conquest than money and political power. They may manage fortunes but are not in it for the money. They have tons of money and manage it as a tool to achieve other things. They are more concerned about a hundred guys putting *tefillin* than receiving a hundred thousand dollars in donations. That, in my opinion, lends a lot of weight to their message. Because, in a deceitful and materialistic world like ours, where everyone wants your money, they are more concerned with the spiritual than the material."

Chapter Twelve

Masters of Repentance: The Baalei Teshuva

> "INSECURITY, VIOLENCE, DEPRESSION, DRUGS, ROB-
> BERIES, CHILD ABUSE, CHEATING, BETRAYAL, LYING, DIS-
> EASE, AND SO ON. THESE ARE THE RESULTS OF THIS SYS-
> TEM OF LIFE: WITHOUT TORAH, THERE IS NO SOLUTION."
> Abraham Leib, *baal teshuva,* Facebook status update

Rabbi on the road

I arrive at the gleaming Beit Midrash Moshe and Julia Saal at the Wolfsohn School at nine o'clock in the morning to interview Shlomo Kiesel.

Shmuel, his son, meets me nearby and leads me to the comfortably furnished room.

"Do you have a yarmulke?" the rabbi asks me, dressed in a tallit.

I say yes and look for one in my backpack, among the many I have accumulated during these months of daily contact with Chabad Lubavitch.

At a long table sits rabbi Shlomo, and his son signals me to sit beside him right where there is an empty chair.

For the first few moments, I feel strange, as if I am defiling the space where some boys in this room still have *tefillin* on their arms and heads.

The atmosphere here is relaxed; the air conditioning is just proper, and the sober and measured lights fit in with the cherry-colored wood of the furniture. The walls are decorated with acrylic boxes displaying ritual and traditional silver objects as if in a museum, all framed by a beautiful abstract mural covered in protective glass on the wall behind the *bimah*. There are some prayer books on the shelves in the background.

A complete breakfast is served on the table. On the other long table are some Hasidim praying; they seem not part of the same space.

"Have you had breakfast?" asks me Rabbi Shlomo.

"No."

"Here, help yourself," he tells me, bringing me a dish with scrambled eggs and sliced tomatoes, crackers, and eggplant. "Do you want coffee?"

He pours me a cup.

A conversation starts about whether or not to get an iPhone based on whether or not the battery can be replaced. Someone says it's built into the device, so if it breaks, you'll have to open the phone, voiding the warranty.

A little boy beside me calls Shlomo "daddy" and asks him for some tomatoes. At least three of the rabbi's nine children are in the Beit Midrash. There is Shmuel Kiesel, whom I have already met, the boy to my left, and another boy, a little older, in front of me. I believe he is also a rabbi's son because he previously asked if he was with the car to take him home later. Shlomo replied he was on the motorcycle.

Someone mentions Google's phone, and rabbi Shlomo replies that for him, Gmail is unbeatable. A big, burly, olive-skinned guy at the head of the table notes that there's nothing like Blackberry for handling e-mails. Kiesel Sr. complains about the sound the messages make as they come in. "It's a peep-peep, peep-peep, all day long! It drives me crazy!" he says, shaking his body with his arms pinned to it.

The rabbi grabs one copy of the book *Tanya* piled up on the table. He opens it and points to a chapter, and several people at our table do the same with the remaining copies. I also grab one copy of the First Lubavitch Rebbe's magnum opus.

The rabbi reads in Spanish with the prosody of a Hebrew chant.

"In other words, what is here beyond God? Nothing," explains a passage and continues reading chapter thirty-three. He reads one more paragraph. "What he is not saying here is a basic fundamental concept of Hasidism. What was *HaShem*'s intention in creating Earth? To have a residence in the lower worlds." The rabbi speeds up the reading, interrupts to add rhetorical inflection, and at one point asks a question, which he answers with a brief chant in Hebrew, which he then repeats in Spanish. "We believe in this unity when, in reality, we are so stupid that we do not realize that reality and what we see and feel is all a lie, all an illusion, it is fleeting, it is the *Matrix*," rabbi Shlomo says enthusiastically. "It is a good movie. Have you ever seen it? It even contains some messianic ideas."

"And who was Messiah in the movie?" someone asks.

"Neo."

"But if he didn't even wear *tzitzit*," says another one.

"It was because he was Sephardic. He had them inside his pants," answers a guy.

"Rent it."

"He was also dodging bullets."

Rabbi Shlomo mimes dodging bullets like in the movie.

"It was a good movie. And the second part was also good. What was the name of the important place in the movie? Zion."

"I watched it twice. The second time, I didn't understand it," says a guy.

"I heard the people who made it studied Kabbalah," the rabbi's son beside me says.

"Sure," exclaims Rabbi Shlomo. "I realized it right away. They discuss the *Matrix*, a dark world, a shell, a lie. Those who were on the outside had to enter the Matrix to do their work."

"The *Matrix* represents the Torah?" someone asks.

"On the contrary," says rabbi Shlomo, "The Matrix hides the truth. It is a lie. They knew where the truth was and that everything in The *Matrix* was dark and wrong. It's a terrific film. You must watch it."

The digression ends, and Shlomo resumes reading the *Tanya* for a few more minutes until the chapter ends. People get up from their seats as he looks up the times to light the Shabbat candles on his cell phone. We are left alone with him, his youngest son, and one of the Hasidim praying beside us.

"It looks like I got a free breakfast and a *Tanya* class," I tell him.

He smiles at me.

Shlomo Kiesel never knew he wanted to be a rabbi. He didn't even come from a Chabad Lubavitch family. His father, an exile from Nazi Germany, was one founder of the Tarbut school, one of Argentina's most well-known and prestigious secular Jewish schools.

Of his father, Shlomo recalls: "He was more concerned with school than with his family and his children, which at the time caused me to distance myself from Judaism. I moved away when I was fifteen or sixteen and didn't see him again until I was twenty-six. The Judaism I had known from the Tarbut, the Hacoaj sports club, had not satisfied me up to that point. They lacked in spirituality."

While Kiesel was not born into a religious or observant family, he acknowledges that his family kept certain traditions. Still, Shabbat dinners, like the holidays, were just excuses for family gatherings within his family. "We didn't keep kosher in my house. We didn't observe any holidays. We didn't say a prayer. There was no fasting on Yom Kippur," he explains.

As a teenager, his spiritual quest led him to travel the world in search of truth. He went through everything imaginable: Christianity, Buddhism, and Islam. Nothing satisfied him.

Those were years of political and social upheaval in Argentina and the world. "When I discovered the Torah, I was twenty-five years old. I remember what it was like to be a young man in the sixties and seventies. What it felt like. It was the flower power, hippie era, and I was among those young people. Fortunately, I got into it because many of my contemporaries in Argentina were involved in politics or the guerrilla, and many of them, as a result, are no longer with us. So God also helped me and showed me a lyrical, idealistic path of searching for love, peace, and truth, which helped me when I discovered the Torah."

His self-discovery process led him to psychoanalysis. He met a Jewish analyst who began lending him mystical books. He discovered the Kabbalah in one of them.

After exploring nearly every other religion, he began his journey into Judaism. He began by exploring Reform Judaism, but he was still dissatisfied. He didn't find his way until a friend invited him to a rabbi's class.

Shlomo Kiesel recalls: "That's where I met Chabad. The first person I met was the late engineer Abraham Polichenko. This was in 1980. Then I met Rabbi Tzvi Grunblatt, with whom I immediately had a strong connection. So much so that I was already putting on *tefillin* the day after I met him. It was fast. It was 1980, 1981. Argentina was going through one of its great crises. As I already had spiritual practices, it was easy for me to adapt to Jewish spiritual practices. I had knowledge of Hebrew because of my studies and because I had been in Israel. I immediately started practicing Judaism. I liked it a lot, and the following year, I traveled to the United States, where I met the Rebbe. He gave me a private audience and instructed me on what I needed to study and what I needed to take care of."

According to the rabbi's story, he met Ana María there. He persuaded her to convert to Judaism and then marry him. The couple moved to Los Angeles, where Shlomo attended Rabbi Chaim Zev Citron's adult *yeshiva*. The couple stayed for three weeks before returning to Argentina. Shlomo devoted himself to Torah study (as the Rebbe had advised him in his private audience) at the Buenos Aires *yeshiva*. They married in 1981 at the Tarbut school his father had founded years before.

Kiesel became interested in becoming a rabbi around this time. He'd been without an Orthodox Jewish education for twenty-five years, so deciding would take a lot of work. The young family returned to Los Angeles, where Shlomo studied for two years until they received the Rebbe's blessing to continue his studies in Safed, Israel.

"I received rabbinical ordination and then returned to Argentina to work," says Kiesel. After he was ordained, Rabbi Grunblatt sent for him to ask him if he was interested in becoming a Rebbe's emissary in Argentina. "That was in 1985. From 1985 to 1987, I worked with Rabbi Grunblatt in what was Chabad Central, organizing activities. Then I was in charge of organizing the first Chanukah public festival in the country," he says.

Shlomo worked alongside Rabbi Grunblatt in Chabad Argentina's headquarters for two years until 1987, when he opened his own Beit Chabad Belgrano. It was the second Beit Chabad to be opened in Buenos Aires City after the Beit Chabad Villa Crespo. Shlomo Kiesel considers this change fundamental for him and his family: "We continued working there until 2004 when the whole Wolfsohn School began."

The school occupies a fundamental place in Kiesel's work in the neighborhood. "We're happy about the school, but now I'm not as involved in its daily running because I want to put my efforts back where they were before, at the Beit Chabad."

He wants me to come with him to see his Beit Chabad.

"Where do you live?"

"Near the botanical gardens. Is your Beit Chabad too far from here?"

"About ten blocks."

"Well, then, I am going to take a cab."

The rabbi's youngest son, who was waiting for a ride on the motorcycle, says he is walking.

We get outside, and he shows me a BMW motorcycle. He puts on a black cap that makes him look like a train driver and tells me, "Up, hold on to me."

I put the yarmulke back in my pocket and climb onto his motorcycle, wrapping my hands around his waist, and we ride away.

The wind hits us in the face.

"How nice it is to ride a motorcycle today, huh?" he says.

I tell him about my experience working at the Argentinian Hebrew Society's library.

"Is it the one on Sarmiento Street?"

"Are you aware?"

"The location, not the library."

"It's a lovely spot. However, it's missing some Jewish books," I tell him.

"Ah, but do you take donations?"

"Books are purchased every two months on a tight budget and tailored to the tastes of a secular Jewish audience."

"Novels?"

"Yes, mostly novels."

"Jewish novels?"

"No, not necessarily."

"So, it's not a Jewish library, after all!"

We take Congreso Street and cross Cabildo Avenue; we do one more block and turn right until the next intersection, where the traffic light catches us.

Another motorcycle is next to us. The guy keeps looking at us and makes me nervous.

"Hey, nice beard you have!" exclaims the biker, pointing beneath his chin with a finger gun. Rabbi Shlomo has a bushy white beard that extends past the middle of his chest.

"Do you like it?"

The light changes, and the motorcyclist goes the other way; we keep going straight ahead.

"This guy must think I'm a ZZ Top instead of a rabbi."

I do not know what he's saying. I won't find out until later that ZZ Top is a blues band whose members are known for their long beards. When I look at their pictures on the Internet, I can see that the rabbi looks a lot like Dusty Hill, the bass player for the bearded bluesmen.

Rabbi Shlomo tells me there are different ways of being in Chabad and that some people are more fundamentalist than others, as in any congregation. He belongs to one of the movement's less fanatical sectors, which causes him some problems. I think he does not always conform to what some people expect of him.

"Being a Lubavitcher for me is not about wearing a uniform," he tells me. "It is a way of life. It allows for individuality."

We ride the motorcycle to the front of a typical Belgrano house, park it on the sidewalk, and get off.

"I never thought that an Orthodox rabbi would take me on a motorcycle through the streets of Belgrano," I tell him.

"I'm sorry I broke your stereotype. We all have prejudices, though. And what is prejudice?" He says this while showing me the way in. "It is a 'pre' judgment. When the person sees it clearly, he gets over it. Every person must face and overcome prejudices. Once someone has passed that test, they can decide. Maybe someone will say, 'They are not so strange here,' or 'they are strange here,' right? People say today that 'Chabad is like Coca-Cola; wherever there are Jews, there is Chabad,' but why is Chabad in so many places? It is so that any Jew can find light and guidance, no matter where they are. Because we all must find our own way and figure out how to deal with this, our identity."

As we walk by, the rabbi instructs a worker to fix the floor and walls. It's a big place with a garden in front with games for kids and another garden in the back. He shows me a small library with prayer books in the living room.

"You told me before that some sectors of Conservative Judaism were 'jealous' of Chabad. To what do you attribute this?"

"What happened was that in the 1960s, the Conservative Jewish movement was powerful," explains the rabbi. "There was no Chabad or open Orthodox presence for people to approach. As a result, all the Jews who had been marginalized discovered in the Conservative movement a way to get closer to religion with few obligations. Conservatism does not impose obligations on you; it does not compel you to comply. It doesn't make you feel like, 'Well, you're at fault if you don't comply.' After forty or fifty years, they now recognize they are in decline and need to move more to the right and become more religious to keep their support base. They realized that being so secular and so light did not serve them. They regard Chabad as fierce rivalry because they recognize modern Orthodoxy has presented them with a match. Because Chabad has so much more to offer. They are naturally jealous now that they are aware of this."

"Jewish Orthodoxy is right-wing?"

"Of course, I believe that Orthodoxy, particularly religious Orthodoxy, leans to the right. Regarding Zionist ideas or Israel, Chabad is always much closer to right-wing ideas than left-wing ideas. Left-wing ideas assert that 'we are all the same; we are not to make distinctions between people,' whereas right-wing ideas acknowledge distinctions. Right-wing ideas support nationalism, Jewish pride, and Israeli pride. For me, 'right-wing' is not a derogatory term. In fact, the Kabbalah considers *chesed*, on the right of the Sefirot tree, to have the attribute of kindness, while on the left is judgment and severity. I prefer to be kind rather than severe. I also believe Chabad leans more ideologically to the right than to the left."

He shows me the books on his bookshelf and then says goodbye. He tells me I should come around here on a Saturday at half past ten in the morning. He says I'll see how nice it is and have a good time.

"Thanks for inviting me, and I'd like to use this chance to ask you one more thing. You've been on both sides, secular and Orthodox. Is there something you miss about secular life that you can't do because you're Orthodox?"

"I understand that neither side of the world is perfect," he says. "Even if they are not religious, some people are sincere and righteous. In the religious world, many people are dishonest and lack the human aspect of being a person. After over thirty years of living here, I can tell you it is good and bad on both sides."

From Marine Corps to Chabad

The house where *Leoded*, the social assistance center run by Rabbi Moshe Blumenfeld is not a modern building, and one can hardly distinguish that it is a center of Jewish life because, embedded in the wall and emerging from the brick, not superimposed on it, there is a *mezuzah*.

On the corner across the street, Tercera Fundación [Third Foundation], a used bookstore that smells like old books, has the *Diaries* of Joseph Goebbels and a first-person account of the Holocaust on display.

Rabbi Blumenfeld opens the door and welcomes me inside. He then takes me on a brief tour of the center in a typical Buenos Aires townhouse.

The office is a bit dark, an effect heightened by the gray paint on the walls. On one side are several phone lines and a laptop that the rabbi constantly checks, tapping a key when the screen saver comes up after a while.

Blumenfeld is a friendly and good-natured man, and, like so many others, he was not born into the Chabad Lubavitch community nor raised in a religious family environment.

"I was an Atlanta fan[1]," he says, "I used to eat pizza at Imperio[2]. Until I was twenty-one, I didn't have a clue. I didn't know anything about religion. But I was already searching. I felt like I owed myself to learn more about Judaism. When I was with my Jewish friends, seeing that they knew and did things I didn't understand bothered me a lot. When I was seventeen or eighteen, I would attend a synagogue with friends, and I wouldn't know how to take the book. I felt very much on the outside. I always had a great desire to study and learn."

He recognizes that there was a strange process from that boy from Villa Crespo whose Judaism comprised cheering for the Atlanta soccer club and eating *pletlzach*, who indulged himself in the neighborhood's most famous pizza corners, to the current Orthodox rabbi.

He is nearly forty years old and belongs to one of the last generations forced to comply with Argentina's conscription, which was abolished in 1994. He was assigned to the Marine Corps in the South of the country: "I found myself in a new scheme of things for the first time in my life. My head suddenly opened up. I began to ask myself questions such as 'Where am I?' and 'What am I doing here?' Being forced to work and survive at minus twelve degrees Celsius changed me. My spirit of survival led me to ask myself how to get out of there," says this man, who decades after the events he describes can be seen in the videos he films and uploads to his blog *Viene Mashíaj* () [Mashiach is Coming.] In those videos, among other things, one can see how he combats the cold in traditional Russian Chabad fashion by drinking vodka.

Back in his days of being conscripted, Blumenfeld started looking for a way out of the Marine Corps. He hit the jackpot when he noticed a legal loophole that would take him out of the freezing temperatures and the forced labor: "I started doing some research, and I came to realize that one way to escape was to become a Catholic seminarist. I sent my parents a letter asking them: 'Where can I study to become a rabbi, so I can leave? I can't stand Puerto Belgrano any longer. Here, temperatures are below zero. They won't let us sleep. They torture us all day long. They keep making us do friction jumping, running, body to the ground...' When I sent that letter, I had already lost thirty-three pounds. I was a skeleton with muscles. We were all little Rambos. The Marines were tough."

---

1. A very well-known soccer team based in the Buenos Aires City neighborhood of Villa Crespo. His fanbase is mostly composed of secular Jews.

2. An historical popular pizza joint in the Villa Crespo neighborhood of Buenos Aires.

According to the rabbi, in these extreme situations, one remembers God: "When I was a kid, I remembered God when I wanted to score a goal in a game of soccer. That was all. When I was getting close to the other team's goal, I would ask him to let the ball in. But when I found myself in the Marine Corps, I connected even more to God; surprise, things happened every time I connected. I had incredible little personal miracles. For example, when my colleagues and I made a mess, I always got away with it."

He took advantage of a visit to his family that he was allowed in his Villa Crespo neighborhood, and it was there that he met Rabbi Birman's Beit Chabad. He approached him and said: "Look, I want to leave the military service. I want to become a rabbi." Rabbi Birman welcomed him and invited him to his Beit Chabad study sessions. It was 1989, and Chabad was slowly expanding in Argentina.

That first contact with the Lubavitch did not convince him: "When I first went to study with them, I noticed all their beards, strange body movements, strange sounds, and hats. It was my first encounter with something like that... I was astounded by what I heard, read, and saw. It wasn't just the time for me, I told myself. Then, I asked myself, 'What's worse? I have just fifteen months left before my discharge from the Marine. But if I stay here, I'll be stuck for the rest of my life.' I convinced myself that I'd rather stay a soldier. After fifteen months, I would be let go and be free forever."

Blumenfeld then returned to the Marine Corps and finished his service. However, he had grown a little enamored with what he had seen during those four weeks when he submerged himself in Chabad Hasidism.

When the remaining fifteen months of his conscription were up, he debated whether to pursue a career in sports journalism or economics or devote himself entirely to that religious life he had briefly glimpsed that piqued his interest. He started small, like many. He began by attending a friend's Shabbat dinner party; then he began to attend the synagogue a few days a week to pray; then he attended Judaic classes; and finally, he discovered he was no longer interested in continuing his college education. "I found answers to every question I had, from the meaning of life to the meaning of being Jewish. I started studying, and I didn't stop. I started from scratch, from nothing, because I wasn't even circumcised, nor did I know a letter of Hebrew. I started reading like a child, one syllable at a time, and in about a year, I could start translating some basic text. Then, it came a moment when I decided, 'Well, I'm going to continue my studies in Israel.' And that I did."

Blumenfeld traveled in 1992. He first went to New York, where he met the Rebbe, and then to Safed in Israel, which, as we have seen, is a place of choice for Lubavitchers to complete their religious education. There, he says, he began his journey to becoming, little by little, a Lubavitch Hassid. His eyes light up when he talks about the Rebbe. He says that he has the stature of a Moses of our times. He recalls that the time he met him was exceptional in the Lubavitch community: "At the time, the Rebbe had already had his first stroke, and he rarely went out. He'd first appear through a small window before being given a small balcony from which to address the public. During his final years, the subject of the Mashiach became a hot topic in the community. Every Chabad rabbi, every Chabad emissary, had to work very hard to prepare the world for his arrival. Those were intense years."

Shortly after his experience in Israel, Blumenfeld returned to Buenos Aires and married a woman who was already in Chabad and came from a religiously observant family.

His behavior and beliefs changed his secular parents: "They didn't have a Jewish upbringing. They weren't observant. At first, when they saw the change, they said, 'My son is going to become an altar boy, a priest. What is he going to do?' All the prejudices. There was a time when, for psychiatry, professing faith was considered a psychiatric disorder, a pathology. Then, my family connected. They began attending the synagogue, going to some festivities, or coming to eat at my house. They lost their prejudices."

Blumenfeld and his wife have eight children, five boys and three girls, who attend Chabad schools separated by gender. They are well aware of their father's search for God while serving in the Marine Corps, looking for ways to escape from the draft.

He tells me about his children: "I teach them we are all equal, that they can talk to others, that they have a lot to offer, that they can connect them, and that they can also learn a lot from others."

The rabbi tells me he has commitments to attend to, so I thank him for his time while he escorts me out. The secretary of the *Leoded* center, who was walking around and setting up offices while the rabbi and I were talking, tries and fails to open the exit door. It's gotten stuck.

Blumenfeld and his secretary take turns trying to open the lock several times, but they can't do it. We get a little nervous: I have to get to work at the library, and the secretary also needs to go out to do some errands.

The rabbi shrugs:

"The only option I see is for you to jump out of the window," he says, "because the locksmith will take at least an hour to arrive."

He opens the blinds, and the secretary steps out onto the balcony.

"Climb up on the railing, sit there, and jump. It's not very high. I did it like that the other day," says Blumenfeld to his secretary, who looks at us terrified.

The rabbi hands her a plastic chair to get on the rail more easily.

While the secretary leaves the room, the rabbi offers to put me on *tefillin* and show me the small temple. He takes me to the back of the townhouse, passing his office through the courtyard that connects the different rooms.

He turns on the lights in a large room with prayer books on shelves, a *bimah*, and the holy ark containing a Sefer Torah written with *Leoded* patients' help. When he tells me the story about it, he says: "I am confident that one of your ancestors was precisely a *soifer*, a Torah scribe."

He puts the *tefillin* on me and asks me to recite the prayer. I repeat the phonetics, and he shows me what I have just said in a book when I finish. When we finish, we go back to the entrance. Nothing has changed there, and the door is still locked, with the secretary on the balcony wondering what to do.

If this situation continues, I will get late for my day job, so I have no option but to jump from the window.

From the sidewalk, a lady who has just arrived at the center's door offers to hold my backpack while I try to put my legs over the railing to sit on it and then drop to the ground.

I've never been an agile guy. The combination of shoes and the heat of the sun on the black shirt I'm wearing makes the situation worse, so when I fall to the sidewalk, I stumble a few steps and drop the yarmulke, which I rush to grab and put back on, as if not wearing it would offend the rabbi.

"You see?" Rabbi Blumenfeld says to me from the balcony, "Chabad is always an adventure."

Sergio fights the Silent Holocaust

The Lubavitch says that for a Jew, there is nothing better than another Jew. They say that no matter how much a member of the people of Israel assimilates, becomes secular, or becomes an atheist, there will always be something in his soul that wants to get out, which will lead him on the right path of the Torah.

They explain *teshuva* as a natural process: a Jew has a spiritual inclination to everything that makes up Jewish life, even if he is unaware of it. For them, if a secular Jew spends an Orthodox Shabbat, starts eating kosher foods, and studies Torah, he will soon feel at home because that is his true essence, and will want to incorporate more and more Jewish life every day until he becomes fully observant of the precepts.

Sergio's small grocery store is the only place in the neighborhood that sells *farfalej*, a type of Ashkenazi egg noodles the size of a grain of rice so delicious that it will undoubtedly awaken the soul of any Jew.

Like any other *baal teshuva*, he was not born into a religious Jewish family. He clarifies, however, that his upbringing was somewhat Jewish traditionalist because he is Sephardic from his mother's side. He remembers how he used to attend his maternal grandfather's house for Yom Kippur. They attended a small synagogue with him that only opened for the holidays.

At thirteen, he had his *bar mitzvah*. This experience deeply impacted him: "I did it with some very nice people, very good people. Then, I told my mother that I wanted to become a rabbi. Then my mother told me: 'Come on! You? A rabbi? No way.'"

After that, although he continued to wear tefillin every day until he was eighteen, he did not continue his Jewish education or feel any interest in his heritage.

"I always felt some interest in everything Jewish. I feel Zionist, on the one hand, and I have always liked everything about Israel. I kept myself informed about things going on over there. However, during my youth years, I dated many girls who were not Jewish. Nonetheless, my primary goal remained to meet a Jewish person. I had a crush on goyim girls, but I knew it wasn't for me. I believe intermarrying Jews is the only way for the Jewish people to survive." Sergio refers to what some call the "Silent Holocaust," the idea that if interfaith marriages continue to proliferate, Judaism may become extinct.

It is hard for me to believe that this forty-four-year-old man, who wears a white shirt, black pants, *tzitzit*, and a cheerfully grown beard, used to play rugby some twenty years ago. On the other hand, his physical build appears to be consistent with his past, and he clarifies that he no longer plays because the matches are always on Shabbat.

Growing up as a Jew in the rugby world wasn't easy, and he had to deal with some antisemitic incidents: "I experienced more problems when I didn't wear a yarmulke than since I started wearing one. I was ten years old when I started playing rugby. I played in a club near my house called Curupaití. I remember that a boy, to insult me, said to me from up a tree: 'Hey, Jew.' And I told him: 'Yes, yes, I am a Jew, come on down, and I will show you.' From that moment on, everybody knew I was Jewish. I didn't make any friends playing rugby at that club."

He went to college after high school and got a degree as an agricultural engineer. There, he met another Jewish boy from his neighborhood. They got together to go to parties in nightclubs that were put on by the local Jewish community.

When he was about to finish his degree, he went to Israel for a six-month work-study program.

Upon his return, he met his friend from college and his friend's sister again. They fell in love and married in 1998 in a Reform Jewish synagogue because Sergio really liked the ceremonial singer, *hazzan*, that performed there.

Around that time, one of his sisters, the closest to him, divorced.

"I have two sisters; one is two years younger, and another is nine years younger than me."

"My youngest sister never experienced any form of Judaism. She didn't attend a Jewish school because there was none, and she didn't live through my grandparents' time because she was young. So, her fate was to become secular. My other sister married a Jew. They did badly and got divorced. She lived in Israel for a while, became a *madrich*, and still attends a Jewish sports and social club. She attended the Maccabean games as a representative of that club. There, she hooked up with the only guy who wasn't Jewish out of the four hundred in attendance."

At that moment, Sergio felt his sister was profaning something very sacred and intimate that perhaps he had not thought about until that moment: "I told her, 'Do what you want with your life. It's your problem. But what example are you giving to your daughters? Because she has two girls, who are now grown up. She said, 'I want my daughters to be happy. We already suffered a lot.' This was because my parents passed away when we were relatively young. My dad passed away when I was fourteen, and she was twelve. My mom passed when I was twenty-four, and she was twenty-two."

It was January 1998 when his sister started her relationship with the non-Jew man. In February 1998, Sergio was in the Hebrew Society locker room, talking with a friend, when he overheard others discussing a meeting in a house with a rabbi. He started a conversation with them, and they invited him to take part in the meeting. He persuaded his wife to accompany him and found exactly what he needed there.

There were several couples and the rabbi. Sergio remembers the occasion: "I felt it as an antibody against what was happening with my sister. The more my sister got involved with that goy guy, the more I observed Jewish practices. Out of anger, to make her angry. What's more, I started using *tzitzit* right away. I would go driving with *tzitzit*, wearing a yarmulke on Saturdays. Or I would go to play rugby wearing *tzitzit*. Then, I studied a little more because I expected my daughter to ask me about Judaism one day. I wanted to be prepared to answer her."

That first meeting in the house of a rugby teammate was with Rabbi Osher Schvertz from Beit Chabad Almagro. That meeting led to several others, some in his own house. In April of the following year, with his wife nearly nine months pregnant, they took another step toward observance by rectifying and homologating the Jewish marriage contract they had made in the Reform temple.

When his daughter was born, Sergio felt as if he had been reborn as well. "The moment you see your child changes your head completely," he says. "I always thought about what I would provide to my children. The Torah says: 'You shall love your neighbor as yourself.' On the other hand, there is what you see on TV nowadays: superficial and sleazy. I don't criticize it. Everyone knows what he wants, but I don't want that for my children or me. Although I miss going to play rugby and meeting the guys after the game, when you choose, you always leave something behind."

Sergio was one step ahead of his wife in his *teshuva* process. "I did not force her. It happened little by little," says Sergio. "For example, I was already wearing a yarmulke but didn't ask her to do anything. She wore pants and didn't cover her hair, but I didn't say anything about it. She also put up some resistance. When I was just starting out, she sometimes came in while I prayed and closed my book. It is hard for people to change their lifestyles. People have a lot of rules, whether or not they believe in God."

Sergio's lifestyle changes affected his family, especially his sister. "I wanted to invite my sister home with my niece for Rosh Hashanah so they could experience it. I told her: 'I ask you a favor, since you are coming home, don't come with pants, come with a skirt.' And she answered me: 'But I don't have a skirt!' I asked her: What do you mean you don't have a skirt? When you go to a party, what do you wear?' She wasn't convinced, and so I told her: 'Listen to me, if you go to a Chinese or a Japanese person's house, and they ask you to take off your shoes, you will take off your shoes because you are respecting the house you are going to, right?' In the end, she did not show up. 'Who is being reactionary, then?' I asked her. 'Is it you or me?'"

Sergio sees Judaism as a heritage that must be preserved. He understands that there will be a struggle to defend it. And, while he discovered that siding with Chabad Lubavitch was the best way for him to engage in that struggle, he understands that someone else may prefer to try siding with other congregations: "Each one has to have his own criteria. What I say is: within the Jewish law, everything. Outside the Jewish law, nothing. I know what I want for my family, and I will look elsewhere if I don't like how things are where I am. But always inside Judaism, never outside."

Sergio and his wife have five children. They send them to Chabad schools, but they also want them to go to schools recognized by the government so that they can choose their own path when they grow up. They know that not everyone in Chabad must become a rabbi or move to Israel, and they want to give them the freedom to decide what they want to do with their lives.

For eleven years, Sergio worked in Buenos Aires public market. When he began his *teshuva* process, he still had to work on Fridays until late at night. But then he began his journey to become religiously observant, and having to work on Fridays became an automatic no-go for him: "My ex-boss is Jewish as well, but he doesn't fulfill the *mitzvot* and is a total atheist. 'What, you used to work until nine o'clock at night, and now you leave at four or five o'clock in the afternoon?' he used to say to me. So, I'd respond, 'How long have I been working with you?' It had been seven or eight years. 'If you trust me enough to delegate money to me, believe me when I say there is no more work to do at five o'clock in the afternoon.' He had to let me work until five because he realized I was right."

In 2002, Sergio grew tired of Argentina's periodic crises. He convinced his wife, despite her resistance, to move to the countryside in Israel. The experience was to last two years. If they did not adapt, they would return.

The family made the journey and lived in a kind of kibbutz, where he worked as a farm laborer, and his wife stayed home and cared for the children.

It did not work out. They returned when the two-year term they had set for themselves was over. Sergio looked for work and had a few interviews until a friend from the synagogue he attended told him he was starting a business to distribute kosher ice cream and asked him to partner with him. He set up a small distributor and soon added sausages and hamburgers to the kosher ice cream distribution. Then, the owner of one of the grocery stores where he distributed offered him half of his business. Sergio agreed, and the two became business partners. Finally, in 2009, Sergio purchased the other half of the business.

Sergio has no regrets about converting from a secular lifestyle to Orthodoxy. He defends his decision: "I am convinced of what I chose, even though I know it differs from what I used to do. This is what *HaShem* asks of us, the *Yehudim*. And it is simple. If you go to a doctor and look at the wall and don't see any diploma, you ask: 'Excuse me, are you a doctor?' If he answers: 'No, but my grandfather was a doctor, and my father was a doctor, and I feel very much like a doctor,' you would turn around and leave. To put it another way, it's nice to feel Jewish, but to be one, you must practice Judaism. You can be a fantastic guitarist, but you'll forget how if you don't practice. Your fingertips will become numb. Let me use a tree as an example to show you this. When you cut off a tree's branches, the tree eventually dries up. The same thing occurs in Judaism. Okay, some parts survive, but more twigs are being cut off than blossoming twigs."

Chapter Thirteen

The Rabbi Who Didn't Believe in God

> "I was born outside. I entered the Platonic cavern and said: 'This is the world.' Until one day I said to myself: 'Wait a minute, I remember that there was something else up there.'"
>
> Rabbi Damián Karo

The first time I met Damián Karo, he was holding a book by the French philosopher Michel Onfray under his arm. I was reading *Despite All Odds* by Edward Hoffman, a classic book on the history of Chabad Lubavitch.

Damián had come to the Hebrew Society library, where I worked, to give a Kabbalah lecture, and we were formally introduced. We shook hands, and when he saw the book cover I was reading, which featured a picture of the Lubavitch Rebbe, he said to me, "I know that man," and smiled.

I told him that the book was mine, not the library's. "Well, that's up to you," he said.

Karo is 38 years old and was a Chabad Lubavitch Hasid for nearly twenty years, from fourteen to thirty-four.

He stands just over six feet tall, has short hair and a shaved beard, and alternates between a modern hat that has nothing to do with the one he wore as a Chabad Hasid and a simple yarmulke. Although he quietly admits that if he still wears something to cover his head, it is only out of a contractual obligation with the synagogue where he now works.

He grew up in the heart of Chabad Lubavitch, was educated in its *yeshiva*, slept in their youth boarding school rooms, and knows the institution like a long lifelong friend: in its good and bad.

Now, working at the Jewish Conservative congregation of Paso Street, he says, "I am the rabbi of Paso. When I left Chabad, I went to work in the Judaica office at the Libertad [Liberty] Street Temple. So, I say it is like this: 'I left Chabad, went to Liberty Temple, and now I'm the rabbi of Paso[1].' Is that clear?"

Karo is fond of puns. This is his way of saying the certainties he once held as a Chabad rabbi are no more. He conceives Judaism as something different: "Just as in Chabad I held certain practices despite no longer agreeing with them until I could free myself, the same thing is happening to me now. I freed myself from the 'house,' now I'm 'in the neighborhood,' but I want to get to the 'city.' I always want it to be bigger. I wouldn't mind continuing to be a rabbi or a teacher if I could tailor it to my feelings. For example, some movements advocate for Judaism without God as a starting point in the United States. They still leave the door open to the possibility of a belief in God. Still, they are focused on what each individual believes. It is an extremely open and liberal Judaism. It's referred to as 'post-Judaism.'"

His practices as a Jew have been liberalized, and now, he does not see them as an end in themselves, so he does not force himself to respect them either. It seems incredible coming from an individual who lived more than half his life complying with the rigid rules of Orthodox Judaism: "The practices, for me, are symbols. Of course, they mean something, but they are a matter of identity. They are neither good nor bad in themselves. And I don't need them. For example, I like candles and keep many symbols, teachings, and examples. Do I light the candles on Shabbat? No, not always. But instead of a table lamp, I have a candle on my bedside table. So, when I go to bed, I stay in the candle's light, which is a different light. Is it necessary for me to rest on Shabbat? No. But I've learned from my daily search for Shabbat to make time for myself, spend time with my family and friends, sleep, read, meditate, connect with other things, and go for a walk whenever possible. I focus on what the *mitzvot* represent rather than the symbols themselves."

---

1. Karo makes a pun that is difficult to translate into English. "Paso" can be translated as "in transit." Karo is then saying something like that he was immersed in Chabad, then was freed when he started working on a synagogue on Liberty Street and now is just a rabbi in transit, meaning that he is a rabbi for now but that he may not be for much longer.

Despite everything, he clarifies he has nothing against Chabad Lubavitch as an institution; that he did not leave at odds with anyone, and that he still has friends inside the congregation. However, he also regrets losing relationships with many people he respects and loves that are still inside Chabad. He also recognizes that he still practices many behaviors that characterized his time as a Chabadnik years after he left.

"In fact, I find myself today analyzing myself and choosing some behaviors or ways of looking at life as very Chabad. I feel like the way I connect to my body, and my clothes are still very Chabad. It's a spiritual exercise that never ends; each person does it from and to wherever he or she can or wants. There are so many parts that you can't cover them all. You have to pick and choose," he says.

His story is not that of a Jew who embraced Orthodoxy and left Chabad Lubavitch to opt for another of the hundreds of more Orthodox offerings. That would be a rather typical story. Karo's path is unique because he started out as a secular Jew. He became interested in the ideas of Chabad Lubavitch and slowly joined until he was one of them. He became well respected in the congregation and climbed Chabad's corporate ladder. Once he was at the top and had gotten the woman who would become his wife, father, younger sisters, and five children to join Chabad, he left the congregation to look into a completely different form of Judaism. He became a *hazara b'she'ela*, an appellative that means "the one who returns to the questions." That is the person who has abandoned the answers provided by dogmatic faith.

His account of his *baal teshuva* period is like that of many others who were dazzled by a form of Judaism radically different from the one they previously knew. "I was born into a 'traditionalist' home. Not religious, far from it, but traditional. On Pesach and Rosh Hashana, we would get together for dinner. On Yom Kippur, my grandfather would attend the synagogue. Still, he was not religious," says Karo, and he recalls that when he was eleven, he began to experience many existential questions, which led him to open up, and to listen to anyone who could answer.

He attended traditional Jewish schools in Buenos Aires in his early years. He attended both a Hebrew school and an official public school for his high school years.

The Hebrew school was enjoyable for him, but it did not yet appear to him as a source of spiritual fulfillment.

On Saturdays, he started attending a Zionist club until after his *bar mitzvah* when a friend began studying with a large, right-wing conservative neo-Orthodox Jewish study group with many high school and college-age followers. "It was a small group, very cool.

They proposed a very serious study of Judaism and a lot of practices. That's where I started, to get to know, learn and study and to develop certain practices: *tzitzit*, yarmulke, kosher, Shabbat," says Karo.

He dropped out of public high school at age fifteen but stayed in Hebrew school. He then started attending Chabad's *yeshiva*. Despite this, he did not see a relationship between his existential search and his Jewish studies. He knew that studying Judaism gave him pleasure, so he simply attended to learn more about it.

"I studied *Mishnah* there, which is like the central part of the Talmud until the *yeshiva*'s director told me: 'I want you to study something for fifteen days. He paired me up with a twenty-something Canadian boy who only spoke English. I only spoke Spanish. We both knew a few words in Hebrew. His was more formal, while mine was more colloquial. The books were written in Hebrew. It was hard for us to talk to each other. However, we sat down and studied. We studied Jewish mysticism, Hasidic philosophy, and Kabbalah. It blew my mind. Then I said to myself, 'This is it. My existential questions are over here, and I'm going this way.' That's when everything fell into place. The search for existential truths mixed with the pleasure of finding oneself, and I was hooked. I began attending the *yeshiva* every day. I had not yet reached Western philosophy in my search. They did not teach it to me at school. I wonder where I would be now if I had known about Western philosophy earlier because it was Philosophy what really interested me. I don't know what I would have done with my life, but I probably would have earned a Philosophy degree or something similar. From then on, I got increasingly involved with Chabad until, a few months later, I moved into the Chabad boarding school. I left aside absolutely everything I had at that moment. I dedicated myself to study."

And so, Damián Karo gradually became Yitzchak Karo, the way he was known within Chabad Lubavitch, following the custom of being called by the Hebrew name given to men after their circumcision.

He spent six years at the Chabad's boarding school for boys. In his twenties, he went looking after an old Hebrew high school classmate. "I looked for her and said, 'This is for you.' She came over with me, studied, and I was not mistaken: it was for her. We got married soon after."

His path already had a rebellious tinge: he imposed his own ways on a tradition that said Chabad Hasidim in Argentina should marry no younger than twenty-four years old and only through arranged marriages.

He started working with his father, making clothes, and stopped studying. He did not last long in that, and soon, they started a daycare center with his wife in their home. That did not last long, either. He went to work as a *mashgiach*, in charge of supervising the compliance with kosher rules of meals and food products.

As *kashrut* supervisor, he was almost self-employed, working wherever he was needed: butcheries, bakeries, and fisheries in Uruguay.

His most stable job then was supervising bakeries, pizza places, confectioneries, and food stores. He wasn't entirely happy with that job, so when the opportunity to travel to Barranquilla, Colombia, as a Rebbe emissary presented itself, he jumped at it.

"A friend of mine had been in Bogotá, and in Barranquilla. They had agreed with the school and the local community to bring a Spanish-speaking couple to take care of the Jewish education at the school. He asked me if I was interested in the position, and I said yes. He recommended us, and we got an offer for a two-month trial period. We stayed for three years before returning to Argentina. I was very young and made many mistakes. Still, overall, it was an amazing experience that led me to learn much," recalls Karo.

Once back in Buenos Aires, he began working part-time at the Chabad Lubavitch headquarters. He stayed there until a new proposal arose: establishing a Chabad Lubavitch summer camp at the *Hacoaj Country Club*. The project was to establish a sort of Beit Chabad in the heart of one of the most relevant secular Jewish country clubs in Greater Buenos Aires City.

"We never received full support for that project from the Chabad board. I was never paid for the entire amount of work I did there. We went through a lot and ended up spending all the savings we had amassed while living in Colombia," Karo says.

The project lasted ten months.

"Did you encounter resistance spreading Orthodox Judaism in a secular Jewish country club like *Hacoaj*?" I ask him.

"I handled the situation. That's what we were trained to do. After fifteen or twenty days of living there, I showed up with a Chabad vehicle. It was a van with a *chanukiah* on top and Chanukah signs on the sides. Just getting in and out of my house attracted all eyes. It was walking out on the golf course during Shabbat, wearing a long black overcoat, and golfers would look at me with paranoia. People would start talking about being unable to play golf during Shabbat anymore. You play with those preconceptions and show off: 'No, look how open-minded I am. You can play during Shabbat as much as you want. I have no problem with that.'"

"Like a sort of provocation."

"To a certain degree, yes. One day, we took some *channukiot* and gave them to families we knew had children. We left them on their doorsteps with a note that looked like my kids wrote it: 'I'll be waiting for you at my house, on such-and-such a day at such-and-such a time, so that we can celebrate Chanukah.' We cooked some food, obviously typical Chanukah food. We brought a giant Chabad dreidel, and we had a great time. The issue was not the ten kids who came. The issue was that a week later, the country's president summoned me to his office. He then asked me: 'My man, what do you think you are doing?' I told him: Nothing in particular. I am but another neighbor here, and my children invited their friends to play at home.' He was a smart guy. He held me there and said, 'Listen, you don't fool me. You are not just another guy who rents a house here. So, let's agree on some common ground because I don't want trouble.' So I told him, 'I am not forcing anyone to do anything they do not want to do. If someone does not like what I am offering, they can decline. It's not that difficult.' He then allowed me to continue doing my thing."

Despite the non-aggression pact Karo reached with the country club's authorities, the project did not last the planned year. After ten months, it was canceled.

"My fourth child was born, and he had a heart defect that needed to be fixed. So, I told Chabad's executive board I wouldn't renew for another year if things stayed that way. They agreed, and we left," Karo says.

The next step in his career within Chabad saw him working at Chabad's headquarters once again. He stayed in that position until he received a proposal to take charge of a synagogue belonging to the Beit Chabad Villa Crespo. Karo accepted the proposal and worked for two years at that synagogue.

"Chabad supports you enough to make ends meet, but it doesn't give you everything you need. The rest you must get yourself. What I ended up doing to cover what I lacked was teaching. I worked in the *Morasha* programs, in *Maianot*, in different Batei Chabad and in several places. In the beginning, I was an entry-level teacher. Then, I made up a name for myself. People began to enjoy my classes. My fifth son was born in the interim."

Those years of working as a Jewish studies teacher and holding various part-time positions led him to be involved in creating *Morasha Universitarios*, which later became ISEJ, as we saw in chapter four. "I gave it its current name. I was one of its founders," he says with a smile. Then, as he was getting close to the top, he left.

His process of leaving Chabad was gradual, and it took him some years to come to fruition. It began "when the existential searches returned to me, as in my adolescence, and I realized Chabad was not fulfilling me anymore. I looked at it critically and realized that it was no longer my thing," he says.

His path towards the exit began with some transgressions, which he says exist within Chabad: "There came the point at which with my wife we started to listen to the radio again. Something forbidden in Chabad if not to listen to Torah's words. We knew the books say you can't, but we listened to the radio, anyway. We didn't do it in the *yeshiva* or during the first years inside Chabad, but I started listening to the radio at one point. I didn't read profane, forbidden books either. But at some point, I started watching movies on the sly. And then, some things made little sense to me at some point. I began to wonder if it was okay for me to ask myself questions. That was around my early thirties. During the last few years I spent inside Chabad, I allowed myself to open some little doors to the outside world. They were minimal doors, as I was still convinced I was where the absolute truth was. Still, I started to go and watch some movies. Many people in Chabad do it as well. I allowed myself to listen to some non-Hasidic music. There are some in Chabad who have DVD players and rent regular movies. And everyone knows it's 'wrong,' but nobody enforces it. Obviously, no one inside Chabad reads Nietzsche or Spinoza. Reading non-sacred books, going to the movies, and listening to music that is not ritual or religious are all forbidden in Orthodox customs. Some people make minor transgressions, but always try not to let anyone notice. I was one of those. At some point, I began to have internal rumblings, and the first question I asked myself was whether I could wonder. And one day, I said: 'Yes, I'm going to allow myself to wonder. There, I started a process that lasted about five years. With myself, with my children's mother, and with my children. I started to dream about a way out. Meanwhile, I began to open myself up to the outside world. I began to speak with other people, see the world differently, think differently, rethink my rituals, symbols, and values, read extensively, and travel to new places."

Karo's departure surprised Chabad's community in retrospect. He kept up appearances as much as he could during those years of thinking his way out of an armed and constructed life.

Of the many rabbis and Chabad people I had contact with during the research for this book, the only one who could express the general mood within the institution in the face of Karo's departure was Rabbi Stawski: "It is a difficult subject. You could see that something was going on with him. But it was very internal to him. We discovered that the procession had been inside him for quite some time. Meanwhile, no one knew; one could be right next to him and have no idea what was happening. Only later did we realize he hadn't been to *minyan* for years. He wasn't even putting on the *tefillin*. How could we imagine? These are things that happen inside. I didn't realize it, and I don't judge him. Each one's relationship with God is personal. But in the end, his departure came as a shock for many. It is a phenomenon that exists, although there are more returnees in Chabad than those who leave. That is why it was so surprising."

Maintaining these appearances while undergoing personal change was not the same for Karo in Chabad as it was inside his family.

His search was of a spiritual order. That pushed him to read at the beginning some oriental philosophies, Zen, Buddhism, and Taoism. His family knew him well. They knew he had always been a kind of rebel within Chabad, with particular issues. "My children's mother told me at one point: 'Relax, you can go to India. It's all right. When our eldest son gets married, I will send you the invitation. Then you can return, and we will accept you with your orange robes.' My answer was: 'No. An orange robe and a black coat are the same things. Why would I exchange one for the other? I am not exchanging one God for another. I am in doubt about God himself.'"

The situation evolved gradually. Karo was unsure about what he wanted for his life; he was looking beyond a life governed by blind faith in the Torah, and he emphasizes that the dialogue with his children's mother aided him in this process.

"During that discussion, she was out of words. But some time later, she understood. It required a long dialogue process because I wasn't clear about my feelings. At one point, she told me: 'You're too caught up in the Chabad knot, in the hurricane's eye. You see many things happening, making you angry and wanting to leave. Because you are extremely sensitive. But what you see is just how organized religion works. However, faith, God, the Torah, and the Rebbe are all something else. You will calm down and return after you leave.' She realized later that it was not the case. You don't leave or stay for one reason. You are a human being, not an accumulation of things."

Damián knows that his decision to leave Chabad was probably influenced by other life events.

The death of Alex (the rabbi who had been left in charge of Beit Chabad Concordia after the departure of the Kapeluschnik family) and his young son in a car accident was one of the most brutal blows he suffered within Chabad. Not only because of the tragedy but also the community reaction: "He was my friend, with whom we even shared a room at the boarding school. The afternoon before the accident, I had talked to him on the phone. He was coming from Concordia to Buenos Aires and was killed on the road. I don't know if it was a crisis or what to call it, but I had a very strong issue with Chabad after his death. I remember talking to a Chabad counselor and telling him: 'I am not angry at God. We cannot revive him, and we have no remedy for death. But the way we are proposing to honor his life, all this thing about praying more, doing more *mitzvot* in his honor, all this idea of keep going forward, is lacking something for me. Can we not give ourselves five minutes, sit down, look at each other, and say: *We are in pain* and cry? Whoever wants to cry can cry; whoever wants to scream can scream; whoever wants to keep quiet can keep quiet, but can't we support each other as people in this shared pain?' I don't even remember what this counselor answered me."

"During that tragedy, I missed Chabad's humanity. The part of grief and pain. I did not get angry with God, I did not get angry with the Rebbe, I did not get angry with the Torah, and I did not get angry with anyone. I did not seek explanations. I was requesting a place for mourning within Chabad."

Karo's next step was to realize that he no longer believed what he said daily, what he preached, and what he taught his students.

"When I allowed myself to ask myself questions, I realized that many of the things in my speech were not as genuine as I thought. I was attempting to persuade young people and the rest of the world, and I noticed myself saying things that had been very clear for me at some point, but that weren't anymore."

"For example, I used to say: 'I do this because I am convinced. If you show me otherwise, I'll change.' But in reality, it was not genuine. I was not open to listening to you to see if you would show me something different. The question came to me: So, do I do it because I am convinced or because I am on autopilot? One question led to the other, and one belief led to the other."

Then, one day, Damián decided to leave Chabad Lubavitch. But he still had a long way to go to detach himself; he depended financially on his work inside the congregation to support himself and his family.

"Life gave me the following challenge: 'If you leave tomorrow, you will be out of work with a wife and five children to support. How will you provide for them?' I answered to myself, 'I'm not fourteen or fifteen years old like I was when I started. So, I'm going to take my time before leaving.' I had some debts. I worked until I could pay them off and put some money away. I spent that long time thinking about my questions, comparing myself and my ideas to those of other rabbis, studying abroad, and putting myself to the test. I stayed in Chabad until I just couldn't do it anymore. The fruit was so ripe that if it stayed on the tree, it would rot. It had to fall off."

Besides the economic difficulties that implied leaving Chabad from one day to the next, Damián also had to face the fact that his five children were still part of Chabad. They were also known as the children of a rabbi of certain relevance within it.

On the one hand, her children found themselves with a father who was changing the cultural habits in which he had raised them: "Of course, it's strange that one day daddy walks into the house without wearing a yarmulke or that starts saying certain things," says Karo, and adds the difficulties at a personal-community level that her children's departure implied for them: "My children saw a change of dad and mom in the house. They saw that Dad's change differed from Mom's. But they also saw that we still cared about the same things. We both believe in love, freedom, respect, and helping people who are in need. We still shared the value of the *mitzvah*. We could share the practice of the *mitzvah* as well. The ritual practice of the *mitzvah*? Maybe not."

May 1, 2006, was Labor Day in Argentina and the first non-working day in Chabad for Karo. Pesach, the holiday of liberation, was ending. He likes to point out these synchronous events: "As soon as the holiday of freedom and liberation was over, I resigned from my positions in Chabad."

The rabbi goes back a few months when his decision to leave Chabad was already made: "In October 2005, I had to undergo surgery on my face, in my mouth because they found I had a dental cyst. They had to take out all my wisdom teeth. In October 2005, I finally lost my wisdom. Besides that, I had to shave my beard for the surgery. I consulted with the rabbinical authority, as Chabad Hasid aren't allowed to shave their beard. He told me it was fine. He explained how I had to shave according to the rite."

"When I had surgery, they took a cyst sample for analysis. I told a friend who knew my intention to leave Chabad, 'So, they sent it for the autopsy.' Knowing I should have said 'biopsy' instead of 'autopsy,' I slowed down, and we both laughed. And he said, 'It's obvious.' I said, 'Well, let's put it into words because we both understood the flaw: Yitzhak's autopsy for Damián's birth.' But it wasn't that Damián came back. It was a new Damián that included Yitzchak and Damián."

When Karo announced he was leaving, it was also a tough moment for him: "First, I thanked the people and the institution for all they had done for me. Then, I said that my way of seeing the world and my beliefs had changed, and I didn't want to hurt or disappoint the institution. I also said that I wanted to live freely with my new way of seeing things, so I was quitting my job and Chabad. We gave ourselves a week to think about the matter. The only thing they heard was that a soul was lost. The whole dialogue was a dialogue of me going back to doing *teshuva* and getting well and that I was crazy and all that. That conversation taught me some interesting things. They said, 'So what happened to all the questions you had when you first came here? Now you're going to run out of all the answers.' And that's where something that was very interesting came up for me. I told them: 'Look, when I came here, I had many questions, and I was looking for certainty. Today, I have certainty, and I am looking for the many questions.'"

His departure had a powerful impact on many Chabad Hasidim.

Some people went from stunned to unable to comprehend his decision.

Within the logic of Chabad Lubavitch, Karo explains his departure as losing a soul, which could ultimately cause the Messiah's non-arrival.

The last exit came to Karo with freedom: "When I left Chabad, since the process was so long and gradual, I felt thrilled. From a hot day, going out in a shirt on the street and saying, 'Wow, this feels so good. How simple life is like this.' To be completely happy. I grew accustomed to wearing a t-shirt, a wool tallit with *tzitzit*, twenty-four hours a day, three hundred and sixty-five days a year, even to sleep. For sleeping, eating, and just about everything."

"Saying hello and giving a girl a kiss on the cheek at first felt so weird, to me, so different."

"Six months after I first shaved, after leaving Chabad, my six-year-old son looked at me and said, 'Now I can see your laugh,' I replied, 'Sure because I cut my beard and you can see my face.' And he replied, 'No, it's because you now laugh.' I met with his mother, who told me, 'Yes, you look happy now.'"

APPENDIX

Brief History of Chabad Lubavitch and of its Arrival in Argentina

What is Chabad Lubavitch, and where does it come from? A brief history

Chabad Lubavitch is one manifestation of Hasidism, a Jewish religious renewal that emerged in the 17th century in Poland under the figure of Rabbi Israel ben Eliezer, also known as the Baal Shem Tov or his acronym *Besht* "The Master of the Good Name."

This movement proposed a new way to practice Judaism that emphasized joy and appealed to the feelings of ordinary people (those who couldn't read or write and weren't part of the strict rabbinical academies of the time). It was a tremendous change for a people who had suffered seven centuries of persecutions, deaths, and pogroms and had seen the promise of the messianic redemption come and go briefly in the form of a sinister character named Sabbatai Zevi. This false prophet persuaded the Middle Eastern Jewish masses that he was the Messiah who would redeem humanity until he was captured by the Sultan of Turkey and forced to convert to the Muslim faith or die. Zevi made his choice and wore the turban, thus dashing the hopes of salvation that millions of oppressed Jews had placed in him.

In this context, Hasidism spread, combining pantheism, a powerful approach to Jewish mysticism (the Kabbalah, also known as "the hidden Torah," that is, the more obscure and hermetic aspects of Hebrew texts that must be interpreted using very specific methods) and hope in the imminent arrival of the redeeming Messiah, a question that had been implanted in the immediate imaginary of Eastern European Judaism.

The conjunction of these elements, coming from various historical processes that had been taking place, formed a coherent system of thought on which Hasidism rested: the fulfillment of the 613 precepts (*mitzvot*), which Orthodox or observant Jews must practice, would be the proper way to achieve the final redemption. Hasidism's core idea was that all Jews, no matter where they stood in society, had to follow the religious rules and be close to God in order to bring the final redemption and the Messiah to the world. This is fundamental to understanding Hasidism and Chabad Lubavitch in particular.

After Baal Shem Tov's death and of his first successor, the Hasidim did not adopt a new unified command but expanded into various groups with their own leaders called *rebbes* (Yiddish for "rabbi," meaning teacher). They carried their particular interpretation of Besht's message throughout Eastern Europe. It was not an easy task, as they faced fierce opposition from other rabbinical sages who continued to understand Judaism through traditional concepts. This branch of Judaism was called *Misnagdim* — opponents — and had its focus in Lithuania under the leadership of the rabbi and sage Elijah ben Shlomo Zalman, the so-called "Gaon of Vilna." They saw in the Hasidim a new incarnation of the false messianism of the late Sabbatai Zevi.

Hasidism's structure around the figure of the *rebbe* created a new way for Jewish communities to interact since these leaders were primarily chosen for their charisma. This was new for Jewish tradition and broke, in some ways, with the rabbinical verticality that had been common until that time. It made it possible for Judaism to become more fragmented and change because disagreements within the Hasidic congregations could split into groups led by a new *rebbe* with his own customs, beliefs, etc.

Thus, Hasidism became a revolution against the "Orthodoxy" of their time, the most conservative expression of Judaism represented by the *Misnagdim*. Today, both Misnagdim and Hasidism have remained as the expressions of Jewish Orthodoxy that oppose the movements of modern Judaism embodied in Conservative Judaism, Reform Judaism, and other liberal movements such as post-Judaism.

Chabad was one of these new expressions of Hasidism that emerged after the death of the Baal Shem Tov. This acronym synthesizes the three fundamental principles of this branch: *Chockhmah* (wisdom), *Binah* (understanding), and *Da'at* (knowledge). Under the leadership of Rabbi Shneur Zalman ben Baruch of Liady, this group expanded throughout Russia (it would later settle for many decades in the Byelorussian city of Lubavitch, which means "The City of Love," from which it took its name) and took on an emphasis on prayer rather than study, in a context in which each branch of Hasidism forged its own customs, forms of dress, beliefs, and peculiarities.

Chabad Lubavitch arrival in Argentina

A kosher butcher shop on the intersection of Billinghurst and Humahuaca Streets in Buenos Aires City announces the history of the Orthodox Jewish movement in Argentina with a sign on the door, next to other billboards that promote meat cuts sales. The sign reads: "Brief approach on the Orthodoxy of the Argentine Jewishness since the '50s, an initiative of a LEADER. For sale here." Inside, the butcher is cutting up a chicken. When asked about the strange ad, he tells me to talk to a man with a long white beard and a sports cap which is sitting in the back under a pencil and charcoal portrait of Menachem Mendel Schneerson, the Lubavitch Rebbe, the highest leader of Chabad, who died in 1994 and has not been replaced to this day.

Isaac Benchimol is the name of the man who is now stroking his beard. He takes orders over the phone and says he sells all kinds of meats, including grilled sausage and *matambre*, which are all kosher. He writes the orders the old-fashioned way: in a small yellow notebook. He says the book he's advertising from the window is about how Jewish Orthodoxy began in Argentina. He goes to the back of his business and retrieves a copy of the book and handles it to me.

The book's cover reads, in Spanish, "Against Wind and Tide. An approach to the work of 'Ribbi' Zeev Grimberg, Z'L," has a picture of a man in a jacket, tie, glasses, and a yarmulke writing on some paper in what looks like a late 1950s office, with a black disc phone to his left. The picture is framed by a wave from the ocean and a blue sky in the background.

The white-bearded man proudly says that he is the author. One pioneer of Jewish Orthodoxy in Argentina, he was also friends with Rabbi Zeev Grimberg and later gave lodging to Dov Ber Baumgarten, the envoy of the Lubavitch Rebbe, who brought Chabad to Argentina.

The smell of blood is powerful here.

"Are you a *shochet*?" I ask him if he is a Jewish ritual slaughterer.

"I am not. My son is."

The book has pictures: black-and-white photos of Jewish families dressed in the style of the 1950s, with gray or black coats and ties, facsimiles of letters written in Hebrew and English, with some rough translations into Spanish on facing pages, though the translations are not always correct and sometimes are cut off before they are finished.

A modestly dressed woman, wearing a colorful blouse, headscarf covering a probably shaved head, and black skirt, enters the shop and talks with the butcher, whom she appears to have known for quite some time. The butcher's shop is half a block from *Beit Chabad Almagro*, one of the Lubavitch "houses" scattered throughout Argentina's capital city and a good part of the country.

The place reeks of blood and dead animals; a yellowish light contrasts with the violet light of the stained-glass windows displaying the pieces of meat.

"The Rebbe himself came to write me letters," says Isaac Benchimol.

"Are you a Lubavitcher?"

"I am now. Yes. I used to be orthodox, but not Lubavitch. See," he says, pointing his finger to a laminated photocopy stuck on the window next to him, so overloaded with pasted papers, blinds, and curtains that it barely filters a little light, "this is a letter from the Rebbe."

The man stops and points to a passage in the book while adjusting his cap.

"All right, tell me how much the book costs."

"Twenty pesos."

"Here you go."

"You know, the other day, I was at the house of a woman who interviewed me because she is writing the history of Chabad in Argentina. She made me draw her a plan of the place in my house where I prayed with Baumgarten."

"Slove Libman?"

His eyes light up.

"Herself!"

The Lubavitch community knows each other. Everyone knows about everyone.

"When did you host Baumgarten?"

He takes a moment to reflect on my question.

"I don't remember exactly... it must have been around '58 or '59, I think. I'm sure it was in the sixties."

He sits down again. The phone rings, and he says goodbye to me while he picks up the call.

What Isaac Benchimol does not tell me that morning is that, besides being a pioneer of Jewish Orthodoxy in Buenos Aires and one of the first to approach Chabad Lubavitch, he is an excellent violinist who performs a beautiful version of the Yiddish song *My Yiddishe Momme*, which I watch on Jabad.tv that afternoon.

***

In the 1950s, Rabbi Dov Ber Baumgarten, the emissary that the Seventh and last Rebbe of Lubavitch appointed for Argentina, arrived in the country from the United States, where the world center of Chabad Lubavitch had been established since the Second World War. Since Menachem Mendel Schneerson, the Seventh Chabad Rebbe, took over as leader, the Lubavitch began an expansionist policy that led this branch of Orthodox Judaism to colonize almost the entire world, even the most remote places.

Baumgarten moved his family to Buenos Aires in 1962.

His son, Pinjas "Pini" Baumgarten, also a *shochet*, tells me about his family's history from an apartment in Once, a heavily Jewish-populated neighborhood of Buenos Aires. He does this in a Spanish sparkled with English and Yiddish words: "My father arrived for the first time in Argentina during the week in which Juan Perón was overthrown, in 1955. That was the first time he came. He came here. What for? Those are God's designs. He came, stayed, went back home, and came back."

Jewish Orthodoxy in Argentina during those years was far from thriving. Assimilationist currents, Zionism, and the gradual political involvement of Jews who had moved to the country over 50 years earlier had led to a "Westernized" Jewish camp.

The researcher Susana Brauner traces these changes in her work *Ortodoxia religiosa y pragmatismo político: los judíos de origen Sirio* [Religious Orthodoxy and Political Pragmatism: The Jews of Syrian origin], where she gives a full picture of the Judeo-Damascene and Alepine Sephardic Jew immigration to Argentina. Around the middle of the 1950s, some of them went back to the way of Orthodoxy. They would serve as the foundation for later Orthodox rabbis, such as the Baumgarten of Lubavitch and the envoy of another Hasidic branch, the Rebbe of Satmer, Eliezer Ekshtein.

The appointment of the Hungarian Amran Blum as Chief Rabbi of the Syrian-Alepine community generated internal dissidence because of his personal and political closeness to the then President Juan Domingo Perón. His community distrusted the government, which it accused of being anti-Semitic. With the 1955 military coup, Rabbi Blum went into exile in the United States. The Aleppine community hired Rabbi Yitzhak Chebehar from Aleppo, who played an essential role in revitalizing observant Judaism within the Argentinian Sephardic community where Rabbi Baumgarten operated. In the words of his son: "During those times, there were few Orthodox Ashkenazi Jews in Argentina. Sephardic Jews are always more Orthodox and traditionalist. They have much more vocation to attend the synagogue and the rites. Unfortunately, the Ashkenazim who came to Argentina were mostly leftists and communists. This was to such an extent that when Ashkenazi parents learned their children would emigrate here, they would mourn because they knew they would be lost to Judaism."

According to Benchimol's description in his book, various Torah and Talmud-nucleated study groups had formed during those years in the Once neighborhood, which already had adequate infrastructure. One of those Orthodox study groups that served as the basis for the later development of Chabad Lubavitch in Argentina was *Shuba Israel* [Return to Israel], led by Rabbi Zeev Grimberg, whose biographical traces inform the butcher's book.

Benchimol relates the encounter with the envoy of Lubavitch: "Rabbi Dov Ber Baumgarten, who was the first Rebbe of Lubavitch' *sheliach* [envoy] to arrive in Argentina, also arrived in these lands around the year '56. During the first six months of his stay, I had the *zejut* [merit] of accommodating him in my apartment, assigning him my children's room. We lived together in perfect harmony, and during that time, I could contemplate and learn how a Hasid conducts himself. Our Shabbat table and Yom Tov were always full of people to get to know him. Others, came to hear him sing with his vibrant voice beautiful *nigunim* (Hasidic songs), which melted into our souls." (22)

Shuba Israel began as a study group. Its members used to meet in a small building on 2300 Viamonte Street. But they grew quickly, leading the community to move to rooms provided by *Agudat Israel* on 2336 Lavalle Street. The organization expanded and attracted many Jews who became *baal teshuvah*.

Many people thought they were close to Hasidism because they were organized around a rabbi, which is like how a Hasidic court is set up.

From *Shuba Israel*, where Dov Ber Baumgarten taught, a group splintered. After internal dissidence, this new group integrated into the original nucleus of Chabad Lubavitch in Argentina. Even though his ideas and plans were well received early on, Dov Ber Baumgarten's first few years in Argentina were tough. He lived in desperate poverty and had to move through several homes of his followers who gave him lodging. In this way, Rabbi Tzvi Grunblatt tells that Baumgarten's income was so low that he could barely buy meat bones to make broth.

Dov Ber Baumgarten had to adjust to a culture that differed from his own. At the time, it was almost impossible to find kosher foods in Argentina, and the few available were almost prohibitively expensive for most people to buy. This was another reason the Rebbe's envoy had an initial hard time living in the country: "We lived at 2581 Cangallo Street[1], fifth floor, apartment K. Bread and milk were delivered on horseback here. It was very different. The doors were always open. There wasn't the violence we know today. It was something else," recalls his son.

Dov Ber Baumgarten was to develop all kinds of activities related to promoting religious observance: "My father came and went and made a *mikveh* (ritual bath) that is still standing today on Helguera Street. He fixed another one in the Barracas neighborhood that was not suitable and did many other little things. There is a lot of history in between, but it is irrelevant. What is relevant is that wherever my old man went, he wreaked havoc because he went with the truth to present *Yiddishkeit* (the quality of being Jewish) as it is," says Pini Baumgarten.

The Lubavitch Rebbe's representative worked as hard as possible to ensure Jewish traditions were followed in Argentina and that the proper infrastructure was built. He turned the successive apartments where he lived into centers for imparting Jewish tradition among the youth of the 1960s. His contribution was fundamental as a trainer of rabbis who succeeded him in his task, not only within Chabad Lubavitch but also in the country's supervision and development of kashrut.

His son says that his father's action received prompt attention from AMIA (The Argentinian Association of Jewish Mutuals), which hired him and the *mynian* (minimum quorum of ten adult men to pray in the synagogue) he had formed to run the *Hogar Israelita* in Burzaco, Province of Buenos Aires, which in those years gave shelter to elderly and orphaned Jewish children:

"My dad took it, but it was all mixed up: meat and milk because nobody cared about anything. And my dad grabbed all his people and told them: 'Let's make it kosher. It was a time of scarcity. There was a lack of flour and sugar. They brought everything from Israel and an old slaughterer, Mr. Pichman, sent meat and chicken to the asylum. My father used to work as well for the slaughterhouse. During those years, everyone did a little of everything. But soon, they noticed that something was wrong. Because tiny portions were arriving at the table of the little ones, and the big ones hospitalized there. They did not

---

1. Cangallo Street name was changed to Tte. Gral. Juan Domingo Perón in 1984.

understand the proportion between what went in and what arrived on the plate. So, my dad entered the storage room and turned off the lights. At 1 a.m., people came in and started taking everything out. Who oversaw the people who were stealing? The head of the asylum. When he saw the lights come on and my dad came out of hiding to confront him, he pulled out a gun. My father opened his shirt and told him: 'If you are *macho*, shoot: are you going to rob old people and orphans?' From there, after my old man complained to the AMIA board of directors, several children were taken out, and some old people were left."

In October 1960, Baumgarten began publishing the magazine *Conversaciones con la juventud* [Conversations with Young People], a modest booklet with Hasidic stories, tales, riddles, and materials clearly intended for a young audience.

It cost ten pesos at the time and was listed as being published by *Merkos L'Inyonei Chinuch Inc.*, the worldwide educational arm of Chabad Lubavitch based in Brooklyn.

Rabbi Tzvi Grunblatt considers that the magazine and Baumgarten's one-on-one approach to his students was fundamental to setting up Chabad's work in Argentina, which was still not institutionalized. Thus, person by person, the first students of the Rebbe's envoy were formed, who would later integrate the original nucleus of Chabad Lubavitch in Argentina. Abraham Polichenko was one of them, and Grunblatt recognises him as one of the early regional successes of Chabad's efforts. Besides this one, among his students was Rabbi Aharon Tawil, one of the first to be sent to finish his rabbinical formation in the central Chabad Lubavitch *yeshiva* in New York City.

In 1967, Dov Ber Baumgarten was appointed director of the *yeshiva Chafetz_Chaim*, belonging to the *Agudat Israel* congregation. Dependant of it was EZRA, a youth Jewish study and action group. EZRA was attended at the time by some young Jews that would later become Chabad Lubavitch Argentina's highest ranks: Jaime Lapidus, the brothers Tzvi and Natán Grunblatt, and Israel Kapeluschnik, among others. As part of his new role at *Agudat Israel*, Rabbi Baumgarten started talking to these young Jews and helping them plan events through EZRA. The organization worked with some methods and objectives like those that guide the work of Chabad Lubavitch today: try to convince Jewish grassroots that were tending towards assimilation to embrace a more religious Jewish lifestyle.

"What did we do?" asks rhetorically Israel Kapeluschnik, "we gathered kids on Saturday afternoons from the different neighborhoods, we took them to a place, which was a temple or a school that they lent us, and we did different religious and game activities with them."

"There was little Torah study," Grunblatt says, "but it was lived Jewishly with prayer and everything. We went to the camps together with Rabbi Baumgarten. We saw in him the personification of the Eternal Jew, the Jew who does not negotiate his Judaism, who does not go to accommodate himself, the Jew where the word of Torah is. Torah, with a capital T. With Baumgartem, we clearly felt like the living heirs of a three-thousand-year-old people. We felt we were and are the personification of Abraham, Moshe, Jacob, and Rabbi Akiva in the 20th century. Rabbi Baumgarten taught us how to feel like Jews and how to act like Jews. With that strength, he laid the foundations of what later became the Chabad movement."

The young Jews who attended EZRA considered themselves oblivious to Chabad's influence. However, Kapeluschnik acknowledges that Rabbi Baumgarten's approach was smart: "It created a relationship between him and us that was very close. We called him *Rebbe*. Any questions we had, any doubts we had, we approached him. We had him at our fingertips. During the week, in the *yeshiva* and on Shabbat, in the *shul*, where we prayed. That created a very close relationship. We still considered ourselves separate from Rabbi Baumgarten or any other rabbi. Yes, we still considered his wisdom. We talked to him, but our motto was, 'We don't depend on anyone.' We were young people in the 1970s, which was an interesting time."

In 1968, Baumgarten began sending his students to complete their training at the Chabad *yeshiva* in New York, following a custom very typical of Chabad rabbis who, to this day, spend their years of training in rabbinical seminaries in the United States and Israel.

Baumgarten arranged these trips for all his interested students and did not require them to be affiliated with Chabad in return, which also helped him gain the youth group's affection.

Abraham Tawil was the first Baumgarten student to travel to the Chabad *yeshiva* in New York to complete his rabbinical training, but so did the brothers Natán and Tzvi Grunblatt, among many others.

In 1973, Baumgarten was expelled from the *yeshiva Chofetz Chaim* for reasons that were never disclosed. Most of the young Jews who met at EZRA decided to follow him as he established Argentina's first Chabad Lubavitch *yeshiva*. He did this in an apartment on Larrea Street that belonged to a follower, Mr. Abraham Aboud, who gave it to Baumgarten for free.

Kapeluschnik remembers it as a critical moment in his life: "He founded the *yeshiva*, practically from one day to the next. He called us and said, 'Look, I am still here.' I believe most of the students continued with him. I also believe it was when God enlightened me to mark my life. It is my case, and I think it is the case of all the other boys who were there: the Grunblatt brothers, the Oppenheimer brothers, Rabbi Rafael Lapidus, Jaime Lapidus, Rabbi Plotka."

At the same time, Rabbi Baumgarten began the arduous task of translating into Spanish the previously mentioned mystical work of Chabad's first Rebbe, the *Tanya*. He did that with the help of what Rabbi Tzvi Grunblatt refers to as "Chabad's executive committee at the time": Hershel Sandhaus, Abraham Polichenko, and Aharon Tawil.

The following years saw the return of Baumgarten's students, who had gone to study in New York. The Lubavitch support base in Buenos Aires had already grown, and the youth group that had followed him continued their efforts to "bring Jews closer together." Grunblatt recalls going to community centers and festivals almost daily to encourage Jewish men over thirteen to put on tefillin.

That same year also meant the official beginning of the activities of Chabad Lubavitch in Argentina. Rabbi Tzvi Grunblatt and another rabbi who Baumgarten had sent to study in the United States, Daniel Levy, started to travel all over the country to expand Jewish observance. They toured ten cities and repeated the experience in 1977, taking the precepts and Jewish observance to unexplored corners.

In Grunblatt's account: "In 1976, we went to Neuquén, Salta. We were received with surprise and skepticism: two boys who arrived with long beards and hats; two Hassidim, arriving and meeting young people. We also traveled to Uruguay. We are talking about the beginning and middle of the Military Dictatorship: arriving in Tucumán, meeting young people, and talking. We did not even know the country was under a 'Dictatorship.' We came and talked about Judaism. We arrived in Mendoza, all over the country, with suitcases full of materials, of Torah and *mitzvot*."

In 1977, with the financial help of the Meir brothers, Jacobo, Isaac, and Enrique Tawil, Chabad Lubavitch acquired its first property in Buenos Aires City (1172 Agüero Street, where its *Ohel Menachem* synagogue and central offices are located to this day.) Up to that moment, the work had been carried out in borrowed places, temples such as the *Beis Yosef*, and the private home of Rabbi Dov Ber Baumgarten.

Rabbi Grunblatt emphasizes the fundamental help of the Tawil brothers in achieving this purchase: "If they didn't put up the money a day before the deed was signed, even the purchase ticket was lost. People think millions of dollars poured out of the United States and into us, but that is untrue. Then, the *yeshiva* was set up, but the money was still tight. There were no desks or chairs in the office, and half of the books in the library came from Baumgarten's own collection."

Chabad Lubavitch's flagship in Argentina had a slow development. Like all the group's undertakings, it started small and expanded. Kapeluschnik relates: "At that time, Beit Chabad central offices, together with the Chabad *yeshiva*, were at 1172 Agüero Street. Soon after a year or two, a family donated the adjoining land, and renovations began."

The institution had to move to a rented building at 300 Jean Jaures Street during the construction work, and the activities were distributed in different centers until 1989, when the works were completed.

Today, 1172 Agüero Street is composed of a building of two interconnected bodies, including its *yeshiva*, a "high school" for boys between the ages of thirteen and fifteen, with a boarding school for those coming from the interior of the country, and a temple with walls made of stones brought from Jerusalem, which was inaugurated in 1996.

But much earlier, on February 23, 1978, at 55, while at his daughter's home in London, Rabbi Dov Ber Baumgarten, the Lubavitch Rebbe's envoy in Argentina, suffered a sudden stroke and died a few hours later in the hospital. He had undergone two complete medical check-ups shortly before, and none had shown anything to worry about. Baumgarten died about five months after Chabad's last Rebbe, Menachem Mendel Schneerson, had a heart attack while celebrating the holiday of *Simchat Torah* on October 4, 1977. Some Chabad Hasidim tell a story that connects the two events. According to his son Pini: "Few people are going to tell you about this, but when the Rebbe had a heart attack, my father grabbed a group of ten people and told them: 'The years that I have left to live, I give them to the Rebbe, so that the Rebbe may live.' They did a writing, an official statement, certified by the ten people there. He and the other ten signed it, and all passed away the same year."

Whether Baumgarten mystically extended the life of Chabad's Rebbe by sacrificing what remained of his life is debatable; what is certain is that he died young, and the event imposed a change of scenery. The one chosen to continue Baumgarten's work was Rabbi Tzvi Grunblatt, who at that time was studying at the Chabad *yeshiva* in New York, developing a work very close to the Rebbe: He was one of those in charge of remembering the speeches the leader gave during Kabbalat Shabbat so that they could be transcribed the next day when the prohibition on working on the holy day of rest (and thus writing) expired.

Grunblatt recalls: "The link of the Lubavitch Rebbe with what was happening here in Argentina was so strong that when Rabbi Baumgarten passed away before the burial took place, he sent for another young Argentinean and me to the office of his personal secretary. He wanted us to contact Buenos Aires to make sure that none of the activities and issues that Chabad had been carrying out or had planned to carry out would be interrupted by the premature and unexpected death of Rabbi Baumgarten. Especially since Pesach was two months away. He wanted to ensure that the shipment of *matzah* that Rabbi Baumgarten brought from there was organized."

In May 1978, Grunblatt was appointed the new envoy of the Lubavitch Rebbe in Argentina. He was twenty-three years old and was engaged to a twenty-year-old Brooklyn-born Lubavitcher, Shterna Kazarnovsky. They were married in July 1978 and arrived in the country in early August. "She agreed to come just three weeks after she got married to a totally unknown country, without us having arranged anything beforehand or with anyone. We did not even have our salary arranged. We only knew that we were coming to fulfill our mission of spreading Judaism here, in Argentina. Immediately, a man from the community approached me and told me he would pay my salary for a year."

Things started to change with Tzvi Grunblatt becoming Chabad Lubavitch's CEO in Argentina. From its humble beginnings, the slow person-to-person work undertaken by Dov Ber Baumgarten and, finally, the acquisition of the building at 1172 Agüero Street, where the first Chabad *yeshiva* was built, they moved on to a second phase that allowed a visible and sped up expansion in the country. In just over thirty years, Chabad Lubavitch has expanded from that single building to thirty-three community centers, sixteen schools, non-formal educational centers, social assistance foundations, a publishing house, seven hundred employees, and hundreds of volunteers. In Grunblatt's words, Chabad now reaches around 45,000 Argentinian Jews. Considering that there are about 200,000 Jews in Argentina, Chabad Lubavitch represents how a quarter of Argentina's Jewish population lives their Jewishness.

I asked Rabbi Grunblatt how Chabad Argentina accomplished all of this under his tenure,

"The impetus for growth came from our *mitzvot* campaigns, especially for each holiday. We started to organize talks, to go out to the street with the Rebbe's message of expanding, crossing barriers, overcoming the *ghetto*, and not isolating ourselves. I contacted, for example, the Maccabi organization, where I started to give talks and leadership courses. These things did not fit in anyone's head. Today, we cannot wait for the Jews to attend the institution. We must take the institution to the Jew. That is the mentality: to break the barriers and the stigmas that there are Orthodox and non-Orthodox Jews. We must reject the notion that there are many Judaisms. There is one Judaism, which is that of the Torah, which we received from God on Mount Sinai, which passed through all generations, and that is what we keep. Perhaps we observe it less because we are unfamiliar with it or not used to it. But that does not take away its strength. Our task is to go, teach, show, and make other Jews taste it. And they will like it. We understand that things have changed. There was a time when Jews had no place to go or gather. It is not like that today, so organizations are no longer necessary for many Jews. It must be then the goal of Jewish organizations to transmit Jewish content. If they do not do so, they have no reason to exist. Today, what is missing are not the spaces for Jews to gather. What is missing is the content in those spaces. Jews meet, and what does the Jew take away from that meeting?"

Epilogue

Sunday, March 28, 2010. A day before heading to Salta to celebrate Pesach with Rabbi Tawil and the Salta Jewish community, I walk around Armenia Square to attend an "urban Pesach" organized by a new Jewish institution making rounds in the local community. They are named *Yok* (in Rioplatense Spanish spoken in Buenos Aires and Uruguay, the name sounds like the phonetic pronunciation of the word "Shock.") They are a liberal, post-Judaic, post-reformist, or a postmodern Jewish institution that uses several marketing tools to sell Jewish tradition, but with a message that is opposed to Chabad's: a Judaism by tradition rather than religion.[1]

A small table filled with Chabad Lubavitch Hasidim sits in a small corner of the square before reaching Costa Rica Street, taken over by a stage and a fair where you can spend a few pesos to play to rescue the Jewish people from Egypt, throw balls to the golden calf and catch the plagues; buy kosher wines, typical food, take pictures in a die-cut that leaves the body of Moses to place your face or listen to the discussion forums.

This is not a party Chabad organized; they even refused Yok's offer to have a table inside the fair. There are Jews around here, and lots of them, more than enough reason for Chabad to come and perform their *tefillin* campaign.

They hand out *matzah* and offer to put on the phylacteries to each man who passes by.

They see me walking; they see my Jewish face and ask me if I've put *tefillin* today. I cannot refuse their request. I didn't come for them and yet feel at fault if I refuse to let them put them on me.

---

1. As to 2023 Yok seems to no longer exist. Chabad Lubavitch, of course, is still going strong.

One Chabad Hasid passes the leather straps over my arm, over my head, and tells me: "Now you are connected in broadband with God, ask him whatever you want. He will listen to you much better."

I stifle a laugh. It's practical, it works, and it creates an ambiguous situation for me: on the one hand, the fun of the mix. I'm sure this Hasid truly believes the words he has just mustered. I'm sure he's aware of the disruptive power that encountering a man dressed in a heavy jacket and a black hat comparing a religious act to going online has for a secular Jew guy like me.

The more I think I know the Lubavitch, their goals, and their ways, the more I feel I don't know them.

I know what they want, what they seek, and what they do to get it. Still, there is a part that defies logic, appeals to the heart, soul, intangible, or whatever is beyond my critical capacity. In moments like this, everything I know about Chabad does not help me explain why this man is putting *tefillin* on me and comparing it to surfing the Internet in the same movement.

***

April 2010. I'm sitting at the desk of a rabbi who organizes one of Chabad's youth education programs in which students are rewarded with a cheap vacation to Israel or New York. This is a sort of intake interview. "Here you sign the declaration where you swear you are a Jew according to the Torah: child of a Jewish womb," he tells me as he checks some data on his PC screen.

I sign reluctantly. I had to take off work to come in for this interview, and they kept me waiting in the hallway for at least an hour until I was served. I realize I have become a very demanding consumer of the Chabad brand.

Another rabbi enters the office. He greets me, looks at me, and says: "I already know him."

I look up and try to recognize him, but I see no resemblance to any of the rabbis and Chabad people I have had contact with in the last ten months.

The person behind the PC screen is silent.

"Yes, he came to my house for a Shabbat dinner," says the newcomer, and for a few seconds, I lose my breath. "After his visit, he wrote some horrible things about us."

I feel like I'm in the worst place at the worst time possible.

The rabbi who just walked in is Moshe, who invited me two years ago to dinner at his house. That was one of my first Chabad experiences.

The rabbi behind the PC looks at me: "So, you're the one who commented about my class? The one who made fun of my explanation about how we have to cut our nails?"

At the time they're referring to, I had a popular web blog, and the experience I described in the prologue of this book was posted there in installments, with a lot of rather cruel sarcasm. I titled each of the six blog posts "Jewish Evangelism."

"I was going through a tough time," I try to explain to them. I genuinely regret making fun of something I didn't know about, which seemed crazy to me the first time I approached it.

Moshe is the more enraged of the two. He claims I made fun of Rivke, whom he describes as someone who works hard to reconnect Jews to Jewish life.

I apologize. I explain that I have changed my mind. This is a genuine thought of mine. I may not have a great deal in common with Chabad Lubavitch; I wouldn't say I like most of their ideological and political positions; I cannot believe in the messianic redemption because I do not find it logical, and I could not change my life to conform to the Jewish precepts. Still, I cannot say that I do not respect Chabad now.

***

This book came from the prejudice I felt during my first time with Chabad when surrounded by people who seemed crazy to me. It also came from the prejudices I repeatedly heard in the Argentinian Jewish community circles I inhabited then.

When I met Damian Karo for the first time, I didn't tell him I was studying Chabad. I was afraid. It took me at least thirty minutes of talking over coffee to explain to him what the project was about.

When I interviewed Damian Setton, I expected him to confirm all the myths about wealthy rabbis, brainwashing, and shady business. At first, it was disappointing to get straight answers that went against the widespread paranoia because it's more exciting to feel like a spy or Private Eye who's going to find out everything that's been kept secret than to show that things aren't really the way people thought they were.

Without a doubt, researching this book allowed me to open up as a human being and as a Jew, finding things I didn't know existed.

I don't want to be an advocate for Chabad Lubavitch, not only because they don't need or want me to be one, but also because I am not interested in that kind of job.

Before beginning each interview with a Chabad representative, I would clarify that the purpose of this book is not to defame anyone or anything. I frequently felt that disclosure was required for them to accept me and engage in conversation with me. Previous works on Chabad Lubavitch, books, myths, hearsay, and communal political issues have marked a twisted path that aggrandized shadows closer to myth than reality about them.

It is also true that the Chabad Lubavitch world is much larger than what I could cover in this book: going through it all would have been an endless task.

When I approached Gustavo Dvoskin for an interview, I told him that the book was not meant to be defamatory, and he responded, "What you have to make is an honest book. That is what is important."

Writing an honest book is what I tried to do at all times, and I hope I succeeded.

I am aware of my limitations. I know that some details about the theology of Chabad beliefs or some historical detail (telling history is not something Lubavitchers engage much with) may be incorrect. This was not done on purpose.

I hope that these pages have shed some light and that the next time an atheist, assimilated, secular Jew like me is confronted for the first time by a man in a black coat and hat, beard down to his chest, strips hanging out of his pants, who invites him to dinner with his family on a Shabbat, he can keep an open mind and spirit in the face of prejudice and sarcasm, which can unknowingly hurt more people than he can imagine.

I really enjoyed reading an idea by Robert Eisenberg, who raises in his book a somewhat disturbing idea for many: the possibility that, based on the statistics of population growth of the Orthodox communities (Hasidic and non-Hasidic) and the decline of the non-Orthodox (Conservative, Reform, etc.) because of intermarriage and assimilation, in about sixty-five years the only Jews left in the world will be only Orthodox.

It is an idea that gives food for thought and opens new questions that will generate discussions and debates. While writing this book, I learned Judaism is also about the permanent contrast of ideas.

I hope the result will be something that can be used in future conversations of this kind.

Buenos Aires, July 31, 2010

Toronto, July 31, 2023 (Translated and revised)

Glossary

Aliyah: Literally, "ascension." It denotes emigration to Israel and refers to the high place where the Temple of Jerusalem was located.

AMIA: Asociación Mutual Israelita Argentina [Israeli Mutual Association of Argentina] is Argentina's biggest Jewish Community Center. Many other Jewish institutions form part of it or are somehow related to it.

In 1994, its headquarters in Buenos Aires City was bombed. To this day, the case remains open and unpunished.

Ashkenazi (pl. *Ashkenazim*): Jews of Eastern European origin.

Baal Teshuva (pl. *Baalei Teshuva*): Name given to a Jew that starts to practice a more traditional religious form of Judaism after being mostly secular.

Baruch HaShem: Expression meaning "Thank God!"

Beit Chabad (pl. *Batei Chabad*): Literally "Chabad House." It is one of the more common forms Chabad Lubavitch establishes its franchises. Generally, a Beit Chabad comprises a synagogue in charge of a Chabad rabbi. They usually offer different activities and programs for the community.

Beit Ha Mikdash: The Holy temple in Jerusalem.

Bubbe: Grandmother in Yiddish.

Challah: A type of braided bread eaten during Shabbat and other festivities.

Chanukah: Jewish holiday that remembers when Jerusalem was taken back from the Seleucid Empire and the Second Temple was rededicated at the start of the Maccabean Revolt in the second century BCE.

Chanukiah (pl. *Channukiot*): A nine-branched candelabrum used specifically to celebrate the holiday of Chanukah.

Challah (pl. *Challot*): A typical braided bread of Ashkenazi origin typically served during Shabbat.

Chametz: Foods containing leavening agents that are prohibited during Pesach.

Farbrengen: Hassidic reunion.

Gefilte Fish: Fish dish typical of Ashkenazi cuisine.

Goy (pl. *Goyim*): Not Jew.

Hasidic: Jewish mystical movement that emerged in the 18th century A.D. It follows the teachings of rabbi Israel ben Eliezer, known as the Baal Shem Tov or his acronym Besht.

Hasid (pl. *Hasidim*): A member of a Hasidic court.

Haggadah: A book of instructions for the Pesach feast.

Hazara b'she'ela: Name given to an Orthodox Jew who becomes secular.

Kabbalah: Branch of Jewish mysticism.

Kabbalat Shabbat: Celebration at the beginning of Shabbat.

Kashrut: Series of prohibitions and regulations that apply to kosher food.

Kehillah (pl. *kehillot*): Jewish congregation.

Kotel: Jerusalem's Wailing Wall or Western Wall.

Kosher: Code of dietary laws that food must comply with to be fit for Jewish consumption according to the interpretations of the Torah (e.g., not eating ham, not mixing meat with milk.)

Keruv: Jewish outreach.

Kibbutz: Community farms. Type of Zionist-socialist social organization of the early years of the State of Israel.

Knish (pl. *Knishes*): A traditional Ashkenazi snack comprising a pocket of thin dough filled with potato and fried onion. It is very typical among Argentinian Jews.

Kosher (*Kasher* in Yiddish):

L'chaim: a toast.

Madrich: Youth counselor.

Mashiach: Messiah.

Mashgiach: Kosher supervisor for meals and food products.

Matzah (pl. *Matzot*): Unleavened flatbread, especially eaten during the Pesach holiday.

Mezuzah (pl. *Mezuzot*): A piece of parchment with Hebrew verses from the Torah written on it. Orthodox Jews put it on doorposts.

Minyan: A quorum of ten men over the age of 13 that is required for some traditional Jewish prayers.

Mitzvah (pl. *Mitzvot*): One of the 613 biblical precepts every observant Jew is expected to observe.

Mikveh: Ritual bath.

Morah (f.) (pl. *Morot* m. *Moreh*): A Jewish teacher.

HaShem: Periphrastic way of referring to God.

Parve: In Jewish food laws, *Parve* is a category of edible substances that do not contain dairy or meat ingredients.

Pesach: Annual commemoration of the Biblical Jews' escape from Egypt under the leadership of Moses.

Pesach Seder (pl. *Pesach Sedarim*): Ritual dinner feast during the Pesach holiday.

Purim: Feast commemorating the deliverance of the Jews from the annihilation decreed by the Persian king Ahasuerus. It is marked by the wearing of costumes and the consumption of alcoholic beverages.

Rebbe: Leader and teacher. In the various Hasidic sects, he is the highest authority figure. He is thought to be in a special relationship with God and prescribes the code of conduct, customs, and general religious direction his Hasidim must follow.

Rosh Hashanah: Jewish New Year.

Sephardi (pl. *Sephardim*): Jews of Spanish and Northern African origin.

Shabbat: Rest Day for Jews. *Shabbat* is observed every week from Friday sunset to Saturday sunset.

Shaliach: A Chabad emissary who encourages people of Jewish background all over the world to practice Judaism.

Shekhinah: The light or presence of God.

Shema Yisrael: One of the main Jewish prayers.

Shul (also *Temple*): Synagogue

Soifer: Yiddish for *sofer*, a Torah scribe.

TAGLIT (also *TAGLIT-Birthright, Birthright Israel,* or *Birthright*): A non-profit organization that sponsors extremely low-cost ten-day trips to Israel for any Jew over 18 and under age 26. They are present all over the world.

Tallit: A fringed piece of clothing that religious Jews use as a prayer shawl.

Terefah: non-kosher

Tefillah: Prayers.

Tefillin: Small leather boxes containing Scripture passages. They're attached to leather straps around the head and left arm. They are only prescribed by the Orthodox for men over thirteen. At the start of the day, they must be put and followed by a prayer.

Tzedakah: The Jewish precept of giving to charity.

Tzitzit: Fringes that Orthodox Jews wear around their waists as a remembrance to fulfill God's 613 precepts.

Yehudi (pl. *Yehudim*): Jewish.

Yeshiva: (pl. *Yeshivot*): "To remain seated." It is the name given to centers for advanced Torah and Talmud studies. They are typically associated with Orthodox Judaism.

Yom Kippur: Day of Atonement. It is one of the most important holidays in the Jewish calendar. It prescribes a day of fasting and reflection.

Zeide: Grandfather in Yiddish.

Zohar: Also called "The Bible of the Kabbalah," it is the most essential textual corpus of this Jewish mystical tradition.

Bibliography

Azar, J. y Schwartzer, M.: *Las formas en la transmisión de religiosidad del Centro para la Juventud de Jabad Lubavitch*, Unpublished research paper.

Benchimol, I.: *Contra viento y marea*, Self-published, Buenos Aires, without a date.

Bianchi, S.: *Historia de las religiones en la Argentina: las minorías religiosas*, Buenos Aires, Sudamericana, 2009.

Brauner, S.: *Ortodoxia religiosa y pragmatismo político: Los judíos de origen sirio*, Buenos Aires, Ediciones Lumiere, 2009.

Buber, M.: *El rabí de la buena fama (El Baalschem Tov)*, Buenos Aires, Editorial Israel, 1938.

———: *Cuentos jasídicos: los maestros continuadores*, I and II, México, Paidós Orientalia, 1990.

Byrne, R.: *El secreto*, Barcelona, Urano, 2007.

Challenge: An Encounter with Lubavitch-Chabad, Lubavitch Foundation of Great Britain, 1970.

Dubnow, S.: *History of the Jews in Russia and Poland*, volumes 1 to 3, Philadelphia, The Jewish Publication Society of America, 1946.

Eisenberg, R., *Boychiks in the Hood: Travels in the Hasidic underground*, Nueva York, Harper One, 1996.

Enciclopedia Judaica Castellana, 10 tomes, México D. F., Editorial Enciclopedia Judaica Castellana, 1949.

Ehrlich, A., *Leadership in the Habad Movement*, online.

Fackenheim, E. L., *¿Qué es el judaísmo?*, Buenos Aires, Lilmond, 2005.

Fidel, C. y Weiss, T.: "Marcos para jóvenes judíos en edad universitaria: objetos de consumo y oferta cultural; modelos institucionales", in *Nuevas voces para una nueva tribu:*

Primer Encuentro de Jóvenes Intelectuales AMIA - 26, 27 y 28 de agosto de 2006, Buenos Aires, Editorial Milá, 2009.

Fishkoff, S.: *The Rebbe's Army: Inside the World of Chabad-Lubavitch*, Nueva York, Schoken Books, 2003.

Foxbrunner, R. A.: *Habad: The Hasidim of R. Shneur Zalman of Lyady*, New Jersey, Jason Aronson Inc., 1993.

Grunblatt, R.; Kinoff de Ruschin, A., y Blank, C.: Alef-Bet: *Mis primeros pasos con las letras hebreas*, Buenos Aires, Editorial Kehot Lubavitch Sudamericana, 2000.

———: *Camino a la libertad: La historia de Pésaj en relatos y juegos*, Buenos Aires, Editorial Kehot Lubavitch Sudamericana, 2000.

Guerreiro, L. "Judíos: Nada cambia para Dios" in La Nación Magazine, Sunday May 16, 1999.

Gutwirth, I.: *Antología del jasidismo*, Buenos Aires, Fleischman & Fischbein Editores, 1978.

Graetz, H.: *Historia del pueblo judío*, Tome VII, México, Editorial La Verdad, 1941.

Harris, L.: *Holy Days: The World of a Hasidic Family*, Nueva York, Touchstone, 1995.

Heilman, S.: *Defensores de la fe*, Buenos Aires, Planeta, 1992.

Heilman, S. and Friedman, M.: *The Rebbe: The Life and Afterlife of Menachem Mendel Schneerson*, Nueva York, Princeton University Press, 2010.

Hoffman, E.: *Despite All Odds: The Story of Lubavitch*, Nueva York, Simon and Schuster, 1991.

Honeg, S. B.: *Vida matrimonial judía: los deberes de la mujer*, Amigos del Movimiento Jabad Lubavitch en Sud América, Buenos Aires, without publishing date.

Jacobson, S.: *Toward a Meaningful Life: From the Wisdom of the Lubavitcher Rebbe*, Harper Collins, 2017.

Kagan, J. (director): *Crown Heights: Nothing is as Simple as Black and White*, Showtime Ent (DVD), 2004.

Keller, W.: *Historia del pueblo judío*, Barcelona, Ediciones Omega, 1984.

Melamed, D.: *Los judíos y el menemismo: Un reflejo de la sociedad argentina*, Buenos Aires, Sudamericana, 2000.

Pincever, Karina (coordinator): *Maltrato infantil: El abordaje innovador del programa Ieladeinu. Aprendizajes de una experiencia integral comunitaria*, Buenos Aires, Lumen, 2008.

Potok, C.: *The Chosen*, New York, Ballantine Books, 1995.

Rabinowicz, H.: *A guide to Hassidism*, London, Thomas Yoseloff, 1960.

Rabkin, Y.: *A Threat from Within: A History of Jewish Opposition to Zionism*, Zed Books, 2006.

Rigg, B. M.: *Rescued from the Reich: How One of Hitler's Soldiers Saved the Lubavitcher Rebbe*, New Haven, Yale University Press, 2004.

Schneider, S., and Berke, J. H.: "Sigmund Freud and the Lubavitcher Rebbe", Psychanalytic Review, 87(1), 2000 (http://www.jhberke.com/Freud_Lub_Rebbe.htm).

Schochet, J. I.: Mashíaj: *El concepto de mashíaj y la era mesiánica en la ley judía y su tradición*, Buenos Aires, Kehot Lubavitch Sudamericana, 1992.

Scholem, G.: *El misticismo extraviado*, Buenos Aires, Lilmod, 2005.

Setton, D.: *Instituciones e identidades en los judaísmos contemporáneos: Estudio sociológico de Jabad Lubavitch, Informe de Investigación N° 21*, Buenos Aires, CEIL-Piette Conicet, 2009.

———: "Las redes de educación judaica no formal y la participación de los jóvenes", in *Nuevas voces para una nueva tribu: Primer Encuentro de Jóvenes Intelectuales AMIA - 26, 27 y 28 de agosto de 2006*, Buenos Aires, Editorial Milá, 2009.

Shapiro, E. S.: *Crown Heights: Blacks, Jews and the 1991 Brooklyn Riot* (Brandeis Series in American Jewish History, Culture and Life), online, 2006.

Sorj, B.: *Judaísmo para todos*, Buenos Aires, Siglo XXI, 2009.

Spollansky, F.: *La mafia judía en la Argentina*, Buenos Aires, Editorial Rubin, 2008.

Sztajnszrajber, D. (coordinator): *Posjudaísmo 2: Debates sobre lo judío en el siglo XXI*, Buenos Aires, Prometeo, 2009.

Topel, M. F.: Jerusalem & São Paulo: *A nova ortodoxia judaica em cena*, Río de Janeiro, Topbooks, 2005.

Universo Jabad: Cincuenta años encendiendo el corazón judío, without a date.

Vigésimo aniversario Asociación Israelita Beit Jabad Belgrano, Buenos Aires, 2007.

Yablonka, I. *Research notes*, Unpublished research paper.

INTERVIEWS

Rabino Damián Karo

20/08/2009; 15/12/2009; 21/12/2009 and 21/01/2010.

Damián Setton

08/09/2009.

Diana M.

05/11/2009.
Dr. Slove Libman
08/11/2009
Gustavo Dvoskin
19/11/2009
Rabbi Shmuel Kiesel
27/11/2009
Rabbi Moshé Blumenfeld
04/12/2009
Jani Gorovitz
10/12/2009.
Rabbi Pinjas "Pini" Baumgarten
24/12/2009
Rabbi Aharon Stawski
05/01/2010
Rabbi Tzvi Grunblatt
08/01/2010
Dr. Gregorio Kaminsky
08/01/2010
Miriam Kapeluschnik
25/01/2010
Valansi Family
January 2010
Pablo Hupert
28/01/2010.
Rabbi Mordejai Birman
03/03/2010.
Rabbi Shlomo Kiesel
04/03/2010
Rabbi Israel Kapeluschnik
10/03/2010
Rabbi Rafael Tawil
31/03/2010
Matthew Paul Miller (Matisyahu)

13/04/2010
Marcela Schilman
27/04/2010
Valeria Marckiewicz and Javier Fajn
05/05/2010
Jésica Azar
07/05/2010
Sergio Moscovich
11/05/2010

CHABAD LUBAVITCH WEBSITES
Argentina
Headquarters
http://www.jabad.org.ar
Beit Chabad Recoleta
http://www.jabadrecoleta.com
Beit Chabad Palermo Soho
http://www.jabadsoho.com
Chabad Palermo
http://www.elshuldepalermo.com
Beit Chabad Congreso
htp://www.chabadbuenosaires.com
Beit Chabad Caballito
http://www.jabadcaballito.com
Viene Mashíaj
htp://www.vienemashiaj.com
Rest of the world
Chabad Lubavitch Headquarters
http://lubavitch.com
Chabad Lubavitch in Spanish
http://es.chabad.org
Crown Heights
http://www.crownheights.info
The Rebbe

http://therebbe.org

Kinus HaShluchim

http://www.kinus.com

Tzivos HaShem

http://www.tzivos-hashem.org

Friday Light

http://fridaylight.com

Chabad Haiti Relief Efforts

http://www.chabadhaitirelief.com

Purim

http://www.chabad.org/holidays/purim/default_cdo/jewish/Purim.htm

The Ohel

http://www.ohelchabad.org

About the Author

A.J. Soifer was born in Buenos Aires, Argentina in 1983.

He immigrated to Canada in 2017, where he earned his Master's and Doctor's degrees in Latin American Literature and Hispanic Studies at the University of Toronto.

www.ingramcontent.com/pod-product-compliance
Lightning Source LLC
Chambersburg PA
CBHW031103080526
44587CB00011B/795